The Gilded Youth of Thermidor

The Gilded Youth of Thermidor

FRANÇOIS GENDRON

Translated by James Cookson

McGill-Queen's University Press
Montreal & Kingston • London • Buffalo

© McGill-Queen's University Press 1993
ISBN 0-7735-0902-X

Legal deposit first quarter 1993
Bibliothèque nationale du Québec

∞

Printed in Canada on acid-free paper

This book is a translation of *La Jeunesse sous
Thermidor*, published by Les Presses Universitaires
de France, 1983. Translation and publication have
been assisted by grants from the Canada Council.
This book has been published with the help of a
grant from the Social Science Federation of Canada,
using funds provided by the Social Sciences and Hu-
manities Research Council of Canada.

Canadian Cataloguing in Publication Data

Gendron, François, 1942–
    The gilded youth of Thermidor
    Translation of: La jeunesse sous Thermidor.
    Includes bibliographical references
    ISBN 0-7735-0902-X
    1. France – History – Revolution, 1793–1796. 2.
    Youth – France – Political activity – History – 18th
    century. I. Title.
    DC185.5.G45313 1993   944.04′4′08351   C92-090712-1

This book was typeset by Typo Litho composition inc.
in 10/12 Palatino.

Contents

Foreword

Rows, fights, brawls, riots – what better raw material for a book full of mud-slinging and stick-swinging? This is what Quebec historian François Gendron offers us in his account of a chapter of the French Revolution.

Awarded a prize by the French Academy when published in Paris in 1983, and now accessible to English readers in a fine translation by James Cookson, this fascinating book chronicles the debates and battles that marked Parisian life following the fall of Robespierre and during the fifteen months of the Thermidorian Reaction. Robespierre was the strongman of the Revolution. He earned himself the terrible but little-known epitaph:

Passant, ne pleure pas mon sort
Si je vivais, tu serais mort
(Passer-by, do not mourn my fate
Were I alive, you would be dead)

Robespierre's presence would be felt looming over the chaos in the capital long after he had been "cut short" by the guillotine, then known as the "national razor." In the shadow of Robespierre the sans-culottes and the *muscadins* fought each other in pitched battles with weighted clubs and cudgels.

The sans-culottes were the *"cul crottés"* [dirty bums] who stormed the Bastille on 14 July 1789. Louis xvi, they said, was "fat enough for what we want to make of him." And along with the monarchy, they also overthrew the elegant aristocracy that carried its rusty swords in the salons. They were called the sans-culottes not because they went around with bare backsides but because they wore pantaloons instead of knee-breeches.

Their enemies were the *muscadins*. It is hard to imagine anything more baroque: a wig powdered with flour, hands whitened with almond paste, poorly cut breeches that made a man look curiously bandy-legged, and a huge stick, the *"rosse coquin"* [nasty bit of work].

Then the brawls begin. Gendron recounts them in minute detail. Fights take place everywhere – in the streets and squares, in cafés, theatres, government offices. And as there must always be a winner and a loser, the extravagant little fops win out over the "good solid family men," or, put another way, the vanguard of the bourgeoisie wins out over the vanguard of the lower classes.

Of course, no one spoke of the proletariat at the time. The lower classes were the rabble, the populace, the riffraff, the mob, the common people. The bourgeoisie were the *honnêtes gens*, the decent people. Today, though the words have changed, it may well appear to historians of the Revolution to be the same old story: the struggle of the poor against the rich, of the have-nots against the well-to-do. And with the same conclusion, too, for it is the rich who triumph, after seizing control of the State.

Indeed, people have been fighting for control of the State in France ever since 1789. And the State has defended itself with the police. It was unbelievable what the State knew about the average man in 1795: his lifelong friends, the women he slept with, his personal idiosyncrasies, his gambling debts. The inexhaustible archives scrutinized by François Gendron recall an observation by Pierre Vadeboncoeur: "We should believe the police when they confess, not believe them when they deny, and realize that when they are not talking about something, there is something they are not talking about."

The Paris that the revolutionaries divided up into 48 sections and that the deputies of the National Convention sought to hold in check by means of the Committee of General Security and the Committee of Public Safety is portrayed here in a vast social panorama in the classical tradition of the historiography of the French Revolution.

This is a definitive work.

Yves Beauchemin

Foreword to the French Edition

We thought that this book should be made available to a wider audience. François Gendron is a professor of history at the Royal Military College in St Jean, Quebec, and his doctoral thesis *La Jeunesse dorée : Épisodes de la Révolution française*, written under the supervision of the late Albert Soboul, was published by the Presses de l'Université du Québec in 1979. This work is based on extensive documentary sources: all of the reminiscences, all of the memoirs, all of the printed matter – newspapers, periodicals, public notices, pamphlets – from that period of gradually regained freedom between July of 1794 and November of 1795, as well as the overwhelming evidence contained in series F^7 and F^{11} of the Archives nationales, have been gone over with a fine-tooth comb. The present volume is a condensed version of the larger work. François Gendron has agreed to some major sacrifices, including all of the critical apparatus and much background material, and in so doing has managed to focus more effectively on the essentials. (Those who wish to explore the subject in greater depth can consult the original edition.) Nothing in this book is asserted in a cavalier fashion. It is the work of a skilled scholar who has taken a sound, meticulous, critical approach to his labour.

It is a pleasure to read Gendron. He has a talent for telling a good story. This narrative, which is of the highest quality, is both valuable and illuminating. But a narrative is not an end unto itself. To understand this story fully, it must be read along with François Furet's outstanding *Penser la Révolution (Interpreting the French Revolution)* and be seen against the background of the events leading up to it – the social and political turmoil which brought the jeunesse dorée of Thermidor into existence as a social group and made it reactionary in the fullest sense of the word. These events comprise the extraordinary ideological chaos whose mechanisms have been analysed by Furet and by Alain Besançon. The Jacobin chaos no longer appears as the initial event in a long, bloody series of events that stretch from 1792 to the present day, from the genocide of the civil war in the staunchly Catholic west of France to the Soviet gulag, the wanton destruction of the Chinese Cultural Revolution, and the self-genocide of the Khmer Rouge in Cambodia. By the time the Thermidorian Reaction began, the "terrorist" ideological chaos had cost some four hundred thousand lives within France, precipitated the departure of part of the élite, driven away currency, disrupted the free play of market forces, and caused an economic decline that would not only wipe out a century of progress but, in times of average harvests, as in 1795, bring about a food shortage so severe that it was more reminiscent of 1693–94 and 1709 than of the grain shortfall of 1789.

Taken out of context, the discourse of the Thermidorian Reaction is absurd and incomprehensible. Only when considered against the backdrop of the bloodthirsty delirium and the cultural, intellectual, spiritual, and moral decline that characterize the course of French history from the September massacres to the Prairial guillotine, only when considered in relation to the stereotyped discourse of the Jacobins, does the stereotyped counter-discourse of the merveilleuses and the incroyables begin to make sense.

Quantitative history also has its merits. For instance, Ronald Seicher has found that in part of the greater Vendée 40 per cent of the population was killed, and 52 per cent of property was destroyed. The massacres in Nantes and the havoc wreaked by Turreau's incendiary columns occurred before 9 Thermidor. In just two years, the Jacobin repression cost approximately twice as many lives as the repression of six centuries of building the territorial state, from the France of the feudal regnum to the administrative monarchy that witnessed American independence.

Without this backdrop, it is impossible to appreciate the Thermidorian Reaction, a reaction which should be seen as an inflamed civil society's rejection of an abnormal, cancerous transplant. This was the inevitable return of the pendulum, bringing back the laws of the market (to a market in the throes of galloping inflation) and restoring to positions of power the literate and educated élite that had managed to escape the death machine operated by the *pères Ubu* of the Republic under the emergency laws.

This is where François Gendron begins his analysis. In the days immediately following 9 Thermidor, a new social group made its appearance in the Parisian revolutionary dialectic: the muscadins. As is often the case in history, the group set itself apart by its manner of dress, carrying on "a tradition of baroque elegance." From the *muguets* to the punks of the 1980s, the tradition is a long one. Yet unlike the other groups, the muscadins played an active part in history. These absentee conscripts of the great mobilization of 1793, endangered sons of a "tertiary" élite soon rejected by the giant senseless death machine, were in the van of the National Guard disarmed during the Terror of the western quarters of Paris, which were held to be suspect by the sans-culottes that dominated the faubourgs. When the economic failure of Montagnard (left-wing) terrorism began to cut increasingly into popular support for the dictatorship of the Committees, allowing a backlash to develop, the coalition that had overthrown Robespierre realized that it needed a militia to protect the Convention against the wrath of the terrorist *sans-culotterie* of the faubourgs – before the transfer of arms from the eastern to the western quarters of Paris brought about a lasting shift in the balance of power within the city. The Parisian bourgeoisie – the intelligentsia, the "tertiary" class of the largest "tertiary" city in Enlightenment Europe – was in a sense represented by the parallel police force formed by the muscadins. The balance of power must have been very fragile for such a minor factor to tip the scales in favour of the west, and of the right. The bourgeoisie's best ally had been the self-destructive rage of the "ideocracy," of which the sans-culottes had been both the instrument and, to almost the same degree as the *collets noirs*, the victim. Yet there is no denying that when the situation became particularly dire – when famine set in, financial channels were destroyed, and the hardships of war began to make themselves felt – the *collets noirs* were no longer powerful enough to contain, not so much a return of deeply loathed terrorist power, but the anomic, aimless, reasonless violence of hunger and despair, born of the frustration of so many foolish dreams. And the uprising of Vendémiaire pointed to the decisive events of 18 Brumaire.

But we are running the risk of not seeing the forest for the trees. Thermidor picked up the thread, so inopportunely broken, of the modernizing Revolution: it would never fully recover from the wounds of the religious war set off by the Civil Constitution of the Clergy and the nit-picking, wilfully offensive way the reform was applied in the west, the gratuitous, nonsensical war waged against Europe, and the mindless genocide perpetrated by a people upon itself. Were they really so vile, these Thermidorians, these republicans of the possible and the happy medium who expressed their ideas in *La Décade*, which has been so well studied by Marc Regaldo?[1] Those who search for intellectual offspring will see the tree that bore the doctrinaires, part of Orleanism, and the opportunist, Comtist republic that, through the educational system introduced by Jules Ferry, brought France slightly more than half of the rich harvest of Nobel prizes reaped by Wilhelmine Germany in the early part of this century.

It would be unreasonnable to accuse the Thermidorians of having failed to heal wounds, still bleeding today, which mark the beginning of France's decline. A study conducted by the Institut national d'études démographiques, corroborated for the Rouen area by Jean-Pierre Bardet, has shown that while the birth rate had been falling since 1770 the first sharp drop in French fertility occurred at the time of the violent de-Christianization campaign of 1793–94. First the rent of 1794, then that of 1797 – Thermidor marks a break with the past. One cannot go back in time. François Gendron is absolutely right: the narrative has its place in history – particularly the narrative set in its long-term context, the narrative integrated into a science "of men in time ... which must constantly strive to connect the study of the dead with that of the living," to quote Marc Bloch's felicitous and still relevant phrase.

Pierre Chaunu
Member of the Institut de France

---

1 Marc Regaldo, *Un milieu intellectuel : la Décade philosophique (1794–1807)* (Lille: Université de Lille III and H. Champion, 1975, 5 vol.).

Preface

An easily discernible tradition of baroque elegance runs through
French history: the *muguets* in the seventeenth century, the *petits-
maîtres* in the eighteenth, the muscadins during the Revolution,
followed, under the Directory, by the incroyables and the merveilleuses, then the fashionables around 1815, the dandies around
1830, the *lions* and the *gandins* during the Second Empire, the *beaux*
of the Belle Époque, the *zazous* of the 1940s, the hippies of the
flower-power generation, and finally our contemporaries, the punks,
whose origins, to be sure, are more English than French.

Of all the Beau Brummells of the past, only the muscadins are still
widely known today. French secondary-school pupils are familiar
with their bizarre attire thanks to Carle Vernet's amusing caricature,
which appears in their third-year history textbook. The Goncourt
brothers' description of their eccentric manner of dress has been
quoted and plagiarized so often in popular histories that their style
has become the very archetype of extravagant elegance and *grand
boulevard* fashion. Then there are the restaurant in Paris's rue de
Richelieu, L'Incroyable, the café in the rue des Petits Champs, Les
Muscadins, and, at the Palais Royal itself, Le Grand Véfour, the
descendant of that meeting-place of the jeunes gens, Le Café de
Chartres, whose name can still be found on a transom window.

The continuing notoriety of the jeunesse dorée stems from the
important role the group played in the political and social history
of the French Revolution, whence the idea for this book. Of course,
the young men of the jeunesse dorée strangely foreshadow the *camelots du roi* of the Action française. This royalist volunteer corps,
made up for the most part of office and shop clerks, craftsmen,
students, and young men of independent means, was seen by Léon
Daudet as the only defence against the Revolution. The *camelots*

attacked democrats in public places with sticks and clubs, smashed all the republican statues they could find, prevented the performance of "subversive" plays, and dominated the debates of the National Assembly until February of 1936, when their organization was dissolved by the Council of State after they assaulted Léon Blum. True, *L'Action française* is not *L'Orateur du Peuple*, Charles Maurras is not Stanislas Fréron, and *La France bouge* is not *Le Réveil du Peuple*, but the parallel is revealing and suggests that at any period in history the disintegration of parliamentary government is accompanied by a rise in political hooliganism.

As for the jeunesse dorée of the French Revolution, a group long neglected by historians, it is certainly time for its story to be told and for an unjustifiable gap in historiography to be filled.

The Sections of Paris Established by the Commune

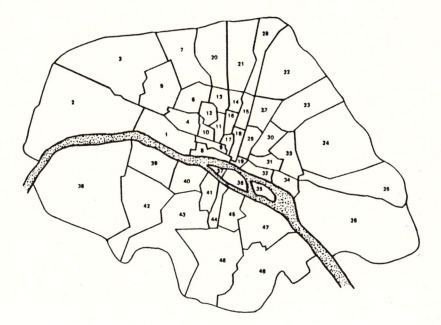

*Portraits of incroyables
and merveilleuses,
1810–1818,
by Horace Vernet*

Horace Vernet del.   *Gatine sculp.*

Chapeau de Paille d'Italie. Echarpe Ecossaise. Broderies à Roues.

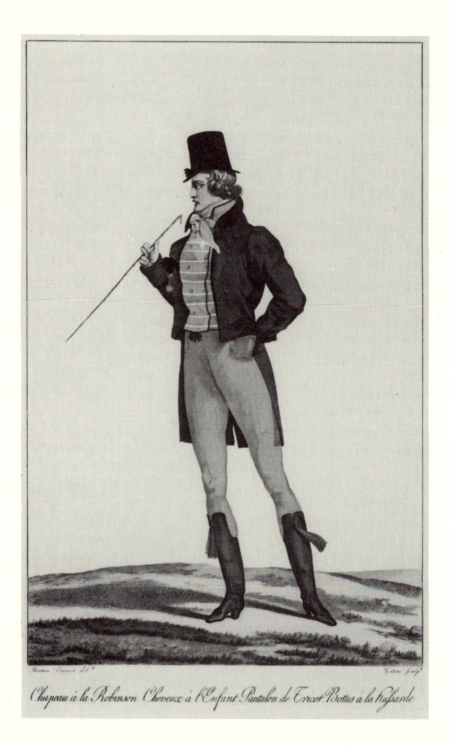

Chapeau à la Robinson Cheveux à l'Enfant Pantalon de Tricot Bottes à la hussarde

Culotte & Guêtres de Peau Couleur de Cuir. Canne à Parapluie

Chapeau de paille d'Italie, par-dessus à la Chinoise.

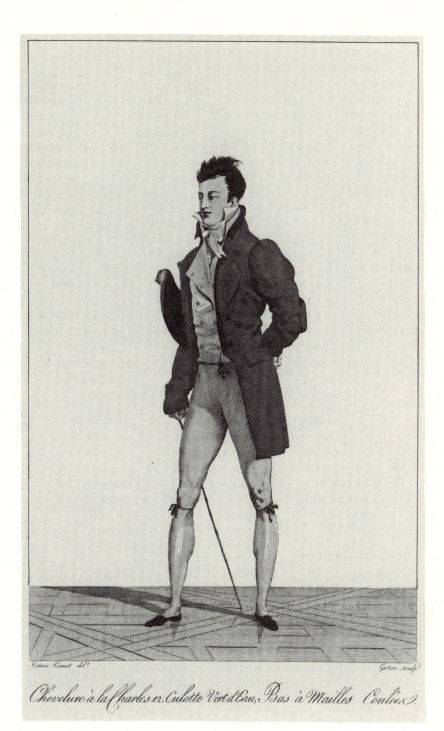

Chevelure à la Charles 12. Culotte Vert d'Eau, Bas à Mailles Coulee.

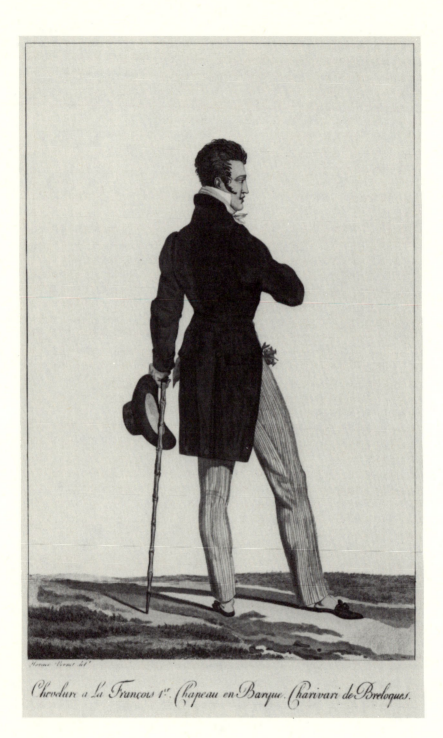

Chevelure a la François 1er. Chapeau en Barque. Charivari de Breloques.

Chapeau en Bateau. Habit Couleur Crotin. Culotte de Peau.

Cravate à Oreilles de Lièvre. Habit Vert Saule. Culotte de Casimir

The Gilded Youth of Thermidor

Introduction

A serious study of the social phenomenon known as the jeunesse
dorée (literally, "gilded youth") had to be based on a thorough investigation of the primary sources. This had never been done and
was therefore an absolute necessity. The results of this research are
presented here.

Standard history has always regarded the jeunesse dorée as the
political driving force of the Reaction, and as the chief instrument
of the Thermidorians, the group of deputies who seized power after
the fall of Robespierre. The jeunesse dorée, most of whose members
came from the middle class of minor officials and small shopkeepers,
was formed in the days following Thermidor. It appointed leaders
and organized meeting places, dominating the political scene until
Germinal and Prairial of the Year III. Members of the jeunesse dorée
hounded the Jacobins in the streets and cafés and forced the Assembly to decree the closure of the Jacobin Club. Then the jeunes
gens drove the Jacobins out of the sections; these fell into the hands
of the Thermidorians, who then purged sans-culotte influence from
government administration. The agitation culminated, in Pluviôse,
in the war of the theatres and in the hunt for busts of Marat. The
removal of Marat's remains from the Panthéon illustrated the abject
depths to which the Convention had sunk in just six months – having
freed itself from the domination of the Jacobins only to fall under
that of the jeunesse dorée.

In reaction to the austerity of the Year II, the jeunes gens – among
whom the police recognized many recently released suspects and
absentee conscripts – became the pillars of the society life that was
returning to the salons. They thus appear as the social and political
antithesis of the militant sans-culottes. By the jocund debauchery
and shameless luxury they brazenly displayed before the stern, des-

titute populace, by the currency depreciation they precipitated through wild speculation in government securities, by their blasphemy against the popular forms of patriotic worship, and by their insolent hooliganism in public places, they acted as a catalyst on the insurrectional energy of the masses. This eventually led to the uprisings of Germinal and Prairial and the resulting eviction of the sans-culottes from the political arena. From this point on, the jeunesse dorée was no longer of use to the Assembly, and even turned against it when the members of the Convention set themselves up as a sort of feudal ruling class in a bid to cling to power. Thwarted in its political ambitions, the jeunesse dorée sought to wrest legislative authority from the "Perpetuals." The army decided the conflict in favour of the Assembly, and thus relegated the muscadins to the role of stylish protesters in a war of words.

Such are the positions and propositions of standard historiography which constituted the working hypotheses of my study, as well as the point of departure of several years' research. The results of this research will, I expect, appear as accurate and well founded to one school as they will appear inaccurate and unfounded to another. No doubt, this is the fate of all historians of the French Revolution.

CHAPTER ONE

The Awakening of Moderate Opinion

9 THERMIDOR, YEAR II, TO 21 BRUMAIRE, YEAR III

When Robespierre was overthrown in Thermidor, Year II, government purges had so reduced popular support for the regime that public opinion was generally indifferent to his downfall. With the successive thinning of Hébertist and Dantonist ranks, the Revolutionary Government had lost the backing of the sans-culottes, who were advocates of direct democracy, as well as that of the moderate bourgeoisie, which was bearing the brunt of the state-controlled economy. The new *maximum des salaires* (law on wages), enacted on 5 Thermidor, had left the Committee of Public Safety bereft of support in the labouring classes, and by 9 Thermidor the only people still in favour of the régime were the Jacobins in the middle and lower-middle classes, amounting at most to a hundred or so men in each section, and they were thrown into complete confusion by the fall of the "tyrant": "We had absolutely no idea what to think or what to do," wrote a patriot of the West Section.

With Robespierre gone and his supporters imprisoned, guillotined, or so dumbfounded that they were incapable of acting, the Assembly drifted aimlessly, disconnected from its social base, as though suspended in a vacuum. But this situation did not last long: the muscadins of the jeunesse dorée – the gilded youth – soon made their appearance, with their square-cut coats, their enormous cravats, and their weighted cudgels – their "executive power," they claimed, quite rightly. A few brawls in the public gardens, such as the one at the Palais Royal, and they were masters of the Paris streets, driving out the last hard-nosed revolutionaries of the Year II.

Meanwhile, in the Convention, a new moderate party, the Thermidorians, had been formed, led by Tallien, Fréron, Barras, and their followers, who saw in the jeunesse dorée a means of applying pressure on the Assembly. A virulent public-opinion campaign was launched against the remaining Montagnards (left-wing people's representatives) and the Jacobin Club, which fell on 21 Brumaire, Year III. The Commune having disappeared in the crisis of 9 Thermidor, there appeared to be no authority that could confront the power of the Convention. Yet this was merely an illusion, for no sooner had the Convention thrown off the Jacobin yoke than it found itself under that of the jeunesse dorée. The Convention thought itself all-powerful, but it was in fact a prisoner of its own troops. In the final analysis, it had simply changed masters.

THE START OF THE REACTION

For Parisians, 9 Thermidor, Year II, marked the end of the "tyranny," which was symbolized, above all, by the inmates of Paris's forty prisons, some 8,500 individuals. Hence the vast movement of public opinion in their favour which spontaneously sprang up on 15 Thermidor in the first general assemblies held since the fall of Robespierre. The moderate Thermidorians, whose ranks had thinned since 31 May, returned in force to the assemblies to call for the release of the detainees. In the Marchés Section, it was reported that more than twice the usual number attended. There was similar agitation in the prisons, where the prisoners were overcome with joy at the news – and where the rage of the Reaction was already simmering. On 16 Thermidor, the inmates at the Lazare prison demanded that they be given wine and threatened to cut the warden's throat. There had been a general uproar at the Anglaises jail a few days earlier: "The prisoners think that the men in power who had them incarcerated are now going to be locked up and that they, the released prisoners, are going to take over from them," wrote the revolutionary committee of the Finistère Section. And the committee was quite right. It went on to explain that several new faces had shown up at the general assembly, "causing trouble and calling for the release of all inmates without distinction."

Initially the Convention spoke out against the demand that prisoners be released, obviously underestimating the strength of public opinion. On 16 Thermidor, the people's representative Goupilleau de Fontenay denounced the unrest in the sections, but it flared up again on the twentieth, with a renewed call for the release of prisoners. On the twenty-second, the people's representatives Jean-Lambert Tallien and Bertrand Barère, who were to become pillars of the Reaction, lashed out against the "incorrigible aristocrats" who were stirring up trouble in the assemblies. The disturbances were still continuing on the twenty-fifth, however: at the Amis de la Patrie Section, for instance, a group of women were calling for their husbands to be set free. This time it was the people's representatives Baudot and Taillefer who denounced the machinations of the "aristocracy." According to Tallien, people's representatives were besieged with requests and crowds gathered at the entrance to the Committee of General Security to call for releases. Barère complained about the avalanche of pleas on 22 Thermidor, and the people's representative Guillaume Vadier did the same on the twenty-sixth. But the protest movement continued to grow.

Overwhelmed by the tide of public opinion, the Convention was forced to make concessions. On 18 Thermidor, it decreed the release of all suspects who did not come directly under the law of 17 September 1793, and, on 29 Thermidor, the release of all those who worked the land, regardless of why they had been arrested. Officially there were still restrictions, and inmates who did not fall into these categories were supposed to remain behind bars. In fact, however, everyone joined in what became a mad dash for freedom. The gates of the prisons were "torn off their hinges rather than opened," the journalist J.J. Dussault reported. Another journalist, Charles Lacretelle, spoke of "long streams of suspects leaving the prisons," and in the Convention on 8 Germinal, Year III, Bernard de Saintes told Barère that in the days following Thermidor the Committee of General Security had spent its entire time, from dawn to dusk, signing discharges.

All of this took place amidst great confusion. Chaos reigned at the Committee of General Security, and the problem was compounded by a company of crooks trafficking in releases. A typical swindler was Jean-Baptiste Romey, of the Brutus Section, a native of Switzerland who speculated on the Bourse, frequented the Café de Chartres, and claimed to have been employed by the Committee of General Security, "though in no specific capacity." The people's representative Louis Legendre, then a member of the Committee, asserted that "this schemer took advantage of the access he had cleverly gained to some members of the Committee to give himself imaginary credit, misuse my name by saying he was my secretary and, with the help of this false title, peddle for a price discharges that the Committee granted only to the legal authorities." On the stairs of the Committee of General Security, another cheat, one Joseph Mailhol, of the Arcis Section, approached a Mme Dufour, who had come to appeal for her husband's release. In her denunciation, she said, "He told me that my husband's case depended on the wishes of Bourdon de l'Oise and Legendre, but that it was very difficult to see these two deputies. He said that Bourdon de l'Oise was a real stickler, but that he would be less expensive than Legendre, whose porter always had to be paid off handsomely." A third, a bailiff of the National Convention by the name of Verdot, "made it clear" to the citizen Galice, who had come to solicit the freedom of a woman, "that the sum of two thousand écus would be required to facilitate her release." Many other cases could be cited, including that of a certain Étienne-Joseph Chevillote who admitted to having received three thousand livres from a Mme Finot to appeal to the Committee of General Security for the release of her husband. In short, a horde of rather unsavoury characters were cheating the common people and selling prison releases by swindling signatures out of the Committee, which seemed to have completely lost control of the whole situation.

In the space of five days, from 18 to 23 Thermidor, 478 suspects were set free in Paris. In the beginning, cheerful groups would gather at the prison gates to see the inmates emerge, and would take them home in joyous processions. But the newly released prisoners quickly seized the opportunity to settle old scores. At the general assembly of the Champs Elysées Section on 15 Thermidor, some members were put under arrest for being "Jacobins." On the same day, the revolutionary committee of the Bonnet de la Liberté Section was subjected to scathing attacks from the Section's general assembly. On 20 and 21 Thermidor, Audouin's *Journal universel* sounded the alarm to the sans-culottes, reporting that the "aristocracy" was stirring up trouble in the popular societies and that public spirit was deteriorating in the sections.

In the Convention, the Montagnards could no longer conceal their anxiety. Everywhere, unrest among moderates was intensifying as the pace of the releases increased. In the Convention, on 23 Thermidor, the people's representative Duhem spoke out against the freeing of aristocrats. On the twenty-sixth, the people's representative Vadier announced that the Duc de Valentinois had been released, along with the Duc d'Aumont, the latter under the name of Gui, labourer in Aumont! They demanded that this rabble be put back behind bars.

But one people's representative, Tallien, had changed his mind. Indeed, his only claim to a place in history was to have realized that people were sick of the Terror, that the inevitable reaction was imminent, and that it was better to be a part of it than to be crushed by it. On 26 Thermidor, Tallien, who had hitherto advocated the "closest possible union ... among the men who had brought down the tyrant," suddenly began to lash out at those who were "carrying on the work of Robespierre." He declared, in a beautiful touch of demagoguery, that he would rather see twenty aristocrats run free than see one patriot in chains and asked, "Are we to believe that the Republic, with its 1.2 million armed citizens, ought to fear a handful

of aristocrats?" On 2 Fructidor he argued that the distinctions between aristocrats and patriots no longer made any sense as the only
types of citizens were good and bad: "What does it matter to me that
a man is born a noble, provided he conducts himself properly? What
do I care that a man is a plebeian if he is a crook?" And again, on
11 Fructidor, he asserted that people had to be brought to love the
Revolution, not to fear it – that justice, not terror, had to be made
the order of the day.

It was around this ideology of indulgence, which allowed the
Committee of General Security to effect mass releases with no more
formality than calling out names, that the Thermidorian party – led
by Tallien, Fréron, Barras, Legendre, Dubois-Crancé, and Merlin de
Thionville – coalesced. The number of inmates had dropped from
8,500 on 9 Thermidor to 4,678 by 17 Vendémiaire and to 4,208 by 13
Brumaire; in other words, some 4,300 suspects were released in the
space of three months – all of them with an unconditional allegiance
to the Thermidorians, to whom they owed their freedom and whose
cause they would espouse wholeheartedly for fear of finding themselves back behind bars. This desire to influence the released suspects explains the ridiculous displays that Legendre put on in front
of the prisoners. As Lacretelle describes, "He visited them constantly. He listened to them; he shed tears for them. He gave them
back to their families. If he turned some of them away, he would
leave much saddened; but he would soon be back to see them,
scolding and weeping at the same time. It was as though he were
chasing them from the prison." A similar description is given of
Tallien's tearful play-acting at the Luxembourg prison:

The people rushed up in a crowd, showered him with blessings, embraced
him, embraced those who had just been released. Do not worry, my
friends, he would say to those he had not yet been able to free from the
house of detention. You will not be yearning for your freedom for long.
Only the guilty will be refused this act of kindness. I shall be back today,
and tomorrow, and we shall work night and day until all patriots unjustly
detained have been returned to their families.

The Thermidorians thus cultivated political supporters who
would back them in the galleries of the Assembly, where a new
moderate claque made up of inmates' relatives and office clerks
was already active. Nicolas Maure, the people's representative from
Yonne, denounced the claque in the Jacobin Club on 7 Fructidor.
Its members were young men who had been called up in the first
conscription – "those known as muscadins," Jean-Baptiste Carrier,

the people's representative from Cantal, explained on 18 Fructidor –
but who had managed to obtain a certificate for some disability or
other from an obliging doctor, thus exempting them from military
service. "They can be recognized by their square-cut coats, their delicate hands, and their pointed shoes," he added. Some lavishly
dressed bourgeois women were even cheeky enough to go and sit
on the benches reserved for the people's representatives, and all
these elegant people would applaud the "moderantist" motions.

Thus, in the Assembly a new political orthodoxy was forming
around the leaders of the Thermidorians, while in the streets a new
solidarity was developing among the militant young men who were
soon to become the Thermidorian movement's zealous defenders.
This was the birth of the jeunesse dorée, as seen by the editor of *Le
Journal des hommes libres*: "Look what is happening around us. Look
at all the schemers and crooks gathering and joining forces. Look at
all the suspect men, known aristocrats, and even disguised aristocrats, joining together to form one large pack that rails against the
revolutionary institutions."

The jeunesse dorée, which according to the police was composed
chiefly of youths released from prison and absentee conscripts, was
active in the first battles fought by the Thermidorians. Thus, when
on 12 Fructidor the people's representative Laurent Lecointre solemnly denounced his fellow Assembly members Barère, Billaud-
Varennes, Collot-d'Herbois, and Vadier, leaders of the left-wing
party, as accomplices of Robespierre, his allegations were declared
slanderous by the Assembly, but struck a responsive chord in the
streets. Dussault recounted, "The Tuileries, the Carrousel, the former Palais Royal, the Place de la Bastille filled with excited crowds.
People were complaining that such a serious denunciation had been
taken so lightly … Some went so far as to say that they would find
a way to force the Convention to deal with the matter."

Battle lines were drawn. Throughout the Year III, the Thermidorians and the Montagnards would vie for the votes of the undecided centrists, while their supporters – the jeunesse dorée, on the
one hand, and the sans-culottes, on the other – fought in the streets.

THE SOLDIER OF THE REACTION: A PORTRAIT

No sooner had Robespierre fallen than the police were reporting
that the cafés, the boulevards, and most notably the Palais Égalité
were "crawling with muscadins." Like all street militias, the musca-

dins had their uniform, described by the Goncourt brothers in a famous and oft-plagiarized passage. Contemporary prints, such as those of Bosio, Isabey and, in particular, Carle Vernet depict them dressed bizarrely in tight-fitting, bottle-green or "dung-coloured" coats, with seventeen pearl buttons in memory of the orphan of the Temple, Louis XVII. On a powdered wig – the hair for which was said to have come from the guillotine victims of the Year II – sits a half-moon cocked hat, posed precariously at a rakish angle. The face emerges from a cornet-shaped, rust-bespeckled piece of muslin called a *cravate écrouélique* (scrofula cravat). Then there are the black-velvet collar, evoking the death of the king, the enormous triangular lapels, the square-cut tails, the tight breeches fastened below the knee in a cascade of ribbons, giving the impression of bandy legs, the chiné stockings, and the open, low-fronted shoes. A huge, insolent monocle attests to the certificate of short-sightedness provided by some obliging doctor. The delicate, feminine hand, whitened with almond paste, holds a weighted stick, a "nasty bit of work." Take a good look at this ridiculous puppet. Try to imagine him in a cloud of musk, prancing about in rapture, repeating in a faint voice, *"Ma pa'ole d'honneu', c'est ho'ible!"* ("Upon my word! How appalling!" said in an affected manner of speech in which the r's are omitted.) There you have a faithful picture of the muscadin. A society soldier? No doubt. But at four against one, they often had the upper hand over the *"te'o'istes."*

The female counterparts of the muscadins were the merveilleuses. Despite their name, they were no *merveilles*. In public they appeared scantily dressed in gauze sheaths, which prompted the remark that the Reign of Terror had given way to "the reign of the gauzy nudes." According to the memorialist Georges Duval, some of them pushed their fondness for the ancient style of dress so far that they would not have had to shed very much to look like the Venus de' Medici. This was in Brumaire, Year III, and female fashion was making a comeback. Modish women took to wearing artistically braided blond wigs. "Women of the lower classes ridicule them," wrote an observer, "and reach out to dishevel their perukes."

Blond wigs and black collars. Picard and Devienne may well have used these extravagant styles as the subject of an operetta, but they amounted much more to a political statement than to simple whims of fashion, as Lebois noted in *L'Ami du peuple*: "The superficial man sees nothing more in this bizarre metamorphosis than the capricious tastes of fashion. The philosopher, in contrast, attributes it to a variety of moral, political, and revolutionary causes." Audouin's

Journal universel commented that "without anyone's realizing it, the vigorous style of the republic is giving way to the syrupy style of the monarchy."

Following standard historiography, the hypothesis can be advanced that, with the exception of a few stray offspring of the nobility, the muscadins were recruited among absentee conscripts, deserters and shirkers from military service, the sons of the bourgeoisie, and, chiefly, men of letters (journalists, poets, and writers of vaudeville), legal officials (clerks of notaries, solicitors, and attorneys), the theatrical community (actors and actresses, conjurers, singers, musicians, and dancers), shop employees (shopkeepers' assistants, clerks, and small merchants), bank employees (brokers, money handlers, stockjobbers, and bank clerks), and government employees (office clerks and other employees, and civil servants). All in all, it was a heterogeneous coalition of social groups, though predominantly bourgeois and united in hatred of the régime of the Year II and in rancour against the Jacobins.

In the final analysis, this deep-seated enmity was the raison d'être of the jeunesse dorée as a social phenomenon: it came into being to fight and crush the popular movement – allegedly the Jacobins – and would virtually disappear with it, after the Prairial insurrection. From this perspective, the young man of the jeunesse dorée appears to be the social antithesis of the militant Parisian sans-culotte. It was in this sense that he was defined by his dress, which was practically a uniform. For instance, Duval writes of the jeunesse dorée that it was not in fact gilded at all, but that it had been given this name because its manners and cleanliness contrasted sharply with "the vulgar ways of the Jacobins and the official slovenliness of their garb." Hyde de Neuville substantiates this observation when he speaks of the muscadins' elegant dress being a form of protest "against the cynical grubbiness that had been affected by the terrorists." In *Le Souper des Jacobins*, a play by Armand Charlemagne, a recently discharged prisoner has the following lines:

Je mettais de la poudre et mon linge était fin
Et mon écrou porta que j'étais Muscadin
On sait qu'il n'en fallait alors pas davantage
Pour aller en charette ou tout au moins en cage

(I put on powder and my finest clothes
And was committed to prison as a muscadin.

That was all it took then to be thrown
In the tumbrel or at least behind bars.)

There is evidence in support of the above thesis in a number of contemporary sources. Standard historiography portrays the jeunes gens as young absentee conscripts from the Parisian bourgeoisie who had been illegally shuffled into safe posts in government administration. Duval, himself a gilded youth, is often quoted on this point: "People pretended not to notice that we were all, or nearly all, absentee conscripts; they thought that we would better serve the public good in the streets of Paris than in the armies of the Sambre and Meuse, the Rhine and Moselle, or the Eastern Pyrenees, and anyone who suggested sending us to patrol the borders would have been very badly received, I assure you."

While everything written by Duval in his *Souvenirs thermidoriens* should be treated warily, this particular statement is corroborated by several different sources. In September of 1793, Dartigoeyte, the people's representative assigned to Gers, had a serious problem with groups of youths aged eighteen to twenty-five who travelled from town to town to escape conscription. In a letter of 12 September, he informed the Committee of Public Safety of a decree he had enacted "concerning the young muscadins who roam about the country to avoid conscription," a decree applauded by the Committee, which in its reply deplored the fact that "in the defence of such a worthy cause as ours, we are forced to employ such contemptible beings as these muscadins."

Similarly, on 27 Floréal, Year 11, the people's representative Bô, on assignment in Lot, advised the Committee of Public Safety of the measures he had taken against "some muscadins who take great pride in having escaped the conscription of last 23 August on account of their age." And on 5 Thermidor, Year 11, Garnier de Xanthes, the representative sent to Bec d'Ambès, announced to the Committee a decree he had enacted against "*muscadinage* and idleness" which required all men called up under the first conscription to register within three days at army headquarters. This measure was designed to deal with "cold, indifferent men who wish to forgo the honour of sharing the laurels of our gallant soldiers" and to make sure that "*messieurs les muscadins* no longer strut about in public, openly defying the law on conscription that calls them to defend our borders." This confirms the remarks of Sébastien Mercier, who saw in the muscadins "a breed of men preoccupied with appearing elegant or absurd and who are transformed into women by the sound of a drum."

Duval writes further that all the young men from the "upper classes of Parisian society" who had suffered in various ways from the Revolution were drawn to the jeunesse dorée. He explains that this took in all the clerks of notaries, solicitors, and auctioneers, virtually all the shop assistants – in short, everyone who belonged to the "honourable bourgeoisie." This observation is corroborated by the memorialist C.-F. Beaulieu, who saw in the muscadins "all the young men who had received some schooling or did not have callused hands"; by Fréron's adjutant, Louis Jullian, who said he was defending the cause "of all property-holders, all honest folk"; by the Montagnard Choudieu, in whose view the muscadins were young men who claimed to be victims of the Terror; and even by a certain Legrand, a former brigadier general, who in a pamphlet against *"les incroyables et les hommes à parole d'honneur"* asked, "And who are these incroyables? None other than our shop assistants whom we used to call *courtauds de boutiques* or *saute-ruisseau.*" While the most common names were jeunesse dorée and muscadins, the youths were also known by epithets such as *collets noirs* (black collars), *collets verts* (green collars), *incroyables* (incredibles), *cadenettes* (braids that hang in front of the ears), *oreilles de chien* (literally, "dog's ears" meaning earlocks), *chouans* (royalist insurgents active in some provinces), *compagnie de Jésus* (Society of Jesus), *million doré* (gilded million), *réveilleurs* (rabble-rousers), *messieurs à bâtons* (gentlemen with sticks), *Royale Cravate* (Royal Cravat), *Royale Anarchie* (Royal Anarchy), *parole d'honneur* (word of honour), *Fréronistes* (Fréronists), *jeunesse fréronnière* (Fréronist youth), and *armée de Fréron* (Fréron's Army).

In total, the jeunesse dorée could mobilize perhaps some two to three thousand young men. Their rallying point was the Café de Chartres or des Canonniers, at the Palais Royal. Jullian wrote, "This was where we gathered to tell one another what we had learnt of the designs of the common enemy, discuss our plans and concerns, draw up our strategies. This was where we set out from whenever we had something major to undertake. This was the daily meeting place of muscadins from all over Paris." Supposedly, a network had even been organized among the jeunesse dorée for alerting agents spread throughout the city in the event of an emergency, but such assertions are impossible to verify.

With two or three thousand men, the jeunesse dorée constituted a large enough force that the Convention could count on it for protection – at least in the first few months of the Reaction – and set it against the Jacobins, if necessary. Indeed, until the Jacobin Club was closed, the jeunes gens proved to be very devoted supporters of the

Committee of General Security, which, instead of putting a stop to their disorderly gatherings at the Palais Royal and the Tuileries, in cafés, theatres, and other public places, encouraged them surreptitiously. In essence, the Thermidorians had enlisted the jeunesse dorée and given it its leaders: Louis Jullian and Alexandre Méchin, the journalists Martainville and Isidore Langlois, the actors Elléviou and Gavaudan, and others. Duval goes so far as to claim that the youths were given regular arms drills in the courtyard of the Louvre and at the Tuileries. Later, in Prairial, the Committees would arm the youths and send them to attack the faubourgs. It thus becomes clear that until about Brumaire, Year III, the jeunesse dorée served as the Committee of General Security's private militia and its "executive power" against the Jacobins. Subsequently, roles would switch, and the jeunesse dorée would become the driving force of the Reaction, imposing on the Committee of General Security and the Convention a policy of revenge and provocation that would lead to the insurrections of Germinal and Prairial.

WINNING OVER PUBLIC OPINION

In *After Robespierre: The Thermidorian Reaction*, Albert Mathiez gives a brilliant account of the degree to which, around mid-Fructidor, the political future of Tallien and Fréron hung in the balance. Both men were included in the motion condemning Lecointre for his denunciation of 12 Fructidor, and as a result all three were struck from the rolls of the Jacobin Club. Billaud-Varennes threatened that they would soon have to answer for the fortunes they had amassed during their proconsulship. The Thermidorians, however, thanks chiefly to the jeunesse dorée, were able to reverse this very critical political situation and win over public opinion in just a few weeks. Their goal was to secure support for their reactionary policies and, at the same time, ensure their own personal safety, which had been in considerable danger.

The rise of the Thermidorians began with an intensely bitter debate over freedom of the press. With the fortune of Thérésia Cabarrus, the émigré widow and banker's daughter, at their disposal, the Thermidorians wanted to use the press to defend themselves and attack their opponents. Since 15 Thermidor, Dussault had been appealing for a free press in the *Correspondance politique*, and at the Jacobin Club Tallien called for "freedom of the press or death!" If the Jacobins were opposed to such freedom, it was because they were afraid of being unmasked, he argued. The Montagnard representative Caraffe replied that freedom of the press already existed for patriots, and that consequently it could be demanded only for aristocrats. That was beside the point, the Thermidorians answered: if the royalists took advantage of freedom of the press, they would be all the more quickly discovered, whence the paradox that the Jacobins were apparently endeavouring to conceal the royalists!

In the Convention on 9 Fructidor, Fréron made the curious claim "that there was nothing more fatal to anarchy than the right to say and write anything," and proposed a decree guaranteeing unrestricted freedom of the press. His motion was rejected after Amar, the people's representative from Isère, quite rightly pointed out that it would legalize royalist propaganda. But, in fact, a free press already existed. On the same day that Fréron's motion was rejected, a pamphlet appeared with the humorous title *La Queue de Robespierre* (Robespierre's Tail – that is, his head had been cut off but his tail [his followers] was still wagging) penned by Méhée de La Touche, which denounced the Montagnards for continuing the work of the "tyrant." Some seventy thousand copies of the tract were printed and distributed throughout the country within a week. It was such a success that an avalanche of imitations were published in its wake, all attacking the Montagnards: *Défends ta queue!* (Defend Your Tail!), *La Queue de Robespierre écorchée* (The Flaying of Robespierre's Tail), *Les Anneaux de la queue* (The Rings of the Tail), *Coupez-moi la queue!* (Cut Off My Tail!), *Renvoyez-moi ma queue!* (Give Back My Tail!), *La Tête à la queue ou première lettre de Robespierre à ses continuateurs* (The Head at the Tail, or Robespierre's First Letter to His Disciples), *La Grande Queue de Barère* (Barère's Big Tail), and so on.

Once the trend had started, Paris was inundated by a deluge of caustic pamphlets, a storm of stinging invective against "the knights of the order of the guillotine, the lovers of mass drownings, and the killers à la lyonnaise." Each day brought a new title, and Tourneux noted more than a hundred. The titles are eloquent in themselves: *Les Jacobins démasqués* (The Jacobins Unmasked), *Les Jacobins convaincus d'imposture* (The Jacobins Guilty of Deception), *Le Fin Mot des Jacobins* (The Truth about the Jacobins), *Les Jacobins à l'eau* (The Jacobins Are All Washed Up), *Le Secret des Jacobins* (The Jacobins' Secret), *L'Agonie des Jacobins* (The Jacobins in Their Death Throes), *Le Contrepoison des Jacobins* (The Jacobins' Antidote), *Les Jacobins sont f... et la France est sauvée* (The Jacobins Are F... and France is Saved), *L'Enterrement des Jacobins* (The Burial of the Jacobins), *Encore les Jacobins, peuple qu'en veux-tu faire?* (The Jacobins Again: What Is to Be Done with Them?), and *Pendant que la bête est dans le piège, il faut l'assommer* (While the Beast is in the Trap, Hit it on the Head).

The tracts contain nothing but broad denunciations. The Jacobins are accused of sharpening their daggers in silence, of deceiving and oppressing the people, of opposing freedom of the press for fear of being unmasked, of wishing a return of the Terror, of having squandered the public wealth, of having cut the throats of over a million people, of distributing white cockades, of being in league with the Jesuits [sic], of having destroyed commerce, of having formed a new aristocracy, of monopolizing jobs, of being the workshop of crime, and above all of attempting to vie with the National Convention. However, since the reader was probably already won over, the content was less important than the style, which consisted of a stream of abuse, calls for murder, and melodramatic lamentations over the September massacres. "The Jacobins must be exterminated unless we want our sons to spit on our graves," Richer-Sérizy asserted. "Hang the Jacobins! String up the rogues!" exclaimed Bouverot. *La Grande Détresse des Jacobins qui n'ont plus le sol* (The Great Distress of the Jacobins Who Have Not a Sou) lashes out at the "tigrocractic government of the infamous head-lopping brothers," while an alleged catalogue of the main works published by the Jacobin Club lists titles such as *Apologie de la Saint-Barthélémy* (Apologia for the St. Bartholomew's Day Massacre), *Inconvénients des réverbères pour les vrais patriotes* (On the Drawbacks of Lampposts for True Patriots), *De L'Utilité des conspirations imaginaires pour cacher les véritables* (On the Use of Imaginary Plots to Conceal Real Ones), *Du Parti qu'on peut tirer des lettres anonymes en matière politique* (On the Political Advantages to Be Derived from Anonymous Letters), *Calcul de la quantité de boue dont on peut être couvert sans perdre la respiration* (Calculation of the Amount of Mud with Which One May Be Covered without Losing One's Breath), and *Les Mille et une Horreurs imaginées pour faire haïr la Révolution par une société de gens de corde* (The Thousand and One Horrors Devised by a Club of Rope Enthusiasts to Make People Detest the Revolution). The author of a play, *Le Club infernal*, sets the story at the Club, describing the scene as follows: "The room is lit by votive candles placed in the skulls of forty-five Farmers General, which shed light redder than the blood of a virgin. At the back, Maximilien Robespierre sits limply on a glowing three-legged stool, holding his chin in one hand, and, with a dagger in the other, traces a vast plan for a universal cemetery."

While most of these pamphlets were published anonymously, a number of them were written by known muscadins, such as the one by Richer-Sérizy cited above and those by Martainville, which are extremely violent in tone. *Les Jacobins hors la loi* (Outlaw the Jacobins) is an example: people found peddling it were put under arrest; the bookseller Maret, of the Palais Égalité, was detained, but Fréron, in a revealing move, had him freed immediately. Martainville's lampoon *Donnez-nous leurs têtes ou prenez les nôtres!* (Off with Their Heads or Off with Ours!) calls for the heads of the "tiger" Billaud, the "sepulchral" Collot, the "dull and disgusting" Barère, and the "aquatic" Carrier, whose only act of kindness his whole life had been to the fish in the Loire. Another text by Martainville, *Les Galbanons de Bicêtre* (The Cells of Bicêtre [a prison hospital for the insane]), parodies a session of the Electroral Club in which no one wishes to take the floor and the debates are obscure because of poor lighting. Other works by this author pen are the twelve issues of the *Journal des rieurs* (The Journal of Those Who Laugh), which is not always funny, and the lampoon *Nous mourons de faim, le peuple est las, il faut que ça finisse!* (We Are Dying of Hunger, the People Are Weary, This Must Stop!), written in a rather plebeian style; those caught peddling the latter tract likewise risked arrest. Evidence from two other sources also suggests that the muscadins were involved in the lampooing: first, an address to the popular societies by the Jacobins on the third *jour sans-culottide* which claimed that "these despicable lampoons" were the work of recently released suspects and originated in courtesans' boudoirs, theatre lobbies, and the Palais Royal; second, an article in *Le Journal de la Montagne* which saw in the Jacobins' detractors "a pack of young men who have managed to secure requisitions for posts in governement administration."

The pamphlets seem to have had a considerable impact on public opinion. On 29 Fructidor, Duhem said that he had been pleased to see good citizens trampling on lampoons that were being distributed for free. "I witnessed sans-culottes refuting the muscadins and women responding to their subtle arguments," he added. But this must have been an exceptional case of indoctrination, for it contrasts sharply with the Jacobins' many protests against "the pamphleteers' too strident trumpets," against "a host of thoroughly disgusting counter-revolutionary pamphlets that are poisoning public opinion," against the "debasement" of prevailing sentiment. At the Jacobin Club itself, members complained that in the public squares and around the Convention the aristocrats were gaining the upper hand and that "by some strange turn of events" patriots were now obliged to whisper to one another or to remain silent.

Like the lampoonists, the periodical press had also embarked on a campaign to influence opinion. On 25 Fructidor, Fréron launched *L'Orateur du Peuple* with tremendous success; on 1 Brumaire, Tallien founded *L'Ami des citoyens*, which was to be written by Méhée de La Touche. From the memoirs of Beaulieu and Lacretelle, we know that the writers of the main newspapers had made it a practice, perhaps at the instigation of the Fréronists on the Committee of General Security, to meet regularly at a restaurant on the Place du Louvre to discuss the political issues of the day and come to some agreement on "opinions that ought to be disseminated to the general public" on specific matters. "A good many ideas that took root in the minds of numerous people in Europe had no other source," says C.-F. Beaulieu. Included in this coterie of journalists were the younger Lacretelle, who admitted to being a member of the jeunesse dorée; Charles His, whom we shall find alongside the muscadins in the brawls against Louvet in Messidor, Year III; Dussault, the editor of Fréron's *L'Orateur du Peuple*; and Richer-Sérizy, the editor of *L'Accusateur public*, perhaps the most virulently anti-Jacobin of all the papers.

In contrast to the weakened, divided leftist press, this rightist press mounted its campaign in an orderly, disciplined manner, with a well-defined goal. As Lacretelle and Beaulieu explain, the aim was to persuade the Convention to go back on the social and political reforms of the Year II. To avoid creating any panic in turning back the clock, it was agreed that the revolutionary laws would be attacked only one at a time and that the faults of repentant terrorists like Tallien and Fréron would be glossed over, but that no mercy would be shown to unregenerate opponents such as Barère, Billaud-Varennes, Collot-d'Herbois, and Vadier.

Both the lampoonists and the journalists of the periodical press were given a golden opportunity with the trial of the ninety-four of Nantes, from which they were able to wring two more trials, that of the Nantes revolutionary committee and that of the representative Jean-Baptiste Carrier. These trials would tip the scales of public opinion in favour of the Thermidorians and discredit the Jacobin Club once and for all. The Club would survive for a few more weeks until the jeunesse dorée raided its meeting hall, using their cudgels to disperse the members, and then convinced the Convention to decree the closure of the Club.

The trial of the ninety-four, who had been arrested by Carrier on the charge of opposition to revolutionary centralism – or, the Thermidorians said, because they were muscadins – and referred to the Paris Revolutionary Tribunal, began on 22 Fructidor. The principal accused, Phélippe, known as Tronjolly, subpoenaed as witnesses the members of the Nantes revolutionary committee, who had also been arrested. He charged that they were guilty of summary executions and of mass drownings in the Loire; they acknowledged these acts but placed the responsibility for them on Carrier. This meant that there were three trials – that of the ninety-four, that

of the Nantes revolutionary committee, and that of Carrier – each revealing ghastly atrocities, which were given wide coverage in the
anti-Jacobin press throughout France. The trial of the ninety-four
was over within a week, resulting in the triumphant acquittal of the
accused, and that of the Nantes revolutionary committee opened on
26 Vendémiaire. A highly excited audience heard horror stories
from the more than 140 witnesses who appeared before the court.
Tronjolly testified that Carrier had ordered over twenty-three mass
drownings in the Loire using vessels with intake valves; in one such
"vertical deportation," some six hundred children had been murdered. Bouvier testified that "republican weddings" had been celebrated by tying young men and women together nude and pitching
them into the Loire. Laënnec testified that "sabrings" had occurred
in the Place du Département and that it had taken three hundred
men six weeks to bury all the dead. Thomas testified that some
forty new-born babies had been drowned in tubs of excrement.
Delamarre testified that after a group of women had been shot by a
firing squad their bodies had been piled into a heap which, in a gro-
tesque joke, had been called "a mountain." Caron testified that, as
an initiation rite, the soldiers of the Marat Company had had to
drink a glass of blood. Forget testified that General Duquesnoy
had proclaimed himself "the butcher of the Convention." Tabouret
testified, "the unfortunate wretches who were taken to be drowned would stick their arms out of the boats' scuttles to beg for
mercy, but the only response they received was to have their arms
chopped off." Moutier testified that he had heard Carrier declare,
in a lower-class quarter of Nantes, that there was no alternative
but to play *boules* with the heads of the city's populace. After the
recounting of such abominable crimes, it was inevitable that Carrier
should appear in his turn before the Revolutionary Tribunal. At each
sitting, an audience of Thermidorians clamoured for him by chant-
ing his name. On 8 Brumaire, the Convention set up a twenty-one-
member commission to look into Carrier's conduct and submit a
report.

Meanwhile, the pamphlet war continued to rage. One tract, entitled *Places à louer pour voir passer Carrier le jour qu'il ira à la guillotine*
(Places to Rent to See Carrier on His Way to the Guillotine), provided the plan for an elaborate ceremonial dinner for the occasion,
for which Barère would sauté gudgeons à la carmagnole and cook
up a fricassee à la nantaise *avec sauce acerbe*, while Collot-d'Herbois
would prepare mincemeat à la lyonnaise, and Billaud-Varennes
smotherings, brainings, and pulps à la septembrise. Another tract,
Le Testament de Carrier (Carrier's Will), portrayed him as the great ad-

ministrator of patriotic baths, commissioner of oaths for celebrating republican weddings, professor of hydrography, and so on. The pamphleteer Ange Pitou had an idea for a spectacular play to be called *La Mort du genre humain* (The Death of the Human Race) – a six-act tragedy with 450 scenes, all finishing in disaster and bloodshed. The main actors never appeared more than once. The set was a public square delimited by two rows of four-bladed guillotines. On one side, vessels with intake valves drifted along the Seine, while centre stage stood a statue of Liberty and an enormous cup bearing the inscription "Parisians, you will all drink from this cup!"

But this was in a humorous vein when compared with the theories of the journalist Gracchus Babeuf, who claimed in all seriousness that the old Committee of Public Safety, on Carrier's recommendation, had implemented a policy of depopulation designed to reduce the number of inhabitants to match available food supplies. Once this was accepted, everything became clear: the insurrection in the Vendée, the war against Europe, the proscriptions, the guillotinings, the shootings, the drownings, the seizures, the maximum law, the conscription – all were the elements of a vast plan of extermination aimed at reducing the total population.

Not just Carrier but the old Committee of Public Safety, the Jacobins, and all the revolutionaries of the Year II were being attacked. Thus, as early as the second *jour sans-culottide*, Year II, *Le Messager du Soir* reported that the Nantes affair had dealt the Jacobins "a terrible blow in public opinion," so that, according to Levasseur, they came to be regarded as madmen and hooligans, if not villains, even by some people who had supported them just a short time before. From that point on, it was only a matter of weeks before the Jacobin Club was disbanded.

THE CLOSURE OF THE JACOBIN CLUB

The hawking of anti-Carrier and anti-Jacobin pamphlets stirred up trouble in public places: on the second *jour sans-culottide*, the first of a long series of street fights broke out in the gardens of the Palais Égalité between supporters of the Jacobin Club and a group of jeunes gens. A fifteen-year-old newspaper vendor, Jean-Louis Brocquin, who hawked Fréron's *L'Orateur du Peuple* and anti-Jacobin tracts, was set upon by what *Le Messager du Soir* referred to as "a mob of revolutionaries armed with sabres and sticks" and taken to the Committee of General Security with two other young men: Nicolas-Prosper Dagaud, a clerk at the post office in the rue

Montmartre, and Jacques-Marie Laporte, a grocer's assistant in the rue St Denis. This sparked wild agitation in the gardens. The jeunes gens, strengthened by reinforcements from the neighbouring cafés, hounded the Jacobins until a detachment of guards arrived and, "with much difficulty," the police reported, managed to restore order.

The following day at the Jacobin Club, the people's representative Lanot told how, between eight and nine o'clock in the evening, at the Palais Égalité, he had got into a row with a "giant of a man whose voice was comparable with his size" – it might have been the street agitator Saint-Huruge – and who in a group of eighty or so people was making derogatory remarks about the Jacobins. Quick as a flash, Lanot had found himself surrounded by some six hundred young men and had to be rescued by the police commissioner, who led him off to the Committee of General Security. Apprehended with him was "a little cravated muscadin, no higher than my chin," who hawked *À bas les Jacobins!* He was twenty years old, had deserted from the Northern Army, and claimed he was the protégé of a deputy. Also at the Jacobin Club, the gunner captain of the Tuileries Section related how, at around ten o'clock the previous day, at the Café de l'Union, he had arrested the brother of the Abbé Royou, who had said exultantly that a Jacobin had just been beaten up at the Palais Égalité, and had added that anyone entering the Club could be sure, even blindfolded, of bumping into a rogue, an assassin, or a counter-revolutionary. The following day, the people's representative Merlin de Thionville had the man released – perhaps in response to pressure from Fréron, who happened to be his cousin – along with the little cravated muscadin.

Also on that day, the affair was taken up in the Convention, where Garnier de Saintes denounced the "insolent individuals" who had been acting arrogantly over the last week and who, the day before, had affronted the patriots at the Palais Égalité – men who thought nothing of paying fifty livres per person for a meal, he added. Bourdon de l'Oise agreed that some of those hawking *Vive la Convention!* were muscadins – that is, "men who, though in perfectly good health, have quit the army under pretence of being ill and who would do better to return to their posts ... However," he went on, "among the hawkers I have also seen men ruined by vice, soldiers of Robespierre who have lined their pockets with the sums he lavished and soiled their hands with the blood he spilt. I repeat what I have already said to the Committee: the hawkers of both sides must be restrained."

This appeal reflected the Assembly's resolve to defend the freedom it had recently won from "the tyrant" and to resist pressure from both the left and the right. "Neither anarchy nor monarchy," was the rallying cry. Merlin de Douai, on behalf of the Committee of General Security, the Committee of Public Safety, and the Military Committee, immediately had a decree passed enjoining all citizens who had not been in Paris before 1 Messidor, Year II, to leave the city; the decree was aimed at both the deserters from the Northern and Eastern armies and the patriots who had fled to Paris to escape the incipient reactionary movement in the departments. On the following day, the fourth *jour sans-culottide*, a group from Marseille bade farewell to the Jacobin Club, and *Le Courrier républicain* of the fifth *jour sans-culottide* noted that it had already become rare in public places to see these "mustachioed figures with their huge sticks, these barbarous henchmen of the last tyrant." Yet while the patriots had to leave the capital, thus depriving the Jacobins of vital support, the muscadins managed to find the means to stay, thanks to the complicity of the Fréronists on the Committee of General Security, who were entitled under a provision of the decree to conscript citizens "for reasons of acknowledged utility or justice." On 16 Brumaire, the police reported seeing large numbers of young men from the first conscription in the cafés, most of them in uniform and all carrying requisitions from the Committees for jobs in arms workshops; the indignant police agent noted that "their hands looked more like those of painters of miniatures than those of smiths or metalworkers." In the end, the decree of the fourth *jour sans-culottide* was, as the representative Rovère de Fontville noted in a letter, a "decisive blow" against the terrorists. Thereafter, the muscadins, with their numbers increasing daily in the streets of the capital, would constantly gain ground at the expense of the terrorists, until by Brumaire, Year III, it had become dangerous to declare oneself publicly to be on the side of the Jacobins. For them, this was the beginning of the end.

With its membership cut to six hundred, the Club found itself in a most ambiguous situation. It persisted in analysing where it had made its mistakes and in repudiating the support it had given to Robespierre on 9 Thermidor: "A session that was not in keeping with the Club's tradition," said Loys, "and that ought to be struck from its records for all time." Moreover, the members were unable to agree on any political program other than a return to the Terror. All they could do, wrote Lacretelle, was bewail the ruins of the scaffold. The Club spoke of "putting a new edge on the national axe," of retapping the old energy of the Revolution; on 15 Fructidor, the representative Joseph Fouché denounced "the false, hypocritical sensitivity" that reigned, and proclaimed the need to re-establish the Terror. For most Parisians, who felt sick at any mention of the scaffold, such prospects were far from exhilarating, and the Club began to show signs of weakness. Its finances were in a disastrous state, and on 11 Fructidor the correspondence committee had to be reorganized because three hundred letters from affiliated societies had not been answered. The session of 9 Brumaire was closed at nine o'clock for lack of work; the public galleries were almost empty. On the eleventh, the speaker's rostrum remained vacant for a few moments because no one wished to take the floor. Finally, under the hail of abuse from the Thermidorian press, which called them, by turns, *robespierrots*, *jacobites*, *jacobêtes*, *jacoquins*, and sundry other names, and accused them of a thousand and one atrocities, the club members began to lose patience. On 23 Fructidor, Duhem had made an unfortunate remark about the centrist representatives, whom he called "the toads of the 'Marsh'"; on 13 Brumaire, Billaud-Varennes asserted threateningly, "A slumbering lion may look dead. But when it wakes, it exterminates all its enemies." These statements left the reactionaries with the impression that the Club wished to save Carrier and that the only way to thwart the plot was forceful action to bring about the Club's closure.

On the evening of 19 Brumaire, young men armed with sticks and sabres gathered in the vicinity of the Palais Égalité and St Roch Church, from where they were led by "the Orator of the Faubourg Antoine," Gonchon, and Saint-Huruge to attack the Jacobins at their meeting hall in the rue Honoré. They numbered a hundred or so, some of them as young as seventeen. Rumours of the raid had been circulating for a few days, but the club members had not given them any credence. The citizen François Queval, of the Tuileries Section, told of a hail of stones clattering against the casement windows and panic breaking out in the galleries.

I went outside to see what was happening. There I saw a large number of citizens armed with sticks, stones, and bottles. Leading this band of rogues was a fellow by the name of Cabacet, a wine merchant in the rue Nicaise, where it joins the rue de Chartres. In one hand he was holding a bottle, and in the other a quarry stone. He was beside himself with rage. He entered the Club by the door that opens onto the rue Honoré, asking how he would get upstairs to clobber the Jacobins, and yelling that they were villains, rogues who deserved to have their throats cut.

According to the citizen Guéret, of the Amis de la Patrie Section, there was a mad panic inside the building. The women in the galleries were screaming "They're trying to kill us! They'll beat us to death!" He went on: "We were all terrified. We thought the only way to save our skins was to run for it." A woman by the name of Candry, from Nantes, who tried to flee after seeing a man "covered in blood," found herself cornered in a cul-de-sac by two hundred men armed with sticks who "threatened to lift up her skirt and whip her." "Ah! You little hussy!" one of them yelled at her. "I'm from Nantes, too. I know you." All of this was accompanied by a few good kicks in the behind. The citizen Massart found himself trapped at the door of the Club, and his assailants struck him on the head and shoulders with their sabres.

Meanwhile, the Committee of General Security, the Committee of Public Safety, and the Military Committee had met and were being kept abreast of developments by reports from the army. However, they did not take steps to intervene until late, after the Jacobins had already been dispersed.

On the morrow, the police reported that "people are extremely worked up, both for and against the Jacobins." A stormy session was held in the Convention. Duhem fulminated against the agitators of the Palais Royal and the rue Vivienne and criticized the Committee of General Security for having released the assailants who had been brought before it. The people's representative Duroy told how, at around eight o'clock, near the Convention, he had run into a woman who was returning from the Jacobin Club "in tears, dishevelled, and her head covered in blood." He immediately went to the Club, where he saw thirty or so "rogues from the Palais Royal who had momentarily ventured away from their den of iniquity" to sling mud at the Jacobins who were leaving the Club and to whip the women who came out. The patrols on the scene simply stood by and watched. If this type of thing was allowed to happen, there was no more police, no more government, he concluded.

No more police, no more government: the people's representative Jean-François Rewbell, who had chaired the meeting of the three Committees the day before, had to assume responsibility. He explained that a group of Jacobins meeting at the Tuileries had incurred the wrath of the populace by shouting "Down with the Convention!" They had been chased to the Club, where they had found themselves besieged. Upon receiving word of what was happening, members of the Committees had rushed to the scene. There they saw Jacobins attacking innocent passers-by with sticks and pushing their bloodied victims into the hall of the Club. Rewbell finished his speech by calling for the closure *sine die* of the Club and, in a stupendously audacious move, the passage of legislation against the slanderers! The motion was referred to the Committees for further study.

On the evening of the twentieth, there was another clash at the Jacobin Club. The secondhand dealer Jolly was seized and dragged into the meeting hall, where he was kicked repeatedly, while women who left the hall were struck and insulted.

On the following day, 21 Brumaire, a delegation from the Amis de la Patrie Section went to the Convention to request enforcement of the law of 25 July 1793, which made disturbing popular societies a crime punishable by death. In spite of stormy speeches by Duhem, the proposal was sent to the Committees for study, and the Assembly refused to give it an honourable mention or insert it in the Bulletin. This amounted to giving the green light to the jeunes gens.

That very evening the youth gathered at the Palais Royal "in greater numbers than usual," wrote Duval, "because of the rumour that the Jacobins were arming themselves for an attack on the Convention that evening and intended to cut the throats of its members who wanted to do away with the Reign of Terror." Fréron was present, and Duval claims to have noted down what he said. The remarks are, in any case, quite in keeping with the logic of the situation: "The Jacobins are discussing whether to cut our throats in the street or in our homes. Let us act while there is still time! Let us close ranks! Let us surprise the beast in its den and render it forever incapable of doing us any harm. Brave young men, let us march!"

The small troop recruited youths idling in the gardens, under the arcades, and in the nearby cafés, and headed for the Jacobin Club to shouts of "Long live the Convention!" and "Down with the Jacobins!" From the original three hundred at the Palais Royal, their numbers had swollen to two thousand by the time they entered the courtyard of the Club. "We were joined by all the worthy young men of Paris who realized the importance of maintaining order [sic]," wrote Jullian, Fréron's right-hand man, who had placed himself at the head of the expedition.

At the Club, the session had opened with the reading of the law guaranteeing popular societies. Then a debate had begun on the attack and the beatings that had taken place two days before. One club member was complaining of having been dragged out into the street when suddenly shouts were heard from the courtyard: the jeunes gens were demanding that the doors be opened. It was eight o'clock. The porter of one of the galleries in the Jacobins' meeting hall, a woman by the name of Lecoq, later recounted that five or six citizens came up to her from inside the hall and ordered her to open the door. When she refused, they set upon her, one of them striking her in the face, another giving her a kick, while a third "hurled his stick at her head with such force that her right eye was injured, to judge by the blackness of the ring around her eye," noted the police commissioner who took her statement, "and she hands over as evidence the said whitewood stick measuring two feet in length." Thereupon the club members rushed to the exit, where a fierce battle began, the two sides laying into each other with cudgels. "Twenty or so of them charged out of the hall," declared one Rambouillet, from the Gravilliers Section. "They started beating me with canes and sticks ... They dragged me inside, where they called me the Marquis de Guise because my hair was powdered. They also accused me of being an absentee from the first conscription."

The club members finally managed to close the door from inside, but the youths started climbing in through the windows, so that the Jacobins had no choice but to flee, leaving behind their coats and red caps. In the rue Honoré, they were forced to run a gauntlet of youths, who showered them with spittle. A slap sent the president's hat flying into the filth of the gutter, and as he bent over to pick it up, he was given a kick in the behind. As for the women who sought to escape by the side doors, Martainville had them subjected to a punishment supposedly designed to avenge the good sisters of L'Hôtel Dieu who had been whipped by the women of the Halle on 7 April 1791 and about whom so many light-hearted songs had been written. This time, assured Duval, "the flagellation was very gentle and only the ladies' modesty was made to suffer." But Lacretelle spoke "of excesses of an abject nature, of ignominious punishment"; Beaulieu, of such vile treatment that the women who were subjected to it no longer dared venture out in their neighbourhoods and were forced to move elsewhere. A pamphlet on this incident entitled *Les Culs des Jacobines visités par le peuple* (The Bums of Jacobin Women Inspected by the People) tells of the expedition of a "horde of counter-revolutionaries who descended from the Palais Égalité to surround the den of the wretched Jacobin rabble." As terrified club members took to their heels, recounts the author, "vigorous athletic fellows with large hands adroitly took hold of the weeping Jacobin women, and without pity for their virtue, without regard for the chill autumn air, uncovered their bound posteriors." No details are given about what ensued, but the pamphleteer claims that "the moon was shocked and withdrew its light from such an appalling spectacle." "Thus," declared Beaulieu in reference to the incident, "was decided the fate of France and even of Europe, for that was precisely what was at stake."

The Committee of General Security, which according to Duval had taken the initiative for this second expedition against the Jacobins and which had more or less directed it from afar through the help of couriers who reported back to it at regular intervals, decided at one o'clock in the morning to close the Jacobins' meeting hall; at four o'clock, the Butte des Moulins police commissioner went and seized the keys, twelve in all, and put a padlock on the main door opening onto the rue Honoré.

The next day, Laignelot, the Committees' rapporteur, explained to the Convention that they had been forced to give in to the pressure of public opinion. Moreover, the Jacobins were not "really a popular society in the true sense of the term." He continued, "In this Club we have seen men who are scarcely known in the Revolution led by a handful of men only too well known, perhaps, and whose influence it is time to curtail, for it could become harmful to the Republic ... Has any well-ordered government ever survived with two rival powers in its midst? Has there ever been a Republic with two parallel governments?" Thus the question was not one of conspiring against the popular societies but one of stifling a source of discord. The Committees' decision ordering the closure of the Jacobin Club was ratified almost unanimously by the Convention, which had finally resolved, explained Isidore Langlois, a journalist with *Le Messager du Soir*, to march courageously onward "without fretting over a few whipped behinds."

Such was the burlesque ending of the great society that had watched over the Revolution at its most difficult moments. The event was of major significance. The Montagnards had lost their prime means of influencing public opinion. Without this important rallying point, the patriots would henceforth face much harsher and fiercer banishment from public places. Already, on 23 Brumaire, a police report noted "that it suffices to look like a Jacobin to be yelled at, insulted, and even beaten." The story was the same in the provinces, where the affiliated popular societies, now adrift without direction, were powerless to defend themselves against the forces of the Reaction. Yet public opinion was in such disarray that the closure of the Jacobin Club was largely greeted with indifference, if not as a fortunate turn of events that went hand in hand with 9 Thermidor. Babeuf himself, consumed by his struggle against the revolutionary government, saw the closure merely as a joke and hurled sarcastic remarks against the "*Jacobinobande* of Maximilien the Headless" and the "blind patriots" of the Quinze Vingts Section who reportedly gave them refuge. The Thermidorian press filled its pages with off-colour jokes about the wife of the deputy from Martinique, Mme Crassous, who had been particularly roughly handled by the muscadins on the evening of the twenty-first. In *Le Messager du Soir*, Isidore Langlois poked fun at "violent M. Crassous, whose energetic half is said to be in bed, lying in a position contrary to the one she prefers." He assured his readers that she intended to produce "the probative evidence upon which is printed in blood the indecency and cowardliness of the criminals who dared to take the sans-culottes from behind." Fréron spoke of "the bruises on Mme Crassous's derrière being reflected in painful lines on her dear husband's ample visage." The jeunes gens were unrelenting in their attacks against Mme Crassous because she was one of the most assiduous tricoteuses at the Jacobin Club as well as in the Convention, where she could always be counted on to applaud the Mountain. In early Brumaire, Fréron had marked her as a prime target for muscadin violence by proclaiming that in the galleries of the Jacobin Club she performed "the duties of a drum major for all the female battalions that pack them." This explains why the muscadins paid her what might be called their most tangible respects.

CHAPTER TWO

The Political and Social Reaction

21 BRUMAIRE, YEAR III, TO 30 PLUVIÔSE, YEAR III

With the closure of the Jacobin Club, the bourgeoisie had its victory, and from Frimaire to Ventôse it was busy consolidating it. In the sections, the government administration, and public places, harassment of the patriots intensified, while in the salons and the dance halls, where the jeunesse dorée shone, the bourgeoisie was once again enjoying a sumptuous, decadent society life. A new symbolic élite, personifying the latest fashionable values, grew up around Thérésia Cabarrus and the singer Jean-François Garat. On 8 Nivôse, Duhem momentarily checked the progress of the Reaction by revealing to the National Convention the royalist writings of Delacroix, but on the twenty-third, Fréron gave it new impetus with his *Invitation à la jeunesse parisienne*. While Duhem ended up in the Abbaye prison, the jeunes gens turned the fête of 2 Pluviôse, which was supposed to commemorate the death of the last king, into an anti-Jacobin free-for-all. Then, in Pluviôse and Ventôse, the whole panoply of revolutionary symbols of the Year II collapsed. This period was marked by disturbances in the theatres, as terrorist actors were banned and Jacobin plays prohibited; by the removal of Marat's remains from the Panthéon, after the Convention had consecrated his name just a few months earlier; and by the sudden disrepute of republican practices such as the familiar *tu* form of address, and of revolutionary symbols such as the patriotic slogans on building façades and the "liberty cap," an essential part of the sans-culotte costume.

Led by the jeunesse dorée, this symbolic revolution reflected the shift in the social structure whereby the rule of the lower classes was giving way to the reign of the honnêtes gens (decent, middle-class folk). Besides illustrating the depths to which the Assembly, henceforth at the beck and call of the jeunes gens, had sunk, the reactionary thrust imposed on Thermidorian politics by the jeunesse dorée stirred the embers of terrorist agitation, which in turn sparked a bout of repression. The jeunesse dorée's driving role in the Reaction thus became clear: by inciting the sans-culottes to violence,

they triggered, and justified in advance, the reprisals taken against them –
in an inevitable chain reaction that eventually led to the explosion of
Prairial. There are even grounds for wondering whether there ever would
have been a Thermidorian Reaction had it not been for the jeunesse dorée.

SOCIETY LIFE AND ITS LEADING LIGHTS

The Comte de Ségur could not forgive the revolutionaries for having
ruined "his" Paris, or, as he put it, "for having transformed the capital of pleasure into a centre of bickering and boredom." In any case,
Thermidor righted the wrong he was done. Once people had "regained their senses," they joined the Abbé Sièyes in congratulating
themselves on having lived through the Terror. With the Republic's
armies victorious, the Vendée under control – or almost – and the
"tyrant" no more, it became clear that the time of great peril was
over. In reaction to republican austerity and the suffocating dictatorship of virtue, Paris was shaken by an explosion of indulgence and
frivolity. With the end of the Reign of Terror came roars of laughter,
a riotous race for pleasure, and a lust for life.

While the cesspit of the Barrière du Trône, where the guillotine
had stood just a few days earlier, was still giving off a putrid stench,
people became obsessed with dancing, in a "sudden, impetuous,
formidable" reaction to the downfall of Robespierre, wrote Duval.
Everywhere, quadrilles and rigadoons were danced to the sounds of
clarinets and tambourines. There was dancing at the Carmes, where
not long before people had had their throats cut, reported Mercier.
There was dancing at the Jesuit novitiate, dancing at the Carmelite
convent – everywhere there was dancing; as though seized every
evening by some sort of choreographic madness, the whole of Paris
turned into a vast dance hall where the guests whirled furiously in
the midst of a musical tempest.

On the right bank, the middle class could be seen at the Tivoli
dance hall and at the Elysée National, where people crowded in to
dance to the orchestra of the Negro Julien, the great popular musician of the day. The fashion merchants of the rue St Honoré and the
rue Neuve des Petits Champs flocked to the dance hall at the Jardin
des Capucines, while bailiffs' clerks and shop assistants thronged to
the Ranelagh, in the Bois de Boulogne. The bal de la veillée, given on
Île de la Cité, was particularly memorable for its "meowing" concert,
in which a harpsichord was rigged up so that the keys moved metal
blades each of which struck the tail of a cat! On the left bank, there
was dancing at St Sulpice Cemetery: at the entrance, a red banner

announcing *Bal des Zéphirs* surmounted a skull and crossbones engraved in stone. Couples danced on the tombstones. At what were known as *bals des victimes*, only men and women who had lost a relative on the scaffold were admitted. Guests showed up with the nape of their neck shaved, as though prepared for the guillotine, and with a red thread around their throat; they greeted one another *à la victime*, by imitating the sudden drop of the head as it is lopped off by the falling blade.

With dancing – "a grave, serious matter," asserted Duval – the Thermidorian Reaction witnessed the rebirth of society life. *Le Messager du Soir* is often quoted on this point: "The charm and laughter that were driven away by the Terror have returned to Paris. Our pretty women in their blond perukes are ravishing; the concerts, both public and private, are most delightful ... The blood-thirsty types, the Billauds, the Collots, and the *enragés* refer to this about-face in public opinion as the counter-revolution."

At the same time the salons were reopening, and in the Year III they were to play a role similar to that of the popular societies in the Year II. Indeed, it was in the clubs, particularly the Jacobin Club, under the unrelenting eye of the infamous tricoteuses, that the policies of the Terror had been devised, policies that the Convention had then adopted as its own. In the Year III it was in the salons, frequented by the recently returned émigrés and by the new bourgeoisie, that Thermidorian policies were decided. And the merveilleuses played no less a role than the Halle market women had played in the galleries of the Assembly just a short time before. As early as Fructidor, Year II, Collot-d'Herbois said to the patriots,"The rogues have promised our heads to their concubines. Your situation is desperate; you are being conspired against in the most despicable places. The fate of the Republic is being decided in courtesans' filthy boudoirs, at the widows' of the émigré general staff, and in the midst of the most disgusting orgies." Babeuf, in *Le Tribun du Peuple* of 19 Nivôse, Year III, wrote:

Fellow citizens, you are once again under the reign of the trollops. The Pompadours, Du Barrys, and Antoinettes have come to life again, and it is they who are governing you. It is they who are largely responsible for all the calamities that have beset you and the deplorable regression that is killing your Revolution ... Why keep it a secret any longer that Tallien, Fréron, and Bentabolle are deciding the fate of human beings whilst reclining indolently on eiderdown and roses, next to princesses?

We shall see whether these comments are nothing more than the wild exaggerations of fanatical patriots. In a letter to a friend, the

Montagnard deputy Soubrany expressed his annoyance at the "official" love affairs: that of Tallien with Thérésia Cabarrus; that of Rovère with the *ci-devant* Comtesse d'Agoult; that of the people's representative Bentabolle with the *ci-devant* Duchesse de Rohan-Chabot; that of the journalist La Harpe with the widow of the Comte de Clermont-Tonnerre; and that of Legendre with Louise Comtat, an actress at the Opéra and former mistress of the Comte d'Artois. The royalist Mallet du Pan, whose remarks can hardly be doubted in this instance, observed that the theatres were full of the deputies' concubine prostitutes who brazenly displayed the jewellery they had stolen from émigré mansions. In public, people grumbled about the "wooers of noblewomen," and it was said that most of the deputies were married to the wives of émigrés. These liaisons were not inconsequential. On 20 Brumaire, Year III, for instance, Duhem stated before the Convention that the previous night's expedition against the Jacobins had been "plotted in the boudoirs of Mme Cabarrus." Indeed, though she aggrandized her role, she did claim to have had a hand in the closure of the Club. We also know, from Lacretelle, that she was involved in the release of hundreds of prisoners in the days following Thermidor and that she provided inspiration for the Thermidorians' press campaigns, rewarding a good article with a kiss. This explains Cambon's indignation in the Convention, on 8 Nivôse, Year III, when he railed against deputies who came to the tribune to "give speeches written in boudoirs, amid men in square-cut coats who attend concerts in the rue Feydeau." The hack journalists of the jeunesse dorée often provided the Thermidorians with prepared speeches, and then later, Lacretelle adds, pumped up their own egos by describing them in their newspapers as splendid examples of consummate eloquence. Dussault, for instance, not only penned all of the articles in Fréron's *L'Orateur du Peuple*, but also wrote the speeches that his employer delivered in the Convention.

The political influence of the Thermidorian salons, which were analogous to the Girondins' *bureaux d'esprit*, cannot be stressed enough. As with the Girondins, young people were warmly welcomed to the salons, and there was always a celebration when the jeunes gens returned from one of their little escapades. "It had never been easier to be a hero," noted Lacretelle. This pervasive influence is shrewdly analysed in a justly famous passage from Thibaudeau. Revolutionaries were enticed to the gilded salons – those of the former nobility, he says – to obtain certain favours, such as the lifting of a sequestration order or the striking of a friend's name from the list of émigrés, or to corrupt their opinions. "First of all, a few joking remarks would be ventured about the Revolution. How could they get cross when the person taking the liberty was a pretty woman?" Then they would be won over little by little, by being brought to mock and show contempt for the democratic institutions. This was how the Republic lost many of its faithful supporters, some of whom sold out entirely to royalism, concludes an embittered Thibaudeau.

In this renascent social life, "in which monarchical refinement tempered, and was tempered by, republican roughness," two figures who had become the idols of the jeunes gens stood out from the crowd: Thérésia Cabarrus and the singer Jean-François Garat. They represented human types then in vogue and personified the values of the day: Cabarrus, indulgence and sweetness; Garat, a sort of decadent refinement.

At twenty-one, Thérésia Cabarrus, the daughter of a Spanish banker, was in the full splendour of her radiant beauty. Observers were unanimous: "A charm that I have seen only in her," wrote the Baronne de Vandrey. "Features of artistic regularity, hair of pure silk, an enchanting smile," added the Marquise de La Tour du Pin. Always "dressed with admirable taste, she possessed both grace and dignity," said the Duc de Raguse. "Perfect harmony in her whole person," observed the Duchesse d'Abrantès. In Thibaudeau's view, she united "French vivacity with Spanish sensuality." All of these compliments are reflected in her portrait by Chassériau in the Musée de Quimper. In 1788, at the age of fifteen-and-a-half, she had married the Marquis de Fontenay, who happened to be "saddled" with a fortune in real estate. After her divorce in 1793, she became the mistress, in succession, of the Lameth brothers, the Duc d'Aiguillon, Félix Le Peletier, Tallien – to whom she was married for a time – Barras, and Ouvrard, and finished what might be called her "career" as the Princesse de Caraman-Chimay.

Cabarrus had been imprisoned during the Terror, but Tallien succeeded in having her released on 26 Thermidor. Finding that she was carrying his child, she agreed to marry him that Christmas, although this union with a former bank clerk, the lowly son of a footman, certainly meant that she was marrying beneath her. She moved out of her rooms in the Chaussée d'Antin and went to live on Cours la Reine, at the Chaumière, a magnificent residence built by the famous actress Mlle Raucourt, which soon became a centre of society life. From here she set new trends for fashion – starting, for instance, the vogue of Greek-style diaphanous tunics during the harshest winter the century had seen. "One could not have been more richly unclothed," remarked Talleyrand.

Though she was adored in the salons, where she was known as "Our Lady of Thermidor," Thérésia Cabarrus was vehemently detested by the lower classes, who were disgusted by her immodest attire. Everyone agreed that the origin of her wealth was more than murky. In Fructidor, Year II, at the Jacobin Club, Levasseur de la Sarthe had asked Tallien to explain his liaison "with an émigré's wife who also happens to be the daughter of the treasurer of the King of Spain." On 8 Nivôse, Cambon denounced her to the Assembly as a new Marie Antoinette. In a letter, the deputy Soubrany waxed indignant: "She makes a display of the most shameless luxury in the midst of the most appalling poverty."

The other idol of the jeunesse dorée, the singer Jean-François Garat, was the "darling of the ladies," and his pronouncements were taken as gospel in the salons. He was the nephew of a minister, and this impromptu about them went the rounds:

Deux Garats sont connus. L'un écrit, l'autre chante.
Admirez, j'y consens, leur talent que l'on vante,
Mais ne préférez pas, si vous formez un voeu,
La cervelle de l'oncle au gosier du neveu.

(Two Garats are known. One writes, the other sings.
Admire, if you will, their highly praised talent,
But should you ever have to make a choice,
Then over the uncle's mind take the nephew's voice.)

Though he had never received any formal musical training and was unable to read music, Garat could charm an audience with his extraordinary vocal range. In one evening he could sing *Sei Morelli*, written for bass; *No Quest' Anima*, written for tenor; a rondo by Nasolini, written for soprano; and the *duo d'Armide*, written for countertenor. In earlier times he had been the favourite singer of Marie Antoinette, who would send a coach and six to fetch him and who had twice settled his debts. Despite being strikingly ugly and extremely arrogant – he pretended to be short-sighted, so that he would not have to recognize anyone – Garat dictated the fashion of the day, as Beau Brummell and Lord Byron would do later. There were coats, cravats, switches, lorgnettes, boots, and sundry other items "à la Garat"; in Parisian society, he was the sole arbiter of good taste.

Thérésia Cabarrus and Jean-François Garat were true sociological phenomena. Around them grew a new élite which, if we are to believe Lamothe-Langon, was the social antithesis of the Parisian *sans-culotterie*:

In opposition to the sans-culottes, who were so dirty, so filthy and hideous, in both aspect and character, a small group of young people from respectable families had formed since Thermidor, most of whom dressed well, in green coats with black collars, carried large canes, and wore their hair in *cadenettes*. The lower classes called them muscadins, while in the upper echelons of society they were referred to as Fréron's jeunesse dorée.

It was up to this new group to define the bourgeois canons of truth, beauty, and good. Sociologists would characterize it as a symbolic élite, and *L'Abréviateur universel* speaks of "a class of persons of both sexes that the rest of the public envies, tries to imitate, flatters, or denigrates, depending on its feelings or the circumstances."

This brings us back to the role of the Thermidorian salons as political laboratories for the debasement of democratic ideas and as social melting pots for the diverse members of the jeunesse dorée, who would eventually become the bourgeoisie of the Restoration.

THE SUBVERSION OF POLITICAL LIFE

The explanation for the events of 9 Thermidor ceased long ago to be a subject of controversy. As Lamothe-Langon wrote, "It was the work of rogues who, fearing for their lives, armed themselves in desperation against other rogues. For them, it was a question of saving their own skins, which were threatened by the restless ambition of Robespierre."

In contrast, interpretation of the first days of the Thermidorian Reaction is less certain. It is possible that initially the centrist representatives thought they could maintain some sort of balance between the left and the right and, by playing off the Reactionaries against the members of the old government Committees, could ensure that they retained control of the reins of power, avoiding the passive role they had played in the past. The centrists' will to achieve emancipation from control by both the left and the right was reflected in Robert Lindet's address to the Convention on the fourth *jour sans-culottide*, a speech which was fair in its treatment of both the terrorists and the Reactionaries, and which was rightly regarded as the political program of the new majority. It was a true masterpiece of intellectual tightrope walking which had something in it for all of the parties and signalled the firm intention of the vast majority of the deputies to free themselves from the yoke of the factions, such as the Dantonists and Hébertists, that had hitherto dominated them.

Power was thus oscillating between "Robespierre's tail" and the Fréronists when the latter group, after making sure that it could count on the "unwavering support of the youth of Paris," resolved to split definitively with its allies of 9 Thermidor. This resulted, on 12 Fructidor, in Lecointre's denunciation of "those who carry on the work of Robespierre." Lecointre had been led to believe that his courage would make him famous and his denunciation win him immortality. But a hue and cry was raised at the Assembly. The denunciation was declared slanderous, and its author deemed a crackpot. That evening, however, so many duchesses, marquis, countesses, viscounts, and former prisoners went to congratulate Lecointre that the rue du Bacq, where he lived, was blocked with carriages. On the other hand, at about half past seven in the evening, at the Jardin National, Justice of the Peace Mathieu spread the news that the Convention had tried to conceal the truth by ignoring Lecointre's denunciation and pressing on with the matters on its agenda, and that "Robespierre's tail was responsible, and would go the same way as the head." The tailor Jacques Poupart was apprehended for having objected to the motion of condemnation brought against Lecointre. Similarly, the *enragé* Varlet, who was in league with the jeunesse dorée, was arrested in the street for praising Lecointre and maintaining, apropos of the deputies, "that they were all guilty, having drunk from the same cup as Robespierre and others, and that they hadn't heard the end of it."

As Thibaudeau notes, the Convention found itself in a very delicate position. If it refused to take action against the terrorists, it would appear to be condoning their "crimes." If it brought proceedings against them, the accused would no doubt defend themselves by saying that they had simply acted according to the Convention's decrees, thereby putting it on trial as well. This explains why, in the early days of the Reaction, the Assembly strove so desperately to remain neutral and to be fair to both the terrorists and the Reactionaries.

A few days after the crushing defeat suffered by Lecointre in the Convention, a deterioration in the Fréronists' political position tested the fragile balance of power within the Assembly. The motion of condemnation brought against Lecointre on 14 Fructidor had also cast a shadow on Tallien, Fréron, and Legendre, the mainstays of the new faction known as the Indulgents; a short while later, the three of them were struck from the rolls of the Jacobin Club, where a menacing Billaud-Varennes announced that they would soon have to account for their actions. In complete disarray, the Fréronists could already see themselves being indicted when, just at the crucial moment, the trial of the Nantes federalists opened. As we have seen, the result of the trial was to swing public opinion back in favour of the Thermidorians. This was also the moment that Tallien chose, in a blatant bit of play-acting, to have himself "assassinated" – an "appalling infamy" that made the public believe that a return of the Terror was possible so long as the "bloodthirsty monsters" denounced by Lecointre, and the terrorists in general, were not crushed. Thereafter, the Reactionaries focused their energy on breaking the resistance of the Assembly. Without the help of the jeunesse dorée, however, they would probably never have succeeded. From the safe posts the Fréronists had given them in arms workshops and government administration, the young men would answer the call from the Thermidorian press to campaign in public places, in the sections, and in the galleries of the Convention. Setting themselves up as the "magistrates of public opinion," they would demand of the Assembly that it go back, piece by piece, on the social and political reforms of the Year II.

As can be expected, this effort to turn back the clock was to meet with plenty of resistance, but first let us look at how the plan was put into action: "The battalions of the jeunesse dorée," wrote Lebois, "are divided into three separate armies. One frequents the Sections, another is active in public places, and the third is present in the galleries of the Convention."

In the sections, the jeunesse dorée took an active role in the general assemblies in order to drive out the "brigands." *Le Messager du Soir* urged the youths on, and *L'Orateur du Peuple* told them how to go about their task: in each section they were to identify the members of the old revolutionary committees, the *gardiens des scellés* (guards of seals affixed to property), the *septembriseurs* (those responsible for the prison massacres of September 1792), the Jacobins, the forty-sol voters, the five-hundred-livre heroes, and the soldiers of the Revolutionary Army, draw up a list of their names, and post it in the meeting hall – not out of a desire for revenge, "for honnêtes gens are incapable of cutting throats," but simply to drive them away from the general assemblies. The campaign soon had its effect. For instance, the lampoonist Jollivet, called Baralère, denounced to the Committee of General Security a number of individuals who had disrupted the Guillaume Tell Section's general assembly on 10 Vendémiaire. On 11 Ventôse four young men from the République

Section went to the Committee to denounce the citizens Racine and Guérault for having insulted them the day before in the section's general assembly by shouting "You royalists belong at the Café de Chartres!" The jeunesse dorée was likewise behind numerous addresses to the Convention against the terrorists: the Temple Section's address of 11 Pluviôse denouncing the members of its old revolutionary committee, "Strike down these tigers!"; that of the Brutus Section on 12 Pluviôse decrying "a terrorist faction stirring up trouble in its midst"; and that of the Montreuil Section on 11 Ventôse giving notice to the Convention: "Why wait any longer to purge the earth of this man-eating scum? Do not their livid complexion and sunken eyes show clearly enough who their foster father was?"

On 10 Germinal, Jullian, representing the Tuileries Section, uttered the following threat in an address to the Assembly: "Accuse the assassins of the people, lest the people join forces and accuse you." And on 10 Ventôse, Year III, Jullian was delegated by the section's general assembly to denounce to the Committee of General Security one Romain Macheret, who had threatened the general assembly by sending it an ear enclosed in a letter. Also worthy of mention is the Fidélité Section, which came to the Convention on 2 Floréal to condemn "the hideous hydra of crime and tyranny ... We shall denounce the agitators to you, and you will punish them," the spokesman said. "Point out your enemies to us, and we shall fight them." Before the Assembly on 21 Floréal, Talma, of the Mont Blanc Section, shamelessly asked for the law of 14 Floréal, Year II, against royalist agitators to be repealed. Finally, one of the most glaring examples of the jeunesse dorée's activity in the sections was *Le Cri de ralliement* (The Rallying Cry), a speech delivered in the Guillaume Tell Section by Souriguère on 20 Floréal; it had been read aloud earlier at the Café de Chartres, and the habitués had voted to have it printed and sent to the forty-eight sections: it was "an appeal to exterminate the cutthroats and usher in the reign of justice and humanity"!

The patriots were now banished from public places – the streets and cafés, the Tuileries and the Jardin Égalité – and *Le Messager du Soir* noted that "Jacobins, highwaymen, and rabid dogs are three maleficent species that are treated equally in Paris." If one is to believe Beffroi de Reigny, it was only fair that this *canaille*, or rabble, should be hunted down, because *canaille*, from the Latin *canis*, meaning "the dregs of the populace and the dross of human society," "well describes the squawking tone of voice, the coarse, vulgar language, the vile inclinations, the foul tastes, the rude manners, the filthy debauchery, and the dissolute orgies that one usually associates with the *canaille*."

This was sufficient reason to arrest the citizen Pierre Lard, the clerk of the Contrat Social Section, who had said that the jeunes gens stirred up trouble wherever they went, and that he found it extraordinary that these men who had been so poorly dressed before 9 Thermidor were suddenly so well clothed, and that he was convinced that somebody was supporting them. It was also sufficient reason to apprehend the employee François-Barbe Laforêt who, according to the fellow who denounced him, d'Arnaudery, must have been a terrorist agent because "he did nothing but make sarcastic remarks about the youths of the Café de Chartres, to whom he referred as Fréron's royal army, and maintained that the muscadins would soon be brought to heel." And sufficient reason to arrest a certain Mme Lemoigne, supposedly "a termagant whose eyes would light up with delight on seeing cartloads of victims," and the citizen Koch, of the Guillaume Tell Section, who reportedly said "that he shat on the Republic." There were many others put under arrest by the many patrols that, according to *Le Courrier républicain*, scoured the streets for Jacobins. *Le Messager du Soir* explained that "they should be given no more rest in public places than exists in their horrible consciences. Wherever they go, public indignation must hunt them down. They must be made to feel all the horror of their crimes, they must come to hate themselves as they are hated by the people."

"Battues" were organized in the cafés of the Palais Royal and vicinity to flush out these "man-eaters" and prevent them from sleeping off the blood they had drunk. A Mme Boudray, a mother of twenty-six children who ran the Café des Bains Chinois, a regular haunt of the patriots, complained that ruffians would come and insult her in her café and that she would have to send for a detachment of the guard, "which, by the way, almost always refuses to help me in such cases." A certain Lemaire, the proprietor of a restaurant in Butte des Moulins and a former commander of a battalion in the Revolutionary Army, remonstrated to the Committee of General Security about being exhibited, made a show of, and slandered on street corners; it had got to the point where he could no longer go out without being insulted, he said.

There was generally plenty of trouble brewing at the Tuileries. On 9 Ventôse the earthenware vendor Jean-Baptiste Gavroy was arrested there by five young men. One of them, the ever-present Jollivet, recounted that he had gone to the Tuileries at around seven o'clock, hoping to meet an acquaintance who would give him a hand in arguing with or arresting the speakers in "the *jacobite* groups." No sooner had Gavroy pointed out the troublemakers than he himself was set upon and dragged off to the Committee of General Security, where he was put under arrest. On 20 Ventôse, the citizen Christine Paquet was "kicked repeatedly in the behind." On the twenty-fourth, one François-Joseph Quentin, the servant of the people's representative Fasillac, was taken to the Committee by two young men for having said "that the muscadins were not patriots." Two days later, again at the Tuileries, the thread vendor Jean-Samuel Arsonnaud, who had been complaining that the émigrés were returning in droves and repossessing their property, and that hence it was not surprising that the value of the assignat was falling, was taken to the Committee of General Security along with a certain Nicolas Bazin, who had spoken out in his favour because, he said, "he did not believe that the youths who were trying to arrest him had the right to do so."

Similar violent scenes took place at the Palais Égalité. On the evening of 14 Pluviôse, at the Passage du Perron, a huge crowd of youths surrounded a house where some suspected Jacobins had taken refuge after being chased for having supposedly shouted in the streets "Down with the muscadins! To hell with the jeunes gens!" Leading the crowd was none other than the editor of *Le Moniteur*, Alphonse Martainville, together with six other furious young men, one of whom scaled the house in pursuit of a "terrorist." On 6 Floréal, one Jean-Romain Druy, of the Le Peletier Section, was attacked at the Palais Égalité by the merchant Louis Pierlot, who called him a villain, a Jacobin, a spy for the former government, an agent of Robespierre, and shouted "Hey! Hey! Here's a Jacobin!"

Daily expeditions through public places were organized for the purpose, said *Le Courrier républicain*, "of hunting Jacobins just as wolves used to be hunted in the British Isles." In this regard, the police had already noted the activity of Saint-Huruge, who "seems to have declared himself the outraged adversary of the Jacobins. He shows all citizens who do not share his views that they are wrong by flogging them and taking them straight to the guardhouse, where he detains them with impunity" – in other words, the jeunesse dorée carried out its escapades with the complicity of the authorities.

The hunt for Jacobins became so fierce that the jeunes gens dared attack representatives of the people in their own homes. This was hardly surprising, however, since pamphlets had been published listing the names and addresses of the "principal" Jacobins. At about half past seven on the evening of 9 Frimaire, a group gathered at the Café Payen, according to a statement made by the proprietress; the leader of the group, a big man of about fifty, drank an eau-de-vie without paying for it and tried to whip her, she said, for being "a Jacobin." Then the crowd, which included many jeunes gens and wigmakers' assistants, went to a café run by a man named Hottot. He testified that his establishment suddenly filled up with people, "some smartly dressed, others very shabbily," who said they were going to cut the Jacobins to ribbons. The crowd searched his house, but, finding nothing, left shouting "Long live the Convention! Down with the Jacobins!" By then it was about eight o'clock, and the people's representative Isoré, from his home in the rue de la Convention, heard "what sounded to him like the noise of a mob" yelling "Long live the Convention! Down with the Jacobins!" A quarter of an hour later the mob was in his courtyard, led by "seven or eight men who looked like those fellows who affect the English style of dress and whom one sees only too frequently now at the Palais Égalité," and was trying to force open his door, bellowing that it would have his head. The people's representative Collot-d'Herbois corroborated this version of events with a similar story: most of the people involved "were dressed in square-cut frock coats, with collars of various colours." The porter Geneviève Barbot said that one of the men had told her to tell her master that he was a villain and a rogue. The matter was reported immediately to the Committee of General Security, which ordered the police commissioner of the Tuileries Section to go and investigate; the Committee also put the deputies' houses under surveillance, and ruled in all seriousness "that the people who had entered the courtyard of the house of Collot-d'Herbois, uttering threats and inciting murder, would be arrested."

But how could the Paris Police Administrative Commission ever carry this order out? The whole affair thus ended on a ridiculous note. When Duhem protested to the Committee, according to Sébastien Mercier in the *Annales patriotiques*, he was told "that it was difficult to prevent Billaud and Collot from being jeered at."

The jeunesse dorée was active not only in the sections and in public places, but also in the galleries of the National Assembly during debates. On 22 Nivôse, André Dumont lashed out vehemently at the galleries, which were packed with militant sans-culottes, calling them a "refuge for the idle." "You are insulting the people!" replied the leftist people's representative Ruamps. "The idle powder their hair. The idle are the muscadins."

That same day, the Convention passed a decree ordering the Committee of General Security and the Committee of Hall

Inspectors to have the galleries policed. Just what this policing amounted to is illustrated below. On 23 Nivôse *Le Messager du Soir* denounced "the three dozen or so harpies who, with their pots and pans between their legs, spew out insults against the Committees," while on the twenty-fifth *L'Orateur du Peuple* maintained that a handful of women drunk on eau-de-vie, "their hideous faces bespeaking dissoluteness, debauchery, and debasement," had been posted in the galleries to disrupt the debates. "If it is another thrashing that these tricoteuses need to be brought to their senses," said *Le Messager du Soir*, "then that is what they will get." The same day, the police reported that Saint-Huruge, armed with a stick, was patrolling the corridors of the Convention, looking for women to flog. On 27 Nivôse, the jeunes gens of the Café de Chartres decided to be more assiduous in frequenting the "convulsive galleries" and driving away "the shrews hired by the bloodthirsty faction." This conflict led to numerous violent incidents. On 20 Pluviôse, Year III, a Mme Dupertois had to use a knife to defend her daughter's honour against seven or eight youths who were threatening to strip off her clothes in a corridor of the Convention. On the twenty-fourth, before the session began, a vicious clash occurred between jeunes gens and Jacobin women in the galleries, and the guards were at great pains to restore order. But this was the last skirmish of its kind, and the youths thereafter reigned as masters around the Assembly. On 22 Ventôse, people complained that the jeunes gens were controlling the seating in the galleries and making citizens pay. On 2 Germinal, the Assembly's sitting opened to the sound of *Le Réveil du Peuple* sung from the galleries; on the morrow, Thuriot had to have the spectators silenced before he could begin the session. "And thus," concluded Lacretelle, "in a two-to-three-month campaign we were able to establish ourselves as the Convention's sole escort. It was finally our turn to fill the galleries."

With the trial of the ninety-four of Nantes, the "assassination" of Tallien, and the relentless agitation of the jeunesse dorée in the sections, public places, and the galleries of the Convention, the Assembly's sovereignty quickly crumbled, so that by 15 Frimaire Lecointre could reiterate his denunciation of the members of the old government Committees. Perhaps this time the Assembly could have had them put under arrest, but, as Lamothe-Langon, the spokesman of the centrists, observed, "What stopped us was the fear of the majority – that if we went too far to the right, we might be carried back toward the monarchy."

Nevertheless, the Thermidorians' thirst for revenge, fuelled by the jeunesse dorée, was insatiable: "Your grave has already been dug, you miserable wretches!" wrote *L'Orateur du Peuple*. "You are struggling futilely on the edge of your tomb ... There can be no peace for France so long as your odious existence pollutes nature!" Thus, on 15 Frimaire, Lecointre's new denunciation – which, curiously enough, was widely distributed to the general public for free – had been referred, this time with supporting documents, to the three government Committees for further study. On 6 Nivôse, the Thermidorian representative Clauzel had a decree passed ordering the Committees' report to be heard on the morrow. On the seventh, the Committees complied with the decree, stating that there were grounds for looking into the actions of four of the seven members denounced by Lecointre: Barère, Billaud-Varennes, Collot-d'Herbois, and Vadier. A twenty-one-member commission, to be chaired by Saladin, a vindictive Girondin who intended to waste no time in conducting the inquiry, was appointed that same evening. However, the Committees made a determined effort to slow him down, and he was unable to submit his report until 12 Ventôse.

In the meantime, "the four guilty ringleaders," as they had already come to be known, were being tried in a battle for public opinion. In *Le Patriote*, Turbat asked,

> Lequel fut le plus sanguinaire,
> De Billaud, d'Herbois ou Barère?
> Lequel des trois est aux abois,
> De Billaud, Barère ou d'Herbois?
> Lequel mérite l'échafaud,
> D'Herbois, Barère ou Billaud?

> (Who was the most bloodthirsty,
> Billaud, d'Herbois, or Barère?
> Which of the three is at bay,
> Billaud, Barère, or d'Herbois?
> Which deserves the scaffold,
> D'Herbois, Barère, or Billaud?)

In *Le Cri du sang qui demande vengeance* (The Cry of Blood That Demands Revenge), one Leboinel recounted the revolutionary atrocities allegedly committed by Collot in Lyon, and stated, "Wandering down by the river, I stepped on skeletal remains; the skulls, legs, and arms scattered among the stones made me shudder with horror." In a *Pétition de tous les chiens de Paris à la Convention nationale* (Petition from All the Dogs of Paris to the National Convention), the representatives of the canine race asked, "Have we ever been seen eating human flesh? Have we ever set up our own public assassination committees?" A tract entitled *Rapport à faire par Barère au nom de l'opinion publique* (Report to Be Submitted by Barère on Behalf of Public Opinion) contained an imaginary speech by Barère to the Convention in which he justified his claims to public contempt and asked to be sentenced to death in the name of the people: "Pass sentence! The people will respect your verdict. Their contempt for me is your guarantee." A *Justification de Collot-d'Herbois* (Vindication of Collot-d'Herbois), by a certain Bozour, was in fact a satiric tract reviewing his "crimes."

Meanwhile, the Montagnards were not simply turning the other cheek. In an *Appel à la Convention nationale* (Appeal to the National Convention), Barère denounced Fréron for being "so humane that he demands nothing more than the heads of the republicans and the blood of his colleagues." With a *Supplément à l'accusation de Laurent Lecointre* (Supplement to the Accusation Made by Laurent Lecointre), he cunningly had reprinted a denunciation against himself found among Robespierre's papers, while R.-F. Lebois, the Friend of the People, likewise denounced the old Committees, which he said were guilty of many military victories!

As with the earlier campaign against the Jacobins, the ultimate effect of this pamphlet war was to disorient the lower classes. "The people," noted a police agent, "seem to have something to say but are afraid to speak. There is a latent discontent that is hard to explain."

Thrice an amnesty for the terrorists was proposed – by Cambacérès on 18 Frimaire, by Lecointre himself on 20 Nivôse, and finally by Boudin on 26 Nivôse – only to be rejected. "An amnesty?" exclaimed Fréron in *L'Orateur du Peuple*. "If the Convention were to grant one, ought there to be an amnesty for it, too?" On the third occasion, on 26 Nivôse, Legendre "regally" had the Assembly override the motion and proceed with the matters on its agenda.

In an even more astounding move, the Committee of General Security attempted to compromise Billaud-Varennes and Vadier on 29 Pluviôse by proposing to them, through a Mme Rousseville, the services of an "emissary in the Faubourg Antoine who would win over public opinion for them." Vadier, who seemed demoralized, said that he appreciated the interest taken in him but nevertheless refused, while Billaud-Varennes, who must have sensed that there was something fishy about the offer, remained silent.

From the viewpoint of the Montagnards, the ideal solution to this turmoil would have been to send the muscadins to join the army.

However, thanks to the Thermidorians, the youths were ensconced in safe jobs in government administration and arms workshops, and even in the case of those whose papers were not in order the military police often had no means of forcing them to report to their army units.

It was common knowledge that government administration was staffed with jeunes gens. In the days following Thermidor, Martainville had urged the authorities to replace the dolts and the scoundrels by "young men with sharp minds." Evidently, little time was wasted, for *Le Journal Universel* reported as early as 12 Brumaire that the only people one saw in government offices were "insolent clerks, well shod, well dressed, well coiffed, who treat citizens haughtily, disdainfully ... and who in the evenings fill the cafés and the theatres." These young men were the "mainstays of the faction that oppressed the patriots," Galizot added the next day at the Jacobin Club, remarking on how "the streets and promenades teem with muscadins who flaunt their idleness after leaving the office." *La Trompette du Père Bellerose* echoed this sentiment on 30 Nivôse: "I would never finish if I were to start in on talking about these smug, idiotic muscadins who are given employment at the expense of so many worthy fathers and their families." And again on 3 Pluviôse: "In government offices I saw hordes of muscadins fooling about instead of getting on with their work. I saw some older father types, with white hair, a little more decent than the others, a few men who were more serious, more assiduous about their work, but I also saw young rascals of fourteen, fifteen, and sixteen who are being paid salaries of 1,800 to 2,000 livres. Does this not amount to stealing these sums out of the mouths of needy fathers and their wretched families?"

The scandalous situation was even more blatant in the arms workshops. As early as Ventôse, Year II, the Committee of Public Safety noted "that many citizens called up in the first conscription have managed to shirk their duty by finding employment in arms production, either with contractors or in workshops." On 28 Brumaire, Year III, a police agent noted that two-thirds of the "workers" from the Réunion workshop who had come to present a petition to the Convention were former conscripts.

In early Frimaire, Year III, trouble was brewing in the Republic's arms workshops as a result of general dissatisfaction with working conditions, pay, and the length of the workday. When, on 4 Frimaire, a group of workers from the Marat workshop delivered an address in the Assembly calling for an increase in wages, a violent clash occurred between the people's representatives Guyomar and

Duquesnoy, on the one hand, who maintained that the arms work-shops were "full of young men, aged nineteen and twenty, who ought to be at the front," and the people's representative Lecompte, on the other, who lashed out at the "miserable uneducated wretches who walk the streets in their red caps and long trousers." This amounted to asking what should be given precedence: the patriotic zeal of the sans-culottes or the "sharp minds" of the jeunes gens. It was a question that Cambacérès, for one, answered in no uncertain terms: "Who cares about the man! It is talent that the Republic needs! Who cares, I say! It is service that the government seeks!"

Shortly thereafter, Montmayau had it decreed that the Committees should take "whatever measures [were] necessary to curb the disorder caused by the troublemakers in the Paris arms workshops." This decree was to have far-reaching consequences: two weeks later, on 16 Frimaire, the Committee of Public Safety used it to order an end to arms production in the Republic's workshops as of 1 Pluviôse, the manufacture and repair of arms henceforth being contracted out to private enterprise, with entrepreneurs given complete freedom to hire whom they liked, including "those pupils who would appear to them to possess the necessary aptitude and who have been conscripted for non-military service."

The sans-culottes feared that they would be dismissed and that jeunes gens would be hired to replace them. When the Committee of Public Safety's decision was posted publicly, on 21 Frimaire, it immediately sparked great agitation in some of the arms workshops. By the next day, the twenty-second, the unrest had spread, and some fifteen thousand workers staged a huge demonstration in front of the Convention to express their fear of losing their jobs just before winter.

Faced with this unrest, the Committee of General Security could think of no better response, over the course of the next few days, than to arrest a dozen or so workers deemed to have "played major roles in the workshop demonstrations." It was most likely this measure that triggered Duhem's fierce outburst at the Assembly on 26 Frimaire: "It is scandalous to see hordes of youths who, on the pretence of doing paperwork, in fact do nothing in Paris while their comrades fight at the front [applause]. These young men are obviously nothing but cowards."

Nonetheless, La Vedette of 30 Nivôse announced the closure of the arms workshops for the following day, with the result, it said, that forty-five thousand workers would be without employment. True, the journalist conceded, these men had had over six weeks to look around, but it was quite possible that many of them had still not found alternative work. A police report of 23 Pluviôse makes mention of "a great many workers who have been unemployed since the closure of the workshops." Two days earlier, on 21 Pluviôse, a carpenter by the name of Degré, of the Homme Armé Section, had been apprehended at the entrance to the Convention after he had protested "very heatedly against the Convention's decision to close the workshops, since it put the workers in a situation where they might easily starve to death." And later, on 1 Ventôse, the police still feared "some sort of reaction" from the workers who had lost their means of livelihood, noting that terrorists everywhere were claiming that "royalists were now doing the work of the dismissed sans-culottes."

A few entrepreneurs did, however, continue to hire sans-culottes, and the attitude of the Committee of General Security in this respect was typical. On 16 Frimaire, the Committee had the owner of a gunpowder factory, Barthélemy de Recologue, put under arrest and ordered the closure of his manufacturing works – to safeguard residents in the neighbourhood against any accident "that might result owing to the sulphurous character of the said Barthélemy." Even more revealing is the case of Jean-Auguste Jullien, the accountant of the Jacobin arms workshop: he was arrested on 12 Pluviôse after being denounced by Alexandre Méchin, who told the Committee that the day before, a dozen or so employees of the workshop gathered at the Café Raisson had said "that they were not part of Fréron's army, that regardless of how rich he was, he could not pay them off because they were above being bribed ... that no one wanted any arms to be produced but that they would manufacture them anyway ... and continued to spew out vulgar abuse against the government, and in particular the Café de Chartres, saying that they would march against Fréron's army, that they would tear the breeches off the muscadins." During all this, Jullien did not say a word, but howled with laughter – unfortunately, this was sufficient reason, in Méchin's opinion, to cancel a contract for the assembly of twenty thousand rifles that Jullien was about to sign with the Arms and Powder Commission. In Thermidor, Year III, Jullien was still languishing in prison and protested "that one must have very little hard evidence against a man to claim that by laughing at remarks made by a drunk, he had committed a crime." Kervélégan, who examined the file, concluded that "a man imprisoned for having laughed cannot be kept behind bars," and a month later Jullien was free again. But there was no trace of his arms workshop, which must have been forced to close.

Still, there was the military ordnance officer Lebas, who was theoretically in charge of sending back to the army "all these young men, in a variety of uniforms, who frequent the cafés, the dance halls, and the theatres." On 1 Pluviôse, the police were planning to round up groups on the boulevard du Temple and take them to Lebas. But what could poor Lebas, with his two clerks and four inspectors, do about all the young men to whom obliging doctors distributed innumerable medical certificates for shortsightedness, pallid complexion, internal pain, excessive stoutness, valetudinarian habits, and so on? "I do not have sufficient resources to keep track of all the soldiers in Paris, not to mention those arriving every day," he wrote to the *agent national* on 16 Pluviôse. In fact, it was hardly worth the trouble, since the Committee of General Security was evidently turning a blind eye to the whole business: it seemed that youths who had already been arrested by the military police commissioner could still be found in public places, thumbing their noses at the inspectors.

Thus, the Committee of General Security, dragging the National Convention along with it, drove the sans-culottes out of government administration and the arms workshops and replaced them with muscadins. The two bodies evidently thought that by surrounding themselves with honnêtes gens they would somehow be safer. Yet at the same time, they sharply increased the number of unemployed workers, and it was in their ranks that the rebels of Germinal and Prairial would find the human resources for their insurrection. As Albert Mathiez has written, "political errors, like moral ones, bear within them their own punishment."

To return to the "four guilty ringleaders," the affair had reached a virtual standstill when the remaining Montagnards decided to risk a diversionary tactic to turn public attention away from the "trial." Before the Assembly on 8 Nivôse, Duhem read out large extracts from a new reactionary journal, *Le Spectateur français pendant le Gouvernement révolutionnaire* (The French Spectator under the Revolutionary Government), in which the author, a jurist by the name of Jacques-Vincent Delacroix, stated, through a fictional character, that he seriously doubted that the people were true republicans, and called for a referendum by secret ballot on the Constitution of 1791. But to call for the Constitution of 1791 was equivalent to calling for the monarchy! This immediately prompted an incredible uproar in the Assembly, and before Duhem could even finish reading, the members had voted to have the author arrested and brought before the Revolutionary Tribunal. The Assembly was still in a state of shock when Cambon, following in the wake of Duhem, decried the influence that the jeunesse dorée was gaining over the Convention. "I say to you quite frankly," he exclaimed, "that we are bowing our heads under a tyranny more oppressive than that of Robespierre." There were murmurings in the hall, then several members cried, "He is right. The tyranny of Fréron is abominable." Picking up the theme of his speech of 18 Brumaire, in which he had lashed out at Fréron and Tallien, whom he portrayed as scurrilous slanderers, Cambon denounced the speeches written in boudoirs, in the midst of men in square-cut coats who prostrated themselves before the idol of the day (an allusion to Thérésia Cabarrus), whose indecent attire suggested a new Antoinette. Cambon's philippic echoed a speech Duhem had delivered to the Assembly on 12 Brumaire:

The Convention has not commissioned Fréron with the express task of calling every day for someone's head. The police should ensure that public opinion is not manipulated the way it is being manipulated at present ... The people are not a party to all the plotting that is going on behind the scenes. Public opinion is not the opinion of the fifteen or twenty thousand muscadins who have managed to leave their army posts and come to Paris on some pretext or other.

In spite of the progress of the Reaction, the danger of being suspected of royalism was still real enough that Tallien and Fréron immediately sought to put themselves on safer ground by going one better: three days later, on 4 Nivôse, they arranged for delegations of young men from the Le Peletier, Butte des Moulins, and Tuileries sections to go to the Convention and congratulate it for having decreed the arrest of Delacroix. During the same sitting, however, Legendre revealed that another book of counter-revolutionary inspiration, *Étrennes aux amateurs du bon vieux temps* (Gifts to Those Who Long for the Good Old Times), had recently been published. Royalism appeared to be a long way from its death bed, and Barras, concerned for his own safety, sought to outdo his rivals by having a decree passed, on 19 Nivôse, instituting an annual holiday to be celebrated on 21 January – that year, 2 Pluviôse – in commemoration of the death of Louis XVI. On 21 Nivôse, delegations from the Mutius-Scaevola and Le Peletier sections went to the Assembly to rail against royalism; on the twenty-fourth and twenty-sixth, at the Palais Royal, youths held a book burning for Delacroix's newspaper.

Within the jeunesse dorée, however, was a strong ultra-reactionary faction that was repelled by such compromises. These hard-liners were not perceptive enough to discern the political stratagem aimed at disarming the Montagnards and refused to have any further truck with the Convention. "They refused for a long time, and would not yield," wrote Duval, and the Thermidorians feared a sudden demobilization of the jeunesse dorée that would leave the Convention at the mercy of the Jacobins. Thus, merely by denouncing Delacroix's newspaper, Duhem would have succeeded in setting public opinion against the Fréronists, thereby re-establishing the political situation of Thermidor, Year ii.

This was the moment – and none too soon – that Fréron chose to publish, in *L'Orateur du Peuple* of 23 Nivôse, his *Invitation à la jeunesse française de sortir de son sommeil léthargique* (Call to French Youth to Wake from Their Lethargy). It was an appeal to citizens who, neither rich nor poor, lay somewhere between "the ostentatious luxury of the one, and the all too common debasement of the other." Were they only good, Fréron asked, for contemplating pleasure, discussing theatre, fashion, and gastronomy, deliberating on the causes and consequences of the Revolution while longing for the triumph of justice? Were they too feeble to take up arms? Then they had only themselves to blame for the dangers threatening them. Were they too cowardly to rebel against the idea of tyranny? Surely not! Moreover, the country's salvation depended on their support. They had already closed the Jacobin Club. Now they would go further: they would wipe out the Jacobins. And Fréron wound up his plea by urging his minions, in the clearest terms, to take the first opportunity to knife any Jacobins they met. The cutthroats had to be exterminated. It was an appeal, wrote Babeuf, to all "the gambling fiends, public thieves, prisoners, relatives of those who had atoned on the scaffold for their crimes against liberty ... and hence the jeunesse dorée, the muscadins, the men with collars and green cravats, *Le Réveil du Peuple*, the Society of Jesus, the *compagnie du soleil* ..."

The jeunesse dorée had, of course, existed well before Fréron's appeal, but he succeeded in infusing the jeunes gens with a new sense of purpose. Though a few youths from the Palais Royal burnt Fréron's paper in response to his taunts, the reactionary movement as a whole was galvanized into action. "On the evening of the day when Fréron's call had resounded through the streets of Paris," wrote Lacretelle, "two to three thousand young men responded enthusiastically." They were given leaders, he added, "to guide them, and to control them," and the Thermidorians saw the jeunesse dorée re-establish their furious street brigades. On the morrow, 24 Nivôse, the police reported "great agitation" at the Café de Chartres, "now raised to the status of a club," and a few days later feared that it might become the focus of an insurrection, considering the vehemence of the diatribes against the Jacobins: "Soon they will stop at nothing less than having them all put to death," the police noted.

On 27 Nivôse, at the Café de Chartres, the Orator of the Faubourg Antoine, Gonchon, had a scribe commit to paper a *Réponse de la jeunesse française actuellement à Paris à L'Orateur du Peuple* (Response of French Youth Now in Paris to *L'Orateur du Peuple*), a veritable ultimatum from the jeunes gens to the Convention, which was immediately placarded throughout the city. If they had refrained hitherto from retaliating against the Jacobins, they said, it was because of their respect for law and order, and not out of cowardice. But could they allow the Jacobins to raise their daggers against them while they, the jeunes gens, proffered a fraternal hand "to the Jacobin hands still dripping with the blood of their families"? Of course not! And so, together with "the brave republicans of the faubourgs," they were going to let the gentle voice of fraternity give way to the terrible cry of vengeance. Clearly it was the Convention's responsibility to avenge the jeunes gens for the massacre of their fathers. Should it show a lack of resolve, they would take the matter into their own hands: "By wreaking revenge on the cutthroats, the Convention will spare us the grisly task of punishing them by their own methods." Such was the tone used in addressing the sovereign authority in the Year III.

Babeuf also replied to Fréron's appeal. If he wanted civil war, he would get it. The sans-culottes were not going to let slip such a wonderful opportunity to put his insolent clique in its place: "So you have told your people to be at the ready. To arms! you cried. We have said as much to ours. Our workers in the faubourgs are already in formation, and are champing at the bit." In *L'Ami du Peuple*, Lebois angrily demanded, "Since when have libertines and thieves been the French people? Since when have whores and gaming heroes been the heroines of the Revolution? I urge the long-eared orator and all gilded citizens who preach justice by telling the people to attack us, I urge you all to think twice about what you are doing. The people do not recognize two kinds of justice ... We are not the aggressors, but we are well able to defend ourselves."

Another patriot who doubtless did not appreciate his "all too common debasement" hurled abuse in a virulent pamphlet:

Rogue! You say that the people are debased! If the people are poorly clothed, poorly fed, if they are wretched, unenlightened, are you not to blame? Is it not your work? The people are debased, you say. What have you done for the people, what are you doing to enlighten them, make them happy, keep them equal with free men, and raise them to the same level of prosperity? You have forgotten, slandered, despised, and betrayed the people; you have destroyed them with want and misery, you have trampled on the rights of the sacred people, and you trample on them still. People, that is your orator!

Lastly, Antonelle, ever clear-sighted and thoughtful, wondered, "Is it not absolute madness the way this frivolous youth is being fanaticized as though for a crusade?"

One could well think that Fréron would have been harassed for what, in the final analysis, was nothing less than a call for murder. But no. Nobody mentioned it at the Convention, not even Duhem, who – as we shall see – was soon to pay for having had the audacity to denounce royalism.

In the meantime, the celebration to mark the anniversary of the king's death went ahead nonetheless, though in a spirit quite in contrast to what one might have expected. While the public was allowed free admission to the theatres, the "festivities" were limited to a concert given in the Assembly by the Institut national de musique, which, curiously enough, played a piece that was so soft and melodious that an incensed Montagnard deputy interrupted in the middle of the performance to ask whether the intent was to deplore the death of the king. In response to this criticism, the orchestra immediately struck up the *Ça ira*, and the conductor, Gossec, explained to the audience that, on the contrary, the intent had been to express "the gentle emotions stirred in sensitive souls by the happiness of being delivered from a tyrant." Then the Assembly went to the Place de la Révolution to take an oath of hatred against the monarchy and returned to the debating hall to hear a hysterical address from the Gardes-Françaises Section against the Jacobins, with the deputy Gérente calling for their annihilation: "They who have corrupted public morals, made a profession of murder, and destroyed entire communes must be wiped from the face of the earth." Finally, on a motion by Tallien, the Assembly more or less repudiated the day's anniversary celebration by decreasing an annual holiday in honour of 9 Thermidor.

As for the jeunes gens, they organized their own celebration. That evening, at the instigation of Gonchon and probably thanks to money from the Committee of General Security, they invited sansculottes from the Faubourg Antoine to meet them at Chez Février. Fréron had given them precise instructions:

Tell them that people are trying to lead them astray and incite them to violence. Tell them that the malicious individuals who seek to fill them with hate and bitterness against the merchants are taking advantage of their good faith. Tell them that dearer foodstuffs are the result of dearer labour, that the merchant who pays higher wages to their brothers, the workers, must necessarily sell at a higher price. Tell them that they are right to ask for much higher wages for their work, that they must be careful not to believe everything people would have them believe, that the least agitation in this time of turmoil would mean the downfall of France.

Upon leaving Chez Février, the youths and their guests from the faubourgs went to the Palais Royal to burn an effigy of a Jacobin; from there they made their way to the courtyard of the Jacobin Club, where the ashes of the effigy were collected in a chamber pot and carried to the Montmartre sewer bearing the epitaph:

Pour m'enrichir au 2 Septembre
De Jacobin je pris le nom,
Mon urne fut un pot de chambre
Et cet égout mon Panthéon

(To get rich on 2 September
I took the name of Jacobin,
My urn was a chamber pot
And this sewer my Panthéon)

Such were the antiroyalist festivities of 2 Pluviôse. The Convention had shown – to its own satisfaction at least – that it did not support the aristocracy. Thus, when Duhem, who had started the whole affair, made so bold as to declare on 9 Pluviôse that the royalists were in the ascendant, he was packed off to the Abbaye prison for having insulted the Assembly! "It is truly remarkable," he declared, flabbergasted. "They would have people believe that I cannot distinguish Fréron's brilliant youth from the young men who are fighting at the front. The gilded nation is waging war against the sans-culottes." And, later: "I repeat what I said. When I spoke of royalists, I referred to the aristocratic theatres, the Palais Royal, and Fréron's youth. These individuals are neither the French people, nor the young men of our armies."

As for Delacroix, he was unanimously acquitted by the Revolutionary Tribunal on 2 Ventôse, after the jury found that it could not be established that his writings tended to support the restoration of the monarchy. Following his acquittal, a "huge crowd of citizens" took him home "to the sound of cheers from all sides."

Thus, legislating according to the dictates of public opinion, the Convention marched to the tune of the jeunesse dorée. As Lacretelle noted, the excesses committed by the jeunes gens often laid the groundwork for a salutary decree on the following day. Indeed, each of the jeunesse dorée's campaigns prompted the Assembly to go a step further on its reactionary course. The fourth *jour sans-culottide*, after the riot at the Palais Royal, saw the expulsion of the patriots from the capital; 21 Brumaire saw the closure of the Jacobin Club and the arrest of Carrier; 20 Pluviôse, the arrest of Babeuf and the removal of Marat from the Panthéon; and 1 Germinal, Sieyès's special police law and the strengthening of the means of repression. The Fréronists, who had sought "to create on the outside a party powerful enough to carry the Convention beyond its wishes," had fully succeeded in their aims. The Assembly, without the least spark of resistance, dismantled piece by piece the political reforms of the Year II: it abolished the law on suspects, allowed the Girondins to return, reopened the churches, amnestied the *Vendéens* and the *chouans*, recalled the émigrés, gave back to the families of condemned persons the personal effects taken from them just before their execution, intensified the campaign to outlaw the patriots, and substituted the Constitution of the Year III for what Fréron referred to as the "scribbled placard" of 1793. The keen observer Mallet du Pan remarked, "The Convention has again become the zealous servant of public opinion ... The power of the Assembly lies outside the institution."

Indeed, this power lay in the hands of the jeunesse dorée. It was henceforth the jeunes gens who formed the sovereign people: judges of all the theatres, oracles of all the cafés, orators of all the sections – in a word, the "magistrates of public opinion."

THE REMOVAL OF MARAT FROM THE PANTHÉON

One major way in which the jeunesse dorée helped the Reaction gain momentum was by turning public opinion against the memory of Marat. In the days following Robespierre's fall, the Jacobins had seen themselves steadily losing ground in public opinion. In a bid to check this slide, if not reverse it, they devised the stratagem of having Marat's remains carried to the Panthéon by virtue of the decrees of 24 Brumaire and 5 Frimaire, Year II, which had never been enacted – apparently because Robespierre had been jealous. It was an adroit move, for to translate Marat, the initiator of and apologist for the September massacres, to the Panthéon amounted, indirectly, to justifying the Terror. If given sufficient pomp, the ceremony might have some impact on public opinion and, by intimidating the Moderates, counter the progress of the Reaction. Thus, at the Jacobin Club on 25 Fructidor, the idea of bearing Marat to the Panthéon was revived; the next day, Léonard Bourdon had the Convention approve a plan for the ceremony, which was scheduled for the fifth *jour sans-culottide*.

Since Marat's remains were still at the Cordeliers Club and the distance from there to the Panthéon was much too short to allow for a long procession, it was resolved that the Montagne Section would first carry the remains to the Convention. The cortège would depart from there, leave the Jardin des Tuileries by the Pont Tournant, cross the Place de la Révolution, take the rues de la Révolution, Honoré, du Roule, and de la Monnaie, cross the Pont Neuf, then take the rues de Thionville, Française, and de la Liberté, traverse the Place Michel, and finally arrive at the Panthéon by the rues Hyacinthe and Jacques. The Public Works Commission advised the Montagne Section police commissioner to see that the streets to be taken by the cortège were "immaculate" and, if necessary, to have them swept clean of any mud or debris. Proprietors and contractors were told to store their goods and materials. Lastly, since Marat's hearse was over thirty feet high, the lampposts had to be taken down to allow it to pass. In short, the route was well prepared for a grand spectacle.

The procession itself, with a cavalry and drum corps leading the way and bringing up the rear, included the representatives of the popular societies, the officers of the sections, pupils of the Champ de Mars, members of the tribunals, artists, the Institut national de musique, citizens – one for every department – carrying baskets of flowers, Marat's hearse, the members of the Convention ringed by a tricolour ribbon, orphans of defenders of France, and soldiers wounded at the front. Some eighteen thousand people were expected to take part. At least that was the number of musical scores that were printed: one thousand for each of the fourteen armies of the Republic, and four thousand for the members of the Convention and the citizens from the various sections. During the procession, the Institut national de musique would play military marches, hymns to fraternity, and, as Marat was carried into the Panthéon, "melodious music so soft and soothing that it would evoke immortality."

Thus, a vast display of pomp and circumstance was to be staged to lend the civic ceremony the splendour and brilliance needed to revive the revolutionary mysticism of the Year II. It is easy to imagine the strategy of covert resistance that the Moderates would adopt to thwart this plan, and the tricks they would think up to sabotage the ceremony. Open resistance was impossible because Marat was still an officially recognized figure.

The first Moderate ploy was a lively, ironic pamphlet by the little-known deputy Couturier, who recalled that Marat had once regarded as a "cruel affront" the idea of ever being carried to the Panthéon, since he held Voltaire and Mirabeau, who were already buried there, to be "distinguished rogues." Then, on 29 Fructidor, Fouché sought to have the ceremony cancelled by alleging that the planned event had more in common with an ecclesiastical procession than with a funeral cortège. His attempt failed, but Thibaudeau nevertheless had it decreed that the people's representatives would not wear ceremonial dress. There were also more underhanded schemes. In the first issue of *L'Orateur du Peuple*, Fréron had pledged that he would carry on the work of Marat, so the "cherished disciple" could not openly object to the proposed celebration. Instead, he started the rumour that the Jacobins were planning to turn the event into a massacre. When the organizers heard this, they clumsily decreed that "all citizens attending the ceremony must be unarmed." In reaction to Léonard Bourdon's proposal that the proper place for Marat's hearse was amidst the people's representatives, Fréron alleged – with the unfortunate support of Collot-d'Herbois – that it was a trick to divide the Convention.

But all these efforts were superfluous, since the ceremony turned out to be a dismal failure. The police reported "that there were fewer people, less gaiety, less enthusiasm than usual." The agent attributed this "to the fear that spread in the days preceding the ceremony on account of the rumours that there might be some regrettable accident ... There were very few people anywhere about." The cortège marched at a brisk pace to the Panthéon, and in the midst of the general indifference the joy of the Jacobins appeared all bluster and affectation. They had an opportunity to see just how much influence they had lost, and Lebois noted in *L'Ami du Peuple* the paradox in translating Marat to the Panthéon at a time when his principles were sinking into general abhorrence.

On the fifth *jour sans-culottide*, Year II, at the instigation of the Jacobins, the Convention had thus borne Marat to the Panthéon with much pomp and circumstance. On 20 Pluviôse, Year III, four months later, it retracted and, under pressure from the muscadins, decreed that he should be removed. It was a degrading recantation, which showed how far the Reaction had progressed and attested to the jeunesse dorée's leading role in the changing political situation.

With the regime of the Year II repudiated everywhere – in both its institutions and its political figures – it was only natural that the statue of Marat should eventually be torn down; in the ideology of liberty, he was the personification of violence, a value typically associated with the populace. The reactionaries regarded Marat as the evangelist of the September massacres, the leader of the bloodthirsty criminals, the man of two hundred thousand heads, and so on. In the eyes of the lower classes, however, the Friend of the People still retained some aura of sacredness, and by attacking his memory the jeunesse dorée was to rekindle the popular movement that had flagged since Thermidor, Year ii, provide a focus for social unrest, and accelerate the pace of the struggle between the classes.

On 18 Nivôse, a few days before Fréron's appeal to the jeunesse dorée, there was talk at the Café de Chartres, amidst praise for Charlotte Corday, of going to the Place du Carrousel to demolish Marat's mausoleum with pickaxes. Well aware of the political consequences that such an act might have, the Committee of General Security reacted immediately and, by ordering the military to arrest the troublemakers, was able to avert it. The notion then circulated, no doubt at the Committee's instigation, that it was "unwise and impolitic" to destroy a still-venerated idol. On 26 Nivôse, the Committee's rapporteur, Clauzel, informed the Assembly that agitators were planning to smash busts in the theatres. In an effort to foil the scheme, he claimed that those planning it were terrorists trying to compromise the jeunes gens. But this was a naïve stratagem. Although he justified in advance the repression against the militant sans-culottes, he also gave the green light to the jeunes gens, who no longer had to fear being accused. That evening, the busts of Marat and Le Peletier disappeared from the Café de la Convention, and on the following day, a bust of Marat was found disfigured at the Théâtre Favart. The *Réponse de la jeunesse française actuellement à Paris à l'Orateur du Peuple*, which in all likelihood originated in Fréron's own printing house, appeared on 27 Nivôse. In a propaganda ploy, Fréron seems to have substituted himself for the jeunes gens so that he could respond to his own appeal, giving "their" reply all the loyal indignation he wanted it to have. *They* overturn the busts of Marat and Le Peletier? How could the government ever accuse them of such a thing? After all, what did it matter to them if Marat was in the Panthéon? The people they had a grudge against were the terrorists. The same idea was expressed in *L'Orateur du Peuple* of 1 Pluviôse, in which Fréron reminded his readers that the memory of Marat deserved respect, since he had been assassinated, and that rather than quarrel over his ashes they should be attacking the guilty who were still alive. Yet what did his death matter, replied *Le Messager du Soir*, if his life, sold to the various factions, had been nothing but a "series of crimes"? And so the campaign against Marat continued, with those who claimed to hold sway over the jeunesse dorée powerless to stop it.

On 12 Pluviôse, in the midst of a great commotion at the Théâtre Feydeau, a bust of Marat was thrown to the ground and smashed to pieces. He had not paid for his season's tickets, it was said mockingly. The Committee of General Security was caught in a bind: it wanted to avoid antagonizing the jeunes gens, but could no longer be a party to these insults to the memory of Marat, who had been solemnly consecrated by the Convention. The following day, the Committee's rapporteur, Laignelot, acknowledged in his report to the Assembly that these actions "in effect debased the Convention," and assured members that the busts would be reinstalled. The youths involved, he said, had been led astray by terrorists and royalists (as if the two could have been confused!) and they had come and disavowed the disturbances. Thus, the Committee still thought that it could force the jeunesse dorée to respect the Assembly's decrees.

Two days later, on 14 Pluviôse, the theatres were in a total uproar. At the Théâtre de la République, Martainville had Laignelot's report read out, and then, as *Le Messager du Soir* put it, "to prove to the government, the Convention, France, and the whole of Europe that it is not just a few individuals, but the entire population that abhors this monster," Marat's bust was smashed to pieces to the paradoxical cry of "Long live the Convention!" At the Vaudeville, Marat's head was knocked off with a club and rolled about on the stage until a supposed moderate kicked it into the audience. There were similar scenes at the Théâtre Favart, the Théâtre des Arts, and the Théâtre de la Montansier. At the Théâtre Feydeau, someone read out the lines

Des lauriers de Marat, il n'est point une feuille
Qui ne retrace un crime à l'oeil épouvanté.

(Not a leaf remains of Marat's laurels
That does not recall a crime to the horrified spectator.)

Meanwhile, at the Carrousel, some forty or so young men "of various ages," among them the *ci-devant* Chevalier de Jean, wanted to demolish Marat's monument. At the Palais Égalité a group of "well-dressed" young men spoke of smashing everything they could lay their hands on, while at the Café de Chartres the Marquis de Saint-Huruge asserted that he would not limit himself to pulverizing plaster heads. In the rue Montmartre, children threw effigies of Marat into the sewer, shouting "There's your Panthéon!"

Overwhelmed by the situation, the Committee of General Security struggled to contain the unrest; on the morrow, 15

Pluviôse, it posted a public notice calling for order, in which it rebuked the jeunes gens for their "imprudent zeal" and threatened them with harsh measures. The very same day, *Le Messager du Soir* lashed out against Marat:

This disgusting cynic lived publicly with the wretched women one meets in the filthiest streets, women a gentleman would not touch with the toe of his shoe. The dealings he had with these vile whores would no doubt have led him to his grave had not Charlotte Corday hastened his death by a few days. Why did such a being not rot to death? Why was Hanriot not left to perish in the sewer where he had taken refuge? Why was the despicable Coffinhal dragged from the latrine pit where he had gone into hiding? Villains ought to die as they have lived – in filth. Our fathers buried murderers and other immoral men in mud, but we set them on pedestals!

The Committee of General Security seemed to have lost all authority. The same was true of the Assembly. On 16 Pluviôse, a mob of six hundred youths went the rounds of the cafés smashing busts, and then invaded the hall of the Convention during its evening sitting, to shouts of "Down with the cursed buveurs de sang! Down with the cursed villains! Down with the bloodthirsty butchers! Down with all the damned rogues! In the sewer with the whole bloody lot!" The debates of the Convention had already lost much of their dignity; now the institution looked like a bear garden.

With busts of Marat starting to become a rarity in public places, all that remained was to demand the demolition of his monument at the Carrousel and his removal from the Panthéon. This was done at the Café de Chartres on 19 Pluviôse in a proclamation that also called on the good citizens to massacre the Jacobins if (admirable precaution!) "they dared to cause the outbreak of civil war."

The Committee of General Security still believed that it could restrain the jeunesse dorée. On 17 Pluviôse, Fréron's right-hand man, Louis Jullian, gave the youths at the Palais Égalité a good talking-to and urged them to remain calm. Agitators had infiltrated their ranks, he explained. In response to the excesses of these agents provocateurs, French youth had to show it was capable of "forceful moderation" and devote its energy above all to informing the Committee about terrorist plots. Fréron himself, in *L'Orateur du Peuple* of 19 Pluviôse, wrote that it was futile to attack a dead man "when so many rogues [were] still alive, insulting the people by their shameless presence in the Convention." But by urging the jeunes gens to remain calm, Fréron put himself in a very awkward position. From the right, a pamphlet soon appeared accusing him of "having written in favour of the bloodthirsty terrorists," while from the left he was excoriated in two vitriolic tracts which it became illegal to peddle. The first tract, *L'Ombre de Marat aux Parisiens* (The Shade of Marat to Parisians), began by portraying France in crisis: the patriots outlawed, the popular societies closed down, the Constitution of 1793 decried as a "scribbled placard," the pamphlets urging gilded citizens to cut the throats of sans-culotte citizens; then it proceeded to denounce the leaders of the Reaction: Fréron, who had had eight hundred people shot in Toulon without trial, who made a scandalous display of luxury, and whose life was one orgy after another; Tallien, who had made a fortune selling prison discharges in Bordeaux; Legendre, who kept an actress, Mlle Comtat; Clauzel, a friend of the merchant aristocracy, and so on. "Certainly I called for the death of the counter-revolutionaries," "Marat" continued, "and the proof that too many of them were spared is that there are still enough of them left to be a threat to liberty."

The second tract, *Le Dernier Coup de tocsin de Fréron* (Fréron Sounds the Tocsin for the Last Time), which the jeunes gens attributed to Chasles and which they burnt publicly at the Palais Royal on 17 Pluviôse, assailed Fréron for his "ferocious desire to destroy the people," lashed out at the "abject cowardice of the gilded young sons of victims of the guillotine" and, in an appeal to the military, pleaded, "Do you not see that they want to make you bow down your brave republican heads, already covered with such illustrious scars, under the arrogant yoke of this Fréronist youth, sullied as it is by vice, prostitution, and the most shameless cowardice?"

There was a real risk that the muscadins' antics would backfire, for the patriots still had a very vivid memory of Marat, the man who had shown himself to be their friend on so many occasions. His bust was everywhere: in the cafés and theatres, on street corners, and in all the sections and popular societies where civic celebrations had been held in his honour at the time of his enthronement. A monument to him stood in the Place des Invalides, and the glory of the Panthéon shone over his ashes. Fréron himself had placed an invocation to the departed spirit of Marat at the head of the first issue of his newspaper; on 2 Vendémiaire, Year III, he had attacked those who had been behind Marat's indictment in 1793. Soon after, Carrier's secretary had asked to have his surname changed to Marat. Many communes in France had taken his name. In short, the figure of Marat, like those of Le Peletier and Chalier, with whom he formed a sort of republican trinity, constituted the supreme civic symbol of loyalty to the new regime and to liberty.

Yet below the surface there was more to it than this. Although by Marat's own admission he was regarded by the Moderates as "a lunatic, an atrabilious madman, a bloodthirsty monster, and the vilest of villains," there was something sacred about his memory in the minds of the common people. In an oration delivered at Marat's funeral, Danton had gone so far as to deify him, while a short time before, the sans-culottes had followed the rites of a genuine liturgy in worshipping him (Albert Soboul has shown the religious nature of this cult). Feudal charters and manuscripts, portraits of famous ancien régime figures, and all manner of objects symbolizing royal despotism were burnt before his effigy. At the Cordeliers Club, now run by Marat's wife and sister, an altar had been erected to him on which, in a precious vase taken from the state furniture depository, his heart was preserved, venerated as if it were a sacred relic. When the altar had been inaugurated, in July of 1793, a speech with the epigraph "*O cor Jesu! O cor Marat!*" had been given, in which a parallel was drawn between the two figures: Jesus with his apostles, for having fought the pharisees and the publicans; Marat with the Cordeliers, for having fought the shopkeepers and the aristocrats. It was ingenuous, not to say completely mad, and a print vendor from the Muséum Section, Jean-Baptiste Penet, protested – because he found the comparison insulting to Marat! Marat's bathtub, lamp, and escritoire were displayed in the Place du Carrousel, and "the harpies went every day to worship his bust and his disgusting furniture," reported a Thermidorian in his memoirs. Virtually all of the Republic's forty thousand or so communes had erected a monument to him on which invocations were said.

Marat was more than a mere civic symbol, he was a sacred figure. And so the jeunes gens' anti-Marat campaign, because it was directed against this political religion, amounted to sacrilegious profanation. In the rue aux Ours, at the corner of the rue Salle au Comte, stood a Virgin called the "miraculous Virgin of the rue aux Ours." Tradition had it that in 1418 a Swiss who had lost everything gambling had stabbed the Virgin in despair and that blood had spurted forth from the wound. The man had been burnt alive, and on 3 January every year until 1790 his effigy was burnt before the Virgin in atonement. On 2 Brumaire, Year II, the statue was removed from its niche and replaced by a bust of Marat. An object of public veneration, this bust was still there when, on 15 Pluviôse, Year III, vulgar jokes about it appeared in *Le Messager du Soir*:

Last night, in the rue aux Ours, a Jacobin passing before a niche where an idol of Marat has been substituted for one of the Virgin Mary surprised a citizen in a most suppliant posture. As it was very dark, however, he mistook what he saw and said to the dishonest comrade, "One does not worship Marat by kneeling, but by preaching his sublime moral doctrine. Marat called for four hundred thousand heads; so far we have collected but two hundred and fifty thousand. Hence we still need another one hundred and fifty thousand. Only by collecting more heads shall we appease his spirit and honour his memory." "You are mistaken," replied the Moderate, without flinching. "I am not on my knees, but I *am* offering a sacrifice to the great Marat. Perhaps you would enjoy the smell of blood more than the smell of the fumes you see rising toward your god. But since you appear to be one of his ministers, you may take your part of the sacrifice." Whereupon he rose and disappeared.

This was all that was needed to provoke the jeunesse dorée to new escapades; at about eight o'clock on 15 Pluviôse the police commissioner of the Lombards Section arrested five men who had just smashed a bust of Chalier in the rue de la Grande Truanderie, and who were intending to vandalize the one of Marat in the rue aux Ours. They were very young, appeared to belong to the same group, and said that they were all honnêtes gens. The next day, however, the Committee of General Security promptly had them released.

The jeunes gens did not stop here. They burnt paper on the pedestals, as though to purify them of the filth left by the busts of Marat. They talked of making him civic crowns out of terrorists' intestines. At the Halle market a butcher covered Marat's bust with blood "to show him with the one attribute that truly suited him." A pamphlet went into great detail in comparing him with Jesus Christ: both had been enemies of commerce, professional agitators, and the objects of superstitious worship, and both had been assassinated. Another pamphlet described Jean-Jacques Rousseau giving Marat a lesson in humanity before a crowd of sans-culottes from the faubourgs gathered one night at the Panthéon, as though it were a great patriotic sabbath. An "impartial" biography, *La Vie criminelle et politique de J.P. Marat* (The Criminal and Political Life of J.P. Marat), declared,

Jacobins, worship Marat if you like. Make a holy shroud of his bloodied shirt, a relic of his bath, a diadem of his old crown, a gospel of his diaries or even of his old monarchical constitution. You are free to do as you wish. The Indians worship the excrement of the great Lama; they even prepare some rather delightful dishes out of it. There is no accounting for tastes!

Indeed, the muscadins offered up excrement in sacrifice to Marat.

In the eyes of the patriots, these carryings-on amounted to blasphemous insults – whence the fears of the Thermidorians and their warnings to the jeunes gens. Fréron, for one, cautioned on 11 Pluviôse, "Take care not to make any reckless moves that might aggravate the virile, truly revolutionary energy of these decent fellows from the faubourgs." And Méhée, the very man who had written *La Queue de Robespierre* (Robespierre's Tail), asked in *L'Ami des citoyens* of 15 Pluviôse, "Are our young men, some of whom have been shaving for a good many years, not already allowing themselves to be driven beyond their self-imposed limits? Will the Convention not become accustomed all too quickly to seeing its decrees disregarded?"

These fears were not unfounded, for, as expected, the muscadins' iconoclastic rampages were stirring up anger and resentment in the populace. In the Faubourg Antoine, the people put a crown on a bust of Marat, carried him in triumph through the streets, and pondered how they could avenge his memory. On 14 Pluviôse, a dozen or so sans-culottes gathered in the Place de Grève spoke of clobbering anyone who dared insult the Friend of the People. On the seventeenth, in the vicinity of the Convention, there was talk of going to demand that his bust be reinstated, while in the Gravilliers Section youths and workers came to blows. The "powder-puff heroes" had taken to their heels, Lebois reported the next day, and "the protests of the gilded army" had been futile. On the eighteenth, the Droits de l'Homme Section prepared an address to the Convention, asking ironically whether it was within the law to violate property by removing the busts of Marat. On the nineteenth, the inmates of the Plessis prison fêted the Friend of the People in the prison courtyard, while in the Faubourg Antoine, workers spoke of going to the Convention to return Marat's and Le Peletier's busts to their rightful places, on either side of the president.

But the Committee of General Security was not prepared to stand up to the jeunes gens and leave Marat in the Panthéon. It was much too afraid of the renewed popular unrest to risk alienating the jeunesse dorée and losing its valuable support in public opinion. As early as 11 Pluviôse, one of Fréron's adjutants, Alexandre Méchin, had advised the Committee of General Security "to take advantage of the considerable force offered by the activity and energy of the young men of this huge commune. They constitute the Committee's only possible counterweight against the faction, and this counterweight is vital because the Committee has no other means of repression, no other armed force that it can really count on."

And so on 19 Pluviôse the Committee of General Security had the busts of Marat removed from the theatres, ordered closure of the Lazowski Club and of the Quinze Vingts Popular Society, where supposed Maratists were allegedly conspiring, and issued a series of arrest warrants, first against Babeuf, and then, in the course of the following week, against fifty or so militant sans-culottes. The Committee instructed the Paris Police Administrative Commission to see that the warrants were "enforced forthwith." In most cases the warrants were for employees of arms workshops, such as the accountant Jean-Auguste Jullien, arrested "for having laughed," and the workshop manager Father Jean, known as Brutus; or else for individuals who professed opinions or principles "contrary to the present order of things," such as one of Babeuf's hawkers by the name of Bouin, known as Little Father Gérard, who was described in his arrest warrant as a "most evil man who is considered to be one of the leaders of the Marchés Section's *jacobite* cabal"; and Marie-Jeanne Dieu, who reportedly said "that she didn't give a hoot about the country, that she was fed up to the teeth with France and the Republic." On the previous day, 18 Pluviôse, all the members of the old revolutionary committee of the Faubourg Montmartre Section had been arrested at one fell swoop.

Next came the disgraceful and cowardly decree of 20 Pluviôse. "Away with these useless shades!" exclaimed André Dumont, and the Convention, which had paid tribute to Marat under an unrepealable law, decreed that the honours of the Panthéon could not be conferred on a citizen, nor his bust placed in the Assembly or in public places, until ten years after his death. As a result, the ashes of Marat, Le Peletier, Dampierre, Bara, and Viala were removed from the Panthéon and returned to common ground. The bust of Brutus was substituted for that of Marat at the Convention, and Marat's monument in the Place du Carrousel was torn down. Duval recounts that while some youths wanted to cast Marat's remains into the river, and others to take them to the Montfaucon refuse dump, some 1,200 to 1,500 of them, at Martainville's instigation, had the vaults of the Panthéon opened and took away Marat's coffin, which they threw down the Montmartre sewer – the opening being wide enough for a coffin, he says. There is no truth to this story whatsoever. Marat's remains were removed from the Panthéon on 8 Ventôse, Year III, and taken to the St. Étienne du Mont cemetery.

On the evening of 20 Pluviôse there were stormy meetings in several sections, though perhaps not quite as stormy as one might have expected: this was no doubt a sign of the flagging spirits of the sans-culotte militants and the fatigue of the revolutionary movement. In the Butte des Moulins, Le Peletier, and Gardes Françaises sections, Marat's bust was overturned without any objections. In the

Fontaine Grenelle Section it was decreed – without opposition, it seems – that the bust of a man "who merited immortality only as a great criminal" be destroyed immediately and that the names of the members of the old revolutionary committee be written in red on a board facing the president. The Mont Blanc, Quinze Vingts, and Temple sections sent appeals to other sections, urging them to knock Marat from his pedestal. Disturbances broke out as a result of some of the appeals, such as the one sent by the Quinze Vingts Section to the Montreuil Section and the one from the Temple Section to the Marchés Section, where a wine merchant named Morel protested against the arrest of the patriots and bared his chest "like a madman," shouting "Liberty or death!" "This would have had quite an effect," the informer explained, "had the Convention's decree not been announced at precisely the same time." The appeal of the Mont Blanc Section to the Muséum Section created a general uproar, which ended in the arrest of the citizens Cousin, Lechard, Leclerc, Lecomte, and Timber. In the Unité Section, seven patriots who "were causing trouble" in the general assembly were apprehended. Among them were a certain Marie-Charles Roux, who was arrested for having tried to prevent the seventeen-year-old apprentice hatter Aubry from reading a paper announcing the Convention's decree, and one Michel Thomas, who argued that this supposed law of the Convention was not known and that it should not be enforced until it was made public. In the Gravilliers Section, unrest "that could take a violent turn" was brewing, and was serious enough that on the twenty-eighth the Committee of General Security thought it worthwhile to recommend vigilance to the watch committee of the 6th arrondissement: "No terrorism, no royalism! Zeal and love for the Republic ..." In the Tuileries Section, a wine merchant by the name of Pierron, a member of the old revolutionary committee who had sought to block enforcement of the decree, was arrested on 26 Pluviôse. In the Droits de l'Homme Section, three young employees, Lefaivre, Marthion, and Goulliart, wanted to read aloud a copy of the Convention's decree, but a hoarding commissioner, Jean-Pierre Carron, threatened to drive his bayonet through the first person who spoke out in favour of overturning Marat, and said that "the only ones in favour were the muscadins."

All in all, unrest was reported in seven of the fourteen sections for which I obtained information. If we extrapolate these figures to the whole of Paris, we can assume there was unrest in twenty-four of the forty-eight Sections. This would explain the apprehension of the Committee of General Security, which had the monument in the Carrousel torn down at dawn the next day and was careful to ensure

that the sentries guarding it did not leave their posts before the demolition crew arrived, so as not to give the jeunes gens a chance to
destroy it themselves. At about a quarter to one, a crowd of workers
began to gather in the Faubourg Antoine, and at half past the
Committee of General Security called out two thousand National
Guards and "as many cavalrymen as possible" to disperse the mob.
This force was demobilized soon thereafter since, as Rovère and
Mathieu explained, "the plots of the malicious schemers [had] been
foiled for the time being."

The pretence of enemy plots could justify virtually any police operation, and the jeunesse dorée did its best to bring plenty of "plots"
to the attention of people closely associated with the Committee of
General Security, thus quickening the pace of the Reaction. For instance, Jollivet asserted that people were trying to turn the porters
at the Halle market against the government. The supposed proof
was that the *décade* (ten-day week) before they had been given only
a small part of the pay that was due to them, and had been told that
there was a shortage of funds. This was obviously untrue, he said;
otherwise, the Committee would have been informed, and, "very
conscious of the inconveniences that might result from the least
delay in the payment of these citizens' wages, would have seen that
funds were made available."

No doubt, the three citizens brought before the Committee of
General Security by Charles-Louis Laneuville and Jean-Louis-Joseph
Broyast on 19 Pluviôse "because they supported Marat" were also
part of a "plot." And it must have been a "plot" that was uncovered
by Cadet Gassicourt on 21 Pluviôse when he denounced to the
Committee the citizen Étienne Feuillant of the Tuileries for having
said to a friend who was going away for five or six days, "The patriots are downtrodden now, but damn it, before you're back they'll be
in control again." Yet another supposed plot was recounted by
Jollivet; he claimed that a fellow had shown up at Fréron's around
ten o'clock in the evening, asked when Fréron would be back, given
two mysterious whistles, and left, mumbling, "We'll find him. We'll
get him dead or alive." Still another plot was allegedly being prepared by the gunsmith Nicolas Servières, who was denounced by
Jollivet for having said, in reference to the removal of Marat from the
Panthéon, "It is the royalists who are doing it all to harass the
friends of the people. It is the federalists who are to blame. They are
obviously at a loss to know what to do. But have patience! It will all
be over soon." Still another "plot" was denounced to the Committee
on 24 Pluviôse by the printer Boulard, who claimed to have over-
heard three disabled veterans at the Café Laflotte say "that it was

time to attack the muscadins, eat up their assignats, and knock their heads off." This, he said, was "a trick of the Republic's enemies to stir up trouble by suggesting that our brave soldiers are mistreated, and perhaps incite some imprudent citizen to let himself get carried away."

Reduced to viewing things through the eyes of the jeunesse dorée, and obsessed by the idea that some group of elusive Jacobins was hatching an evil plot behind the scenes, the Committee of General Security was no longer able to recognize that the jeunesse dorée was provoking the ire of the common people. For it could only be called provocation when young men were permitted to perform dances on Marat's grave on 21 Pluviôse, yet the next day sansculottes from the Faubourg Antoine were arrested for carrying his bust in triumph through the streets, or when the tracts of Maton de la Varennes recounting *Les Crimes de Marat et des autres égorgeurs* (The Crimes of Marat and Other Cutthroats) were allowed to be sold in the Place du Carrousel, where the mausoleum of the Friend of the People had stood only a few days earlier. And there is no other word than provocation for the volume entitled *Assassinat de Marat en vaudeville* (Assassination of Marat in Vaudeville), a collection of couplets to be sung to well-known tunes, or for the song *Marat dépanthéonisé*, which was heard in the theatres on 21 Pluviôse:

Marat dont les anarchistes
Prônaient la divinité
Par les Français athéistes
Est dépanthéonisé.
Eh aye! eh hu! et aye! eh pouss!
Eh aye! eh hu! et v'la comme il arrive!
Le Jacobin enragera
Et le républicain rira,
Le beau contraste que voilà:
Dépit par ci, gaieté par là
De voir ainsi son culte à bas.

(Marat, who the anarchists
Claimed was a god
By the French atheists
Is removed from the Panthéon.
And heave! And ho! And out he goes!
And heave! And ho! And so it goes!
The Jacobin will rage
And the republican will laugh,

Oh what a lovely contrast:
One resentful, the other joyful
To see his cult thus felled.)

It was obviously a clear provocation, too, to ask disingenuously, once Marat had been *dépanthéonisé* (i.e., removed from the Panthéon), how one was going to *démaratiser* the Panthéon. Or, to cap it all, to suggest carrying Charlotte Corday to the Panthéon.

In *L'Ami du Peuple*, Lebois called on the sans-culottes to respond to these provocations: "The rogues are in their niche. You know who they are. Now is the time to smash them to smithereens just as they smashed the bust of the Friend of the People." But it was still too early. The fire had to be stoked some more. Not until later, in Germinal and Prairial, would the anger of the populace boil over, and the removal of Marat from the Panthéon seems to have played no small role in bringing it to the boil.

THE WAR OF THE THEATRES

In September of 1793, the performance of a moderate play, *L'Ami des lois*, had brought about the closure of the Comédie Française, 113 years after its founding. The actors of the Théâtre de la Nation were banned from the stage and outlawed, with the exception of their leading man, Molé, who had had the foresight to have written on his door, "The republican Molé lives here." The patriot actors who had rallied around Talma and who had left the Théâtre de la Nation to found the Théâtre de la République had been allowed to continue performing.

In the days following Thermidor the release of the actors of the Théâtre de la Nation gave rise to a revival of moderate comedy. On 24 Thermidor, Year II, after six months behind bars, the actor Larive returned to the stage in *Guillaume Tell*; on the twenty-ninth, Louise Comtat, Dazincourt, Naudet, and Fleury appeared in *La Métromanie* and *Les Fausses Confidences*. Audiences were soon applauding the passages that recalled the fall of the tyrants. Solidarity among moderates was experiencing a rebirth. Then the theatre-going public started the fad of throwing notes onto the stage and asking the actors and actresses to read them out. In late Brumaire, in *Le Journal des rieurs ou le Démocrite français*, Martainville published some couplets celebrating the closure of the Jacobin Club, which the Committee of General Security prohibited from being read out at the Théâtre de la République. Subsequently, however, a certain tolerance developed, and the fad became common practice in all of the theatres. According to the police, the notes that were cast onto the stage were first taken to the Café de Chartres to be censored by the jeunes gens, who rejected all but calls for the murder of terrorists. The theatres thus grew more and more agitated every week, and by early Pluviôse performances could easily have been confused with general assemblies, with the stage as the speaker's rostrum.

The war of the theatres had begun. The aim of the jeunes gens was to force actors who had lent their talent to the regime of the Year II by appearing in "Jacobin" plays to atone for their sins. As an act of contrition, most of them were required to sing *Le Réveil du Peuple*, "an unimaginative, ridiculous glorification of the Convention," which protested against the "barbarous slowness" of the Reaction and urged the representatives to hasten punishment of the terrorists. The words are by Souriguère, the music by Gaveau:

Peuple français, peuple de frères,
Peux-tu voir sans frémir d'horreur,
Le crime arborer les bannières
Du carnage et de la Terreur?
Tu souffres qu'une horde atroce,
Et d'assassins et de brigands,
Souille par son souffle féroce
Le territoire des vivants!

Quelle est cette lenteur barbare?
Hâte-toi! peuple souverain,
De rendre aux monstres du Ténare
Tous ces buveurs de sang humain.
Guerre à tous les agents du crime!
Poursuivons-les jusqu'au trépas
Partage l'horreur qui m'anime;
Ils ne nous échapperont pas.

(People of France, fraternal people,
Can you look on, without shuddering in horror,
As crime raises the banners
Of carnage and Terror?
You allow a gruesome horde
Of butchers and brigands
To run amok through
The land of the living!

Why this barbarous slowness?
Make haste, sovereign people,

To return to the monsters of Taenarum
All these drinkers of human blood.
War on all the agents of this crime!
Let us hunt them till death
Shares the horror that possesses me;
They shall not escape us.)

Le Réveil du Peuple was sung for the first time by Gaveau at the general assembly of the Guillaume Tell Section on 30 Nivôse, Year III. The words were published the next day in *Le Messager du Soir*, and this hodgepodge of trivialities soon became *La Marseillaise* of the Reaction and enjoyed an immense success. Indeed, it was so successful that as early as 8 Ventôse Gaveau asked the Butte des Moulins police commissioner to confiscate what he claimed was an unauthorized edition of *Le Réveil du Peuple*, saying that he was now the sole author, Souriguère having sold him his rights. Every evening in the theatres, according to the *Gazette française* of 6 Germinal, the verse "Quelle est cette lenteur barbare?" met with thunderous applause, in protest against "the slow, stumbling progress of the Reaction."

But let us return to the terrorist actors. Beginning in early Pluviôse, the jeunes gens demanded that they make amends, and this created further unrest in the theatres. The actor Vallière agreed to go and plead his case at the Café de Chartres, but only after Gaveau had tried in vain to argue for his vindication at the Théâtre Feydeau. Fusil, who had been Collot-d'Herbois's assistant in Lyon, was appearing in *Crispin, rival de son maître*; the jeunes gens first asked him to sing *Le Réveil du Peuple*, but then changed their minds, fearing that his "foul mouth" would defile the cherished hymn. He was expelled from the Théâtre de la République on 5 Pluviôse after a spectator, standing on a bench in the orchestra, read out a document bearing Fusil's signature which sentenced his father to death. Another actor, Dugazon, refused to go to Canossa and left the stage of his own accord, pitching his wig and costume at the audience in a gesture of defiance. Lays defended himself in the pamphlet *Lays, artiste du théâtre des Arts, à ses concitoyens* (Lays, Actor of the Théâtre des Arts, to His Fellow Citizens). Trial, a former member of the Le Peletier Section revolutionary committee, which refused to deny its alleged involvement in the "murder" of the citizen Saint-Amaranthe, was banned from the stage and actually died as a result, "deeply distressed and seething with rage," according to Duval. Lastly, Talma, who had been interrupted in the middle of a performance by a group of young men who claimed that he was a terrorist, silenced the audience and, with incomparable dignity, declared that he had always loved liberty and hated murder: "The Reign of Terror caused me much bitter grief," he said. "All my friends died on the scaffold!"

Every evening in the theatres a new actor had to beg pardon. The increasing unrest came to a head on 18 Pluviôse with the performance at the Ambigu Comique of a play by Périn and Commaille Saint-Aubin entitled *Le Concert de la rue Feydeau ou la folie du jour* (The Concert of the Rue Feydeau, or the Folly of the Day).

The concerts given at the Théâtre Feydeau were definitely the folly of the day, with "all the muscadins and muscadines, formerly known as élégants and élégantes," crowding to get in, according to *La Vedette*. Why the crush? To hear Garat, "the Orpheus of our times," or to catch a glimpse of the beautiful Thérésia Cabarrus, who was literally idolized, as though having pretty eyes and a lovely smile amounted to saving the French Republic, *L'Abréviateur universel* commented wryly.

The play, a sort of bourgeois version of *The Marriage of Figaro*, in which good, solid middle-class citizens scoff at their own shortcomings, began its run on 15 Pluviôse. In it, a pretentious, lazy little muscadin ridicules the faubourgs and speaks pompously of the Palais Royal. One of the concluding lines of the play is "Let us leave these idle rich to conceal their uselessness with shameful luxury."

On 17 Pluviôse, the jeunes gens invaded the theatre and, in the midst of a great uproar, brought the performance to a halt. The authors and the theatre director were called upon to make amends. There was talk of burning the play on the stage. Finally, the Temple Section police commissioner, wearing his sash, managed to restore order by promising to bring the play before the Committee of General Security. However, the Committee sent a letter to the theatre director authorizing performance of the play, and the letter was read out to the jeunes gens by the police commissioner the following evening. They had crowded into the theatre in great numbers, intending, as Saint-Huruge said, to teach some Committee members a good lesson. Yet no sooner had the police commissioner finished reading the letter than a Donnybrook broke out on the stage between spectators from the boxes and others from the orchestra, the two sides laying into each other with sticks and clubs. The youths tore the play out of the prompter's hands and drove the actors from the stage. Then, reported the police commissioner,

The citizen Audinot, the director of the theatre, seeing the utter chaos, his theatre overrun by young men on a rampage, and believing that a full-scale brawl was about to begin – which could have caused unimaginable calamity

– said to me that since it was already quite late in the evening … and he feared that the play might serve as a pretext to an eruption of the ill will that seemed to have spread throughout the theatre, he had decided that the play would not be performed.

The jeunes gens appeared to have carried the day. Yet appearances were illusory: while the free-for-all was going on inside the theatre, the Military Committee had had the building surrounded by close to a hundred soldiers. When the audience emerged, some two hundred youths were arrested and taken to the administrative headquarters of the 6th arrondissement, in the Gravilliers Section, where a force of two hundred was needed to maintain order. Martainville, who must always be read with good-humoured distrust, gave the following report of the interrogation to which he was supposedly subjected:

"Do you know the Chevalier Dejean?"
"No."
"But you do frequent the Café des Canonniers?"
"What does it matter to you?"
"You visit the galleries in the Convention, don't you?"
"Your wife goes there to knit, doesn't she?"
"Were you at the meal for the jeunes gens?"
"I'm going to demand that you tell me where *you* eat every evening."
"You belong to this so-called brilliant youth that has been bribed by Fréron and that shouts 'Long live the Convention! Down with the Jacobins!'"
"Fréron doesn't have enough money to bribe anyone, and young Frenchmen aren't so base as to let themselves be bribed. I'm sure you would rather hear us shout 'Down with the Convention! Long live the Jacobins!'"
"You are insolent."
"Do you find the truth offensive?"
"What does 'brilliant youth' mean to you?"
"Youth that shines through its virtues and its love for the Convention."
"Let's see your hands."
"Look at my fingers: they are stained with ink."
"Where did you dine?"
"There is no point giving you the address of my restaurant. It is very expensive and has little to commend it."
"Do you know Saint-Huruge?"
"If I didn't, I would be the only one in Paris."

The jeunes gens protested vehemently, in an address to the Committee of General Security which appeared in *Le Moniteur* of

24 Pluviôse, probably on Martainville's initiative. They had gone to Audinot's, they said, "to enjoy an evening of innocent entertainment," but had been astonished to find that the same play was going to be performed that had caused such an uproar the night before. The sole aim of the play was evidently to set citizens at odds, as the main character was a young aristocrat, called a muscadin, who had been conscripted to serve in the military hospitals and who held the faubourgs up to ridicule while praising the Palais Royal. When the curtain had risen, all the young men, out of solidarity with their friends of the faubourgs (why else!), had begun booing the play and shouting "Down with the Jacobins! Long live the National Convention! Long live our brothers of the faubourgs!," whereupon "some Furies of the guillotine and four or five brigands," high up in the gallery, had dared to insult the Convention. The jeunes gens had immediately overrun the theatre, taken control of the stage, and halted the performance. A police officer had come and read out an order of the Committee of General Security stating that the play was not banned. He had been heard out respectfully, the youths went on, but that could not prevent the public, "the natural judge of dramatic works," from decreeing that the play should not be performed. It was then that the spectators learnt that the theatre had been surrounded by the military. As they left the building, their papers had been checked and some arbitrary arrests had been made. The jeunes gens had been insulted, and sabres had been drawn against them; they had even been shot at, but the pistol had hung fire. Under a hail of curses from furious women calling for the guillotine, they had been taken to the guardhouse, and from there to the watch committee of the 6th arrondissement, in the Gravilliers Section. To add insult to injury, Léonard Bourdon had then arrived at the watch committee to try and incite the populace against them – and against some brave sans-culotte locksmiths with whom they had been fraternizing. In short, the attempt of the authorities to cool the ardour of the jeunes gens had only succeeded in incensing them further.

This pantomime was still too tame for an inveterate storyteller like Martainville, who immediately published his own version of the events, a farrago of farcical jokes entitled La Nouvelle Henriotade. The Ambigu Comique, he explained, had put on a play that was "insulting to moral standards, to French youth, and to all members of the fair sex." Hence it was understandable that, outraged by such a shameless act, "citizens who upheld the law" should rush to the theatre to prevent the performance of this "immoral rhapsody." But while "the enemies of discord" were putting a halt to the performance, "a horde of ferocious men" had perfidiously ringed the theatre and, as the jeunes gens came out, dragged them off to the watch committee under the gibes of a jeering "mob." At the watch committee the youths had been interrogated by "lugubrious-looking men" (the revolutionary commissioners of the 6th arrondissement). Martainville stigmatized their "*jacobite* insolence" – reminiscent, he said, of the tribunal of 2 September – but finally admitted that the young men had soon been released, without further ado.

In fact, the jeunes gens never were interrogated. The 6th arrondissement watch committee simply examined their papers and then sent them to their respective watch committees. The story about Léonard Bourdon's attempt to rouse the "mob" against the young men was equally false. Bourdon did put in an appearance at the watch committee at around midnight, but the committee itself acknowledged that he "had not meddled in any way at all, and had left shortly after he had arrived." So the jeunes gens spent the night in committee custody and were released the next day. It was at least a warning to them, and perhaps for the first time it could be said that the Committee of General Security had not given in to the jeunesse dorée's blackmail.

But it did not give in to the terrorists either: on 20 Pluviôse, Mathieu announced on behalf of the Committee of General Security that it considered the young men's conduct at the Ambigu Comique to be "more a case of rash irresponsibility than evil intentions." Indeed, far more dangerous in the Committee's view was the activity that had been observed in the Faubourg Antoine, where "depraved men were seeking to lead weak, credulous men astray," where the passing of the tyranny was lamented openly in public, and where the national representatives were the object of slanderous attacks. Then he announced the arrest of Babeuf and the closure of the Lazowski Club and the Quinze Vingts Popular Society, and secured passage of a decree removing Marat from the Panthéon. The role of the jeunesse dorée thus became abundantly clear. Agitation originated on the right; the Committee of General Security struck on the left. The jeunes gens revealed themselves as the driving force of the Thermidorians' campaign against the populace.

As for *Concert de la rue Feydeau*, which had been put back on the theatre's program on 22 Pluviôse and which the jeunes gens, led by Martainville, were preparing to disrupt once again, the Committee of General Security banned it at the last minute, and no effort was made to revive it. To mark the victory, Martainville dashed off an anti-Jacobin response to the original play entitled *Le Concert de la rue Feydeau ou l'agrément du jour* (The Concert of the Rue Feydeau, or the Pleasure of the Day), which was put on at the Variétés Montansier in early Ventôse. The jeunes gens turned out in droves to applaud it, for, as the author remarks,

> ... tyran, voleur, assassin,
> Par un seul mot cela s'exprime
> Et ce mot là, c'est ... Jacobin!

> (... tyrant, thief, murderer,
> May be expressed in a single word
> And that word is ... Jacobin!)

Spectators asserted that the rogues should be shown no mercy, "that they would have their arms and legs broken, and that people would soon be walking in their blood." This was not a figure of speech.

THE DESTRUCTION OF REVOLUTIONARY SYMBOLS

Scarcely had the decree of 20 Pluviôse, Year III, consecrated the victory of the jeunesse dorée over the busts of Marat than they were on the warpath against two other symbols: the revolutionary slogan "Fraternity or Death," which was written on the façades of public buildings, and the red cap which had hitherto been de rigueur for the true sans-culottes. At times it even appeared that the Convention was trying to outdo the jeunes gens. For instance, in response to a request from the Halle au Blé Section, it decreed on 2 Ventôse that monuments in the shape of a mountain would be demolished. In vain the people's representative Gaston berated the Assembly, calling on it to show "respect for the French people" by refusing to destroy its symbols; Mathieu replied that a mountain was nothing more than "an eternal protest against equality," whereupon the decree was promptly passed.

On 13 Ventôse, the police reported that there appeared to be a desire to obliterate the word "Death" from house fronts, "since it recalls the reign of terror and blood"; that evening, at the Théâtre Louvois, the jeunes gens wrote "Peace" in its place on the curtain. At the Théâtre du Vaudeville the youths forced the director, Barré, to cross out the inscription, and on the fifteenth the *Gazette française* opined that the slogan was "more suited to be the epitaph of the human race than to cement the links of fraternity." On the eighteenth, acting on a decree from its general assembly, the civilian committee of the Théâtre Français Section encouraged citizens, to the sound of the drum, to erase the inscription from house façades. On 30 Ventôse, the general assembly of the Bonne Nouvelle Section voted unanimously to replace the word "Death" with the word "Humanity." "If tigers had had inscriptions at the entrance to their caves, would they have had any other inscription than this?" it was asked rhetorically in the preamble to the decree.

The campaign against the red cap caused more of a stir, resulting in scuffles with two people's representatives, Armonville and Guffroy, and in a short but very bitter quarrel in the Assembly. Armonville was very attached to the red cap. On 9 Nivôse, Year III, he had mounted the speaker's platform of the Assembly wearing his cap. "Down with the cap!" people had shouted, "Down with the Jacobin symbol!" But he had refused to take it off, whereupon the people's representative Charlier had cited the rule dictating that deputies had to speak bareheaded, and Armonville had been reduced – a suggestion whispered to him by Duroy – to putting his cap on the head of the bust of Marat. "The red cap has fallen into total disrepute," remarked *La Vedette*. "It is rarely seen in Paris now." On 26 Nivôse a red cap that the actor Grammont had put in a conspicuous spot in the Café de Chartres was covered with a tricolour sash. "People believed that the red cap had been reddened by the blood that dripped from Grammont's hands rather than by the dyer's mixture," explained *Le Courrier universel*. Another, more serious incident occurred on the evening of 16 Ventôse. Armonville was sitting with Léonard Bourdon in the Café Payen, in the National Convention building, when a gang of hooligans came in singing *Le Réveil du Peuple* and shouting "Down with the buveurs de sang, the red caps, the Mountain, and the Crest!" The jeunesse dorée was making one of its "civic outings." Catching sight of Armonville, the young men surrounded him and demanded that he take off his cap. Of course he refused and, reported a police agent, "dared to make disparaging remarks about the youths and call them counter-revolutionaries." Since the quarrel was becoming quite acrimonious, the guards were sent for; they took Armonville under their protection and put five of the young men under arrest.

While Armonville was squaring off with the jeunesse dorée, Léonard Bourdon managed to escape. He burst into the Assembly, where the sitting had just begun and members were voting on whether to renew officers' terms. "Members of the National Assembly are being insulted near the place of these deliberations!" he cried.

The deputies of the Left immediately came down from their benches. "We must go and see what is happening!"

But Legendre was quick to respond: "You who murdered the fathers of nine families, nine good citizens of Orléans, are complaining that you have been insulted!"

And someone interjected: "It was Armonville who insulted the citizens! He was drunk!"

The Assembly decided to carry on with its proceedings. A moment later, however, Duquesnoy raised the matter again, demanding that the deputies who had just been insulted be allowed to speak. But Legendre countered, "I demand that the floor be given to those who claim they were insulted. When they have been heard, they will be told that it is their own base conduct that invites insults. It is their drunkenness ..."

The people's representative Gaston rose angrily and drew his sabre. Members formed a circle around him, held him back, and finally persuaded him to take his seat again.

Things had gone too far, and the Committee of General Security had to promise to investigate the incident and prepare a report. A short while later, Clauzel went to the Café Payen to find out the names of the young men who had insulted Armonville. The jeunes gens denied having insulted anyone, but remarked "that the representative in question would perhaps be well advised to give up the cap that has been so dishonoured by the bloodthirsty men who had worn it." Gaston, who had accompanied Clauzel, got into a quarrel with one of the youths, and the two of them were led off to the Committee of General Security. As for the report, it was never mentioned again – at any rate, it did not appear in Le Moniteur. However, I did find the joint statement of the five jeunes gens who were apprehended by the guards:

Earlier today, a large group of young men went, as usual, to the Café Payen to give chase to the buveurs de sang who go there daily and who have sworn, by their daggers, to massacre the people's representatives who value humanity and the law. Just as we got there, the people's representative Armonville arrived, wearing his red cap. Immediately, all the citizens present, as if by natural impulse, began singing Le Réveil du Peuple. The citizen Armonville, sitting next to the stove where Le Réveil du Peuple was being sung, took a lorgnette from his pocket to look at one of the citizens who was singing. This fellow, who had just arrived in Paris from Lyon, did

not know the citizen Armonville, and spoke to him very sharply ...
Someone shouted "Down with the red cap!" ... Armonville replied that
only rogues refused to wear the red cap. Several citizens pointed out to him
that the cap was an object of discord and that he ought to sacrifice it for the
sake of peace and replace it with another in the colours of liberty.

The Committee of General Security must have been satisfied with
this statement, since the youths were subsequently released. Not
that they had repented, however. Three days later they were again
plotting against Armonville. Knowing that he regularly crossed the
Pont National, they planned to wait for him on the bridge and,
when he happened by, grab his cap, throw it in the river, and give
him another hat more to their liking. On 19 Ventôse, the police,
which had got wind of what was up, intended to inform Armonville
and suggest that he remove his cap "at least while he was on the
bridge." This must be what transpired, for there is no record of such
an incident.

The Committee of General Security had shown poor judgment in
playing down the Armonville incident. The next day, one of its
members, Guffroy, was set upon by the jeunes gens. This was all
the more surprising because Guffroy did not appear to have anything in common with the so-called terrorists. In fact, he was one of
the most unrelenting reactionaries, and his printing house turned
out scores of anti-Jacobin pamphlets. Nonetheless, some of the
young men must have recalled certain issues of his newspaper
Rougyff ou le Franc en vedette, in which he had revelled in blood only
a short time before: "If the fluid of the body politic is vitiated, it cannot be purified, and must be let. This is the only remedy ... And
here is my recipe: Come, Lady Guillotine, amputate all these enemies of France! Faster! Faster! Don't bother to count! Heads in the
sack!"

On 17 Ventôse, passing by the Palais Égalité, Guffroy encountered a group of jeunes gens, who tore the small red cap he was
sporting on top of his hat and trampled it in the mud. Four or five
of them were arrested, while the others went to sound the alarm at
the Café de Chartres and in the theatres. At the Vaudeville, the performance was interrupted. Someone announced that at the
Carrousel men armed with large sabres were attacking the jeunes
gens, whereupon, noted the police, the curtain was lowered and
everyone left. A dozen young men were delegated to go to the
Committee of General Security to demand that their comrades be released, but they in turn were apprehended. There was a great commotion in the theatres. Citizens were being arrested arbitrarily, it

was shouted. A crowd of youths set off for the Committee of General Security. As it was feared that they might ransack the Committee's offices, Merlin de Thionville and Legendre hastened to cut them off and urged them to go no farther, arguing that the public would soon be saying that the youth of France was dictating the law to the government, and promising them that justice would be done. At around eleven o'clock, the young men who had been detained were set free. One might have expected them to go quietly home. But no, they immediately began their rounds of public places again, hunting for more red caps.

Nevertheless, the jeunesse dorée did not form a homogeneous bloc, and on the morrow, the eighteenth, there were many regrets at the Café de Chartres; according to an observer, the conduct of the jeunes gens was genuinely disapproved of by the rest of their comrades. A delegation was sent to Guffroy to disavow the incident of the day before and to apologize for "the thoughtlessness of these young hotheads." Guffroy replied in a letter, read out at the Café de Chartres, urging the young men to stay within the bounds dictated by good principles. Naturally, Armonville did not receive an apology.

The attitude of the reactionary press to the incident showed that the jeunes gens could not necessarily count on its uncritical endorsement, nor did they enjoy the unconditional support of the middle class. *Le Messager du Soir* approved of their actions, as did *La Gazette française*: "To judge by the inane admiration that has been shown for red caps, one would be inclined to think that the Revolution was the work of galley slaves. In ancient Rome the cap of liberty was white. William Tell's cap was brown. Why did we choose red? Was it to tell other nations that liberty could be won only by showering its altars with human blood?"

L'Orateur du Peuple, on the other hand, accused them of waging war on bits of clothing, and *La Vedette* thought that they had gone too far: "In our opinion, the jeunes gens are too zealous. Before, they were oppressed; now they are doing the oppressing. Everyone must be free to wear whatever he likes on his head. When shall we know the price of that liberty which consists in being allowed to do whatever does no harm to others? A red cap is not sufficient reason to disrupt law and order."

The gilded youth were indeed going too far, attacking all the Montagnards they could find. On 1 Ventôse, fingers were pointed at Choudieu at the Théâtre des Variétés: "He murdered Phélippeaux," it was shouted, and he was left sitting alone. "People seemed to be afraid that if they went near him they might be poisoned by the contagious fumes given off by his body," wrote *Le Messager du Soir*, adding that the same evening, a void also formed around the deputy Bassal, or "Father Bassal." On 8 Ventôse, Duhem was baited at the Café Payen by young men singing *Le Réveil du Peuple*. On the tenth it was "Léopard" Bourdon who was insulted on his way to lycée "with his pack of buffoons": "Rogue! Butcher of Orléans," youths shouted at him. The same day, two deputies were thrown out of the Café Payen by jeunes gens from the Café de Chartres after they had declared themselves to be Jacobins. "We wanted to find out their names to denounce them to the people," the young men explained. On 14 Ventôse, Vadier was arrested in the Faubourg Antoine. *Le Messager du Soir* reported gaily, "He was led home in disgrace, like a fox that has just had its tail cropped. But Vadier has yet to lose his." On the 22nd, Albitte was booed at the Café de Chartres. While the jeunes gens claimed that they were the Convention's honour guard, it was obvious that they considered this to apply only to the "healthy part" of the Assembly!

The incident involving Armonville convinced Fréron of the urgent need to curb the activity of his minions, and he admonished them, in the pages of *L'Orateur du Peuple*, to be more prudent in future. It was all very well to wage war on the terrorists, but was this war ever going to end? Were they not in danger of becoming terrorists themselves? And were not these calls to arms over plays or bits of clothing rather trivial in the end? One did not carry out a revolution just for the fun of it. Moreover, "the part of the population that remained silent" was becoming annoyed with such childish pranks, and the Jacobins were simply waiting for them to make a mistake so that they could turn it to their own advantage. And this was not to mention the royalists, who were also seeking to use them to further their own aims. Fréron went on:

Will this or that coat, this or that physiognomy, this or that hat be today's reasons for proscription? And will you wage war on unpowdered hair and trousers the way the followers of Robespierre waged war on tight breeches and powdered hair? Do you wish to take their conduct as a model for yours? Will you disturb the peace over a red cap? Will you expend such energy in quarrelling over bits of clothing? I repeat: this is not the way to consummate a revolution.

In conclusion, if they loved their country, they should take care not to jeopardize it.

The lower classes regarded this war over "bits of clothing" as an insult, for through the red cap the jeunesse dorée was in effect attacking republican values and the whole ideology of liberty. Fréron had grasped this. He saw that the Jacobins might seize the opportunity to revive the flagging popular movement. He also saw that by its ceaseless agitation in public places the jeunesse dorée was alienating its own base of support, "the part of the population that remained silent" – that is, the bourgeoisie. He saw that if the Committee of General Security was ever put in a situation where it had to take harsh measures against the jeunes gens, it would no longer have a force it could use as a counterweight to the sansculottes. But Fréron had little control over his fops save when he incited them to revenge; while the police noted that on 19 Ventôse the young men of the Café de Chartres agreed to comply with his wishes and not to cause any more disturbances in public places, in reality their agitation, far from subsiding, actually increased.

The jeunesse dorée did not seek counsel solely in *L'Orateur du Peuple*. They also followed the advice proffered by Isidore Langlois in *Le Messager du Soir*, and their activity can be traced in greater detail in its pages. Thus, while Fréron was urging them to remain calm, Langlois was again calling on them to act. A horde of Jacobins, he said, their pockets bulging with gold, their hands dripping with blood, were protesting against the high prices of basic necessities in order to lead "simple men" astray and incite them to pillage shopkeepers' establishments. There was every reason to fear that an explosion was imminent. Some people wanted a return to the butchery of Collot, Marat, and Carrier. The jeunes gens had to recall the oath they had sworn: to perish rather than to fall under tyranny again, and to avenge the heinous crimes committed against their families.

I say to you, youth of Paris, do not let down your guard! Stand and be counted! Form the vanguard of the National Convention! There are villains plotting your demise. The future will show how wrong they are. You shall live to protect persons and property. You shall live to defend the Convention against these cutthroats. You shall live to support, from within, the cause of liberty for which your young friends are fighting so courageously on our frontiers.

Le Messager du Soir thus took over from *L'Orateur du Peuple*, and it was in vain that Fréron disowned the jeunes gens. The connection had already been created. Henceforth, people would speak increasingly of Fréronist youth, of Fréron's army, of Fréron's soldiers. It was a situation that made Mirabeau's words ring true: "When one takes it upon oneself to lead a revolution, the problem is not to keep it in motion, but to hold it in check."

CHAPTER THREE

The March toward Insurrection

1 VENTÔSE, YEAR III, TO 30
FLORÉAL, YEAR III

The months Ventôse, Germinal, and Floréal offer clear evidence of the jeunesse dorée's involvement in Thermidorian politics. They had been recruited into a parallel police force set up by the Fréronists on the Committee of General Security. According to the Fréronists, the jeunes gens inspired many of the Assembly's policies and served to keep the "wild sans-culotte mob" at bay.

There were good reasons for this arrangement. In the queues that gangs of jeunes gens, armed with weighted sticks, drove away from shop doors, and in the groups that gathered at the Jardin National and on the boulevards, propaganda in support of a revolt against the Assembly was increasing, heightening the political consciousness of the populace and preparing the mobilization of the masses. In late Ventôse, in the midst of a worsening food shortage and in the wake of a flood of insurrectionary pamphlets, a rash of street fights occurred in various parts of Paris, culminating in the violent clash of 1 Germinal between sans-culottes and muscadins. This clash was significant for a number of reasons: it revealed the secret dealings between the National Convention and the jeunesse dorée; it provided a clear picture of the social groups that were in conflict; and, since the jeunesse dorée got the worst of it for the first time, it furnished proof that they were no match for the common people when they rose up in revolt. No longer able to count on its praetorian guard, and in spite of a special police law against seditious mobs, the Assembly was thus at the mercy of a new revolutionary uprising.

The jeunesse dorée held such sway over government action – it was they who forced the arrest of the "four ringleaders" (Barère, Billaud-Varennes, Collot-d'Herbois, and Vadier) on 12 Ventôse – that members of the Convention spoke of dissolving their assembly and transferring it to Châlons sur Marne. The honnêtes gens then tried a new tack, seeking to appease the sans-culottes of the faubourgs with friendly dinners, exchanges of delegations, and notices calling for a united front against the Jacobins. But the strategy failed. The sans-culottes had little interest in fraternity when they were starving, and they could see that repression was intensifying in the sections. The implacable antagonism between the bourgeoisie and the lower classes was evident in an address of the Tuileries Section threatening the Assembly with retaliation if it granted an amnesty to the "four ringleaders"; this address was mirrored by one from the Quinze Vingts Section, in which the sans-culottes asserted that they would "stand up for the Republic and for liberty."

The first hunger riot took place on 12 Germinal. The sans-culottes occupied the Assembly, but were then driven out by a detachment of three hundred jeunes gens led by Legendre. He was subsequently put in charge of escorting to Fort du Taureau a number of deputies who had been arrested for allegedly conspiring with the rioters. From Germinal to Prairial, the food situation in Paris deteriorated from scarcity to famine, and the contrast between the luxury of the few and the destitution of the many sharpened dramatically. Social unrest continued to grow, and the Committee of General Security did not succeed in building a force capable of containing it. Some 1,600 terrorists were disarmed, but the key step – reform of the National Guard – was a dismal failure, and the Committee, in the hope of rallying some support among the common people, suddenly began to crack down on speculators. The sole result of this was to alienate the jeunes gens. In Prairial, at the decisive moment of the popular uprising, the Assembly would thus find itself without support, and only at the last minute would the jeunesse dorée agree to rush to its defence. The two would settle their accounts later, in Vendémiaire.

THE ARREST OF THE "FOUR RINGLEADERS"

On 12 Ventôse the Commission of Twenty-One was scheduled to submit its report to the Convention on the conduct of Barère, Billaud-Varennes, Collot-d'Herbois, and Vadier, following their denunciation in the Assembly on 15 Frimaire on charges of having conspired with Robespierre. The Fréronists were calling for their heads. The centrists were hesitating. Would the purge go further? What people's representative had not voted in favour of terrorist measures in the Year II? The fate of the "four ringleaders" was thus hanging in the balance when the jeunes gens decided to impose their own verdict. The day the report was due they would take over the Convention's public galleries and chase out any Jacobins who were there. The National Convention would not dare acquit the four "master criminals" in the presence of its praetorian guard. On the evening of 9 Ventôse, at the Vaudeville, *Le Réveil du Peuple* was sung. When the singers came to the words *"Périssent les assassins!"* (May the murderers perish!) someone shouted, "They only have three days left!" These three days – 10, 11, and 12 Ventôse – brought the jeunesse dorée back to the forefront of parliamentary affairs; once again, the Assembly's dependence on the jeunes gens was clear for all to see.

On 10 Ventôse, Boissy d'Anglas, the people's representative responsible for Paris food supplies, expressed to the Convention his concern about the crowds that gathered daily outside bakeries. Every day, he claimed, strangers arriving in Paris insinuated themselves into these crowds to stir up trouble. Villetard made a show of supporting him, saying that the Committees should disperse the crowds. Then he cleverly associated the jeunesse dorée with the unrest: "For the last four months, twenty or thirty young men from the first conscription have been arriving in the city daily. What are they doing here? This bears out the government's claims that eventually there will be unrest in Paris." The remark was astute: the jeunes gens were thus held to be behind the disturbances that had been feared might result from the famine. They were the ones who, since they had no ration cards, were unduly swelling the queues in front of bakers' shops.

But Bourdon de l'Oise was quick to retaliate: "The cutthroats are trying to stir up trouble. And a crafty attempt has been made to throw you off the scent with talk of the young men from the first conscription who are in Paris on leave ... These young men are not the ones queuing up in front of the bakeries; the ones queuing up are the followers of Robespierre, the men who were in his pay." Rewbell added that while there might be twenty or thirty young men arriving in Paris daily, an equal number left every day; moreover, inspectors checked their papers when they arrived and refused entry to those whose papers were not in order. "The young men are not the ones causing unrest in the markets," he said. "They are not the ones who whisper to you as they pass by, 'What is eight and a half and eight and a half [a reference to Louis XVII, the dauphin imprisoned in the Temple]?' It is the Jacobins in league with the royalists."

Then Rovère divulged "the key to the mystery": a major report was due to be presented on the twelfth, he said, and the Jacobins were planning to take over the public galleries for the occasion. Police agents had naturally accused the jeunes gens, but, Rovère went on, "You must realize that there are two types of police officer: some are honest citizens, but others are still agents of Robespierre. The Committee of General Security has been forced to organize a counter-police force because the officers in the first force blamed everything on the muscadins and the royalists, and never said a word about the plots of the cutthroats and Robespierre's disciples."

The Committee of General Security thus admitted that a parallel police force, financed with public money, had been set up and that it was the chief source of intelligence about threats of insurrection. The Committee had created the force by decree on 11 Nivôse, Year III, because it was felt that the reports submitted by the official police were "frequently untrue." The new force reported to the Committee at noon every day. It was headed by a thirty-eight-year-old émigré, Charles Villambre, of Halle au Blé Section "crippled and able to walk only with difficulty, his left hand paralyzed." Little is known about the members of this parallel police force, but evidence suggests that they were recruited from among the jeunesse dorée.

The next day, 11 Ventôse, Fréron gave a speech in the Convention, probably written by Dussault, which any other assembly of legislators would surely have taken as an insult to its sovereignty. Fréron could not have been more forthright in his contempt for the powers that be. He said that they had lost all control over the course of Thermidorian politics, which was now being dictated entirely by "this general insurrection of public opinion and this seething desire for national revenge" – in other words, the jeunesse dorée. He continued,

While your wise Committees and brilliant minds are busy debating the law, it escapes your grasp and is laid down by public opinion, which sometimes anticipates your actions. If this overwhelming activity often robs you of the glory of being able to take the initiative, it nonetheless gives you the pleasure, so precious to loyal representatives, of knowing that you are of one mind with the people and that you are just as intelligent.

But the Convention so revelled in its own debasement and subservience that it welcomed these remarks about its servility, even applauding and voting to have them printed.

That same day, in the cafés of the Palais Égalité, the jeunes gens complained that they were being unjustly accused of royalism and of stirring up trouble in the sections and the theatres, and proposed presenting an address to the Convention in which they would reassert their respect for the institution. In the Bon Conseil Section an announcement was made, "inviting citizens to go to their section to present an address." The ex-Jacobin Jean-Baptiste Loys, a former secretary of the Jacobin Club who had already been arrested once following a denunciation in *L'Orateur du Peuple* of 2 Vendémiaire, Year III, remarked, "Only schemers are going to go," and was promptly arrested a second time.

As planned, the young men delivered their address to the Assembly the following day, 12 Ventôse, when the Commission of Twenty-One was due to submit its report. Apprehensive about the situation, the government had put the military on alert early in the morning. A sizeable crowd had gathered and was milling about outside the Convention. Soldiers at the Jardin National were saying that no one should be fooled by all the talk, that the men who were shouting so much abuse against the terrorists and the buveurs de sang might be in a position to do much worse, and that if something happened, they would run and hide as they had always done.

The jeunes gens picked a quarrel with a soldier, who said he had returned from his army post, calling him an agent of Robespierre. Wanting to prove his identity, the soldier took out his papers, but the young men paid no attention and went on insulting him. Losing his temper, he went for one of them and sent him tumbling into the garden. "The spectators approved of this punishment," said a witness.

The galleries had filled very early. "The terrorists were in the minority," wrote *Le Courrier républicain*. This was corroborated by the police: "Many citizens who are accustomed to finding a seat in the galleries could not conceal their resentment at being turned away." The citizen Pierre Roumy, who was heard praising the Jacobins in the corridor leading to the public galleries, was thrown out. A commissioner of the National Lands Office, Jean-François Carton, decided to take him away to the Committee of General Security "in the interests of keeping the peace." "I only managed to do so with great difficulty," he added, "although I was helped by several young men who happened to be there."

In the Assembly, Saladin was presenting the report of the Commission of Twenty-One. He recalled the Reign of Terror, referred, in passing, to the arrest warrant issued for Thérésia Cabarrus, citing it as an example of the irregular warrants that had been issued at the time, and concluded that the arrest of Barère, Billaud-Varennes, Collot-d'Herbois, and Vadier was justified. Young men hastened to the Théâtre de la République to break the news, to shouts of "Long live the Convention!" The jeunesse dorée had won. Could any other outcome have been expected? The Convention gave official sanction to the arrest of the "four ringleaders" without any opposition, and immediately afterwards, several young men of the first Paris conscription addressed the Assembly.

Duvoisin-Calas, the deputation's spokesman, explained that they had come to respond to the slurs cast against them in the Convention. They were being called deserters and royalists, when in reality they had rushed to their country's rescue. They swore to fight tyranny to the death, "whether it be symbolized by a crown or a red cap, a throne, or a mountain." Rallied around the Convention, they were determined to defend it, even if they were still covered in the blood of their brothers and friends. The cutthroats should not hope for an easy victory. Duvoisin-Calas wound up his speech with the customary calls of "Long live the Republic! Long live the National Convention! Down with the buveurs de sang! Down with the Jacobins!"

That evening, to celebrate their victory over the Assembly, the jeunes gens organized a "battue" in the patriot cafés. The tailor Michel Quarré, who was heard saying in the Café Payen that the jeunesse dorée would not show up, that it was all talk, that he could tell the difference between a turned-down collar and a turned-up one, and that if the jeunes gens were good citizens they would be at the front, was led off to the Committee of General Security by six youths, including a certain d'Ocagne, one of the men who had signed the petition. The widow Payen corroborated the charge, adding that Quarré had said two days before, in reference to some youths who were singing *Le Réveil du Peuple*, that within three weeks "these rogues, these Fréronists in the pay of the Committee of Public Safety, [would] not be singing that song any longer." Similarly, the citizen Jean-Baptiste Vingtergnier, a brigade leader in the Army of the Sambre and Meuse, was arrested the next day at the Café Payen and dragged off to the Committee of General Security by seven young men. He, too, was accused by the proprietor, Mme Payen, of having said "that the young men of Paris were all scoundrels who needed to be taught a good lesson, and that they'd soon be getting one, and that on his own he could send twenty of them packing, with a few good kicks in the arse." These were not empty threats, and the day was coming when the sans-culottes would wreak their revenge. In *L'Orateur du Peuple*, Dussault, who ghostwrote Fréron's arcticles, made determined efforts to incite social strife, whipping up the jeunesse dorée against the "rabble" – the "do-nothings reduced by their own laziness to the most contemptible misery." "Young republicans" he wrote, "vanguard of the standing army composed of all the enemies of the decemviral tyranny, it is you who shall assist the representatives of the people in times of crisis. It is you who shall silence the cries of the wild mob and keep it at bay. Your hour has come. Stand and be counted."

But the sans-culottes also read *L'Orateur du Peuple*, or had it read to them. How long would they let themselves be called "rabble" and "wild mob" without reacting?

THE DETERIORATING SOCIAL SITUATION

The "great" Committee of the Year II had managed to feed Paris thanks to institutionalized terror and a complicated system of enumeration, requisition, taxation, and rationing, using vouchers and cards. With the fall of Robespierre, the regime lost its driving force, and the swing back from a controlled to a free-market economy was inevitable. But the return to liberalism occurred in such chaos and confusion that it led directly to the economic depression of the Year III.

For the common people, the depression meant unbearable misery – inflation, unemployment, and food shortages in the midst of the harshest winter of the century. From Nivôse to Prairial the ration of bread, the staple of the populace's diet, declined regularly, dropping to just two ounces per person by late Floréal. Moreover, ration shares varied from section to section, and sometimes misappropriation or pillaging of flour stocks meant that nothing at all was distributed. The Seine had frozen over, preventing transportation of the wood and coal needed for heating. Many of the poor were out of work, following the purges that had been made since Thermidor in government offices and the arms workshops, which had been turned over to private enterprise. The effects of inflation forced them to sell their furniture, their personal effects, and even their clothes to survive, leaving them totally destitute.

Beginning in early Nivôse, queues formed in poorer areas of the city at around two or three o'clock every morning in front of shops distributing wood, candles, coal, bread, meat, and oil. Women from the lower classes would wait six or seven hours, often with a swarm of children around them, for a few meagre ounces of bread, and even this they were sometimes refused. And what bread! Black, fetid dough that would stick when thrown at the wall, remarked Duval in his memoirs.

The jeunes gens also queued up – but in the evening, outside the theatres. The contrast between the morning queues and the evening ones was striking: in the morning, haggard faces, ragged clothes, and vulgar swearing; in the evening, elegant dress and joyful bursts of laughter. From the latter, the bourgeoisie had nothing to fear; from the former, everything. The crowds of miserable, hungry wretches, numbed by the cold, often drunk, might turn into an un-ruly mob at any moment. The sight of these queues – almost as long as Halley's comet, Duval joked – filled the honnêtes gens with dread. One journalist wrote, "There is every reason to do away with this immoral practice, which makes people waste much valuable working time, encourages laziness, ruins morals and health, and furnishes seditious elements with a prime opportunity to spread their destructive principles."

When rows over who was before whom, indecent acts, pickpock-eting, or political quarrels sparked by insurrectional propaganda stirred up too much trouble in the morning queues, groups of jeunes gens would arrive with their clubs to disperse the crowd. Duval records that several times a week the call to arms would sound in the bourgeois districts of the city, summoning the young men to their sections, whence they would be led to the rue Beaubourg, the rue des Gravilliers, or the rue Grenier St Lazare to drive the Jacobin firebrands away from the queues. And so the win-ter passed, with near-riots and minor revolts serving to crystallize the antagonistic social forces and keep them in a state of confronta-tion. Then came the spring, and things reached the boiling point.

As the social struggle clarified, the lower classes became more aware of their political situation. Sincere patriots who had allied themselves for a time with the Moderates in the fight against the Jacobins realized, once the Jacobin Club disappeared, that they had been tricked. In a letter to a friend which, intercepted by the police got him thrown into prison, Boucher, called Vive l'Amour, a father of five, wrote on 3 Ventôse, Year III, "Fréron, the Orator of the jeu-nesse dorée, and Tallien, the husband of Thérésia Cabarrus, will not be as successful as they had hoped. The true friends of France whom they led astray momentarily with their foul pamphlets and lampoons have just recently opened their eyes and are starting to see how things really stand."

Acts of provocation by the jeunesse dorée continued. At the Palais Égalité, young men asked passers-by, "What are fifteen and two?" They threw a wounded soldier out of a café, forced innocent people to shout "Down with the Jacobins!," and attacked terrorists at the Jardin National. But the sans-culottes were beginning to realize that things could not go on much longer the way they were. "The patri-ots are being taken to task," said a hunchback in the Jardin des Tuileries on 15 Ventôse, "but have patience! The people are suf-fering, and *Messieurs les muscadins* will not get away for long with insulting them in their misery."

Arrests continued, on the most arbitrary pretexts: "irredeemable wretch," "unruly firebrand," "admirer of Robespierre," and "cut-

throat" appear on the warrants. But, in contrast to the days following Thermidor, mass releases could no longer be used as a means to
divert the public eye from the arrests, and common people like the
carpenter Loison suddenly came to the realization "that patriots
were being put behind bars more than ever before."

The propaganda campaign continued. According to some rumours, the terrorists had set up workshops in Meudon for producing human leather. But this was too much to swallow, and even *Le
Courrier républicain* called it ridiculous. Fréron appealed to the
"brave, patriotic inhabitants of the faubourgs" to beware of tricks by
the Jacobins to turn them against the young men of Paris and make
them believe that the jeunes gens were effeminate cowards.

Naturally, the Thermidorians pretended to know nothing about
the jeunesse dorée, though it was obviously responsible for the deteriorating situation, and Fréron, playing with words, asked in a
speech to the Convention, "Where is the aristocracy? Where is it
hiding? What resources does it have? What armed strength? What
hopes? It is nothing but a ghost, and we are not visionaries." This
was a red herring. The men the patriots were denouncing as aristocrats were not the *ci-devant* nobility, but the muscadins. Regardless
of how often the patriots pointed them out, and of how much the
muscadins drew attention to themselves with their self-indulgent
lifestyle and their provocative tactics, the Thermidorians stuck to
their strategy of asking where the aristocrats were. In response
Lebois, in *L'Ami du Peuple*, wrote, "They are at the Palais Royal, in
the cafés, in the theatres of the rue Feydeau and the rue Nicolet;
they are at the Carrousel and in the galleries of the Convention, at
the doors of the Committees; they are marching under the flag of
the jeunesse dorée; they are the gilded million, the people of the
boutiques." The patriots did not deny knowing who they were.
Jacquet, the storekeeper of the Opéra, always carried two pistols "to
serve Fréron" if he ran into him; the printer Rohait swore that he
would "exterminate all the jackass aristocrats, and all the muscadins."

Tension heightened suddenly in late Ventôse. Supplies had more
trouble reaching Paris and the crowds outside bakers' and butchers'
shops grew larger. In the Convention, Boissy d'Anglas cynically
praised the "gilded million," without which, he said, the people
would have no more army to defend them, nor commerce to feed
them. Then, unafraid of contradicting himself, he had members
vote in favour of a decree reducing the bread ration to one pound
per person. With this measure the Assembly seemed to accept responsibility for all the misery of the food shortage, admitted its im-
potence, and gave the impression that it had no desire to improve

matters. In the days following this admission, Paris was to see a further rise in popular unrest.

A poster campaign launched at about the same time was a significant factor in the growing agitation which mobilized the common people against the jeunesse dorée and the Convention. On 22 Ventôse a bill headed "People, awake, the time has come!" was posted around Paris. The police described it as "a spark thrown with criminal treachery to light a huge conflagration." The time had come for the people to stir, the author explained. While they were dying of hunger, their enemies were growing fat. "Go and see the Tallien-Cabarruses, kings Bourdon and Fréron, the Legendre-Comtats, and all the rest of our ruling class in the restaurants of the *Palais extrêmement royal* and elsewhere, and you will see their tables piled high with beautiful cuts of meat ... you who can barely afford vegetables!" The poster had a considerable impact, causing crowds to gather in the Faubourg Marceau on the day it appeared. At the Café de Chartres there was talk of an excursion to the faubourgs to tear it down.

The authorities were not long in reacting. On 25 Ventôse, searches were made of bookshops and printing shops in at least eighteen sections. A fellow by the name of Collignon, called Dumont, who said he was a public reader for the sans-culottes, was apprehended as the presumed author. Then Augustin Donnier, Babeuf's printer, was arrested. Both were false leads. The poster may have originated with erstwhile members of the defunct Electoral Club. In any case, the author was never discovered.

On 29 Ventôse, the police reported that another bill, this time with the ironic title "Advice Given to the Sans-Culottes by Guffroy to Save France," had been "posted in all the streets, and notably in the markets and other places where people congregate." The author exclaimed, "Down with the muscadins! Down with these b---- swaggerers who stink of musk from head to toe! Down with these powdered rogues! I cast b---- powder in your eye! Down with the muscadins! Down with them, I say! Wherever they are, they are your enemies!" The poster caused a terrific stir in public opinion. *Le Messager du Soir* reported "that a great number of workers assembled by wild termagants and well-placed criers read the poster or had it read to them."

The public-notice campaign helped spread the mood of revolt. Rows and brawls became more frequent in the vicinity of the Convention. On 26 Ventôse, the habitués of the Café de Chartres decided that they would make regular visits to the Jardin National to disperse groups gathered there. There were numerous complaints about the Fréronist youth, "young swaggerers who come to the Palais Royal to carry on the counter-revolution." The next day, the twenty-seventh, the Finistère and Observatoire sections – composed almost exclusively of labourers who worked on the river, noted an observer – appeared before the Convention. "We do not have enough bread," said the spokesman. "We are beginning to regret all the sacrifices we made for the Revolution. Do not allow the spectre of famine to walk in our midst. Use every means that the people have put in your hands, and give us bread. Eight hundred of our comrades await your reply."

The reply was to expel the petitioners. Outside in the garden, the jeunes gens were waiting for them. One young man approached and called them scheming scum. Twice, at four and at seven o'clock, the jeunesse dorée returned, wielding sticks and clubs, to break up the gatherings of petitioners. In columns, four abreast, they rushed through the groups, singing as they scattered their enemies. They silenced the tricoteuses, and the "men with the large sabres" were dragged through the mud and taken to the Committee of General Security. A forty-four-year-old roofer from the Piques Section, Mathieu Lefèvre, was arrested by a gang of about thirty young men who, according to him, were no older than twenty-two or twenty-three; they led him off to the Committee, roughing him up along the way. He maintained that they had arrested him merely for saying, "It is a pity that we cannot agree, and that there are so many different parties." The interrogating officer, François Girard, refused to believe him "because such a trifle would not have provoked such a strong reaction from the young men." Similarly, Anne Digaud, a hosiery vendor from the Cité Section who said that he had passed by the Convention at around five o'clock to find out the result of the petitions, was attacked by some sixty jeunes gens, who ordered him not to take part in any gathering. When he replied that he was not taking part but was merely having a look, they set upon him, calling him a terrorist, a rogue, a buveur de sang, and hauled him off to the Committee of General Security. "At the same time, just a short distance away," Digaud stated, "some of these fellows were murdering a man. He was struck over the head viciously with a sabre and knocked off his feet."

The same violent policing went on in the galleries of the Assembly. On 29 Ventôse a father of four, Jean-Louis Deschambres, caught criticizing the "big merchants," was put under arrest by men armed with sticks who seemed to be both patrolling and stirring up trouble simultaneously, and who spent their time concocting crimes to pin on peaceable citizens. On the morrow, the thirtieth, the jeunes gens sauntered through the Jardin des Tuileries, elbowing the workers who were there and stepping on their toes. On their own authority, they arrested the shoemaker Pierre Rivière, the kitchen helper Michaud, a former monk by the name of Douche, and the jeweller Jarlat. The Committee of General Security asked the Paris Police Administrative Commission for hourly reports on the political situation in the Faubourg Marceau, and called up a reserve force of one hundred men in each section.

The Thermidorians, however, pretended that nothing was amiss. When Duhem accused the Committee of General Security of protecting "Fréron's youth," Delecloy responded innocently, "The Committee has asked me to tell you that it is not aware of any army or group of youths belonging to the people's representative Fréron." This was easier than explaining why, when jeunes gens were taken to the Committee, they went in by one door and out by another, while when patriots were led there, they were kept behind bars to perpetuate the Reign of Terror. But the sans-culottes were at the end of their tether. The jeunesse dorée was not a figment of the imagination, and they were going to prove it by teaching the fops a good lesson.

THE CLASH OF 1 GERMINAL

Primidi, 1 Germinal, was petition day, and the Montreuil and Quinze Vingt sections went to the Convention to call for implementation of the Constitution of 1793. A number of clashes occurred between the petitioners and the jeunesse dorée near the Palais National; in its consternation the Assembly, instead of considering the political demands of the sans-culottes, lurched to the right and passed a special police law against seditious gatherings.

The Assembly's sitting had opened in the afternoon, with the appearance on the rostrum of the mother of Girey-Dupré, the editor of *Le Patriote français*. She asked for a pension to compensate her for the loss of her son, who had been "slain by the tigers." The deputies then applauded the Arsenal and Le Peletier sections, which had called for punishment of the "terrorists," but refused to hear petitioners from the western departments who had come to report some alarming news about the "war against the royalists." This attitude was a clear sign of what was to come. A deputation from the Montreuil and Quinze Vingt sections was shown in – "a troop of petitioners who claimed they could barely stand, they were so starved – but 'so drunk' might have been a more accurate description," wrote *Le Journal de Paris*. The group's spokesman, the saddler

Cochery, explained that he had not come to make flowery speeches: the people were suffering. The Constitution of 1793 had to be put into force immediately.

The president's reply was cautious, if not threatening: the National Convention had long had to compete against powerful rival organizations (an allusion to the Jacobins). Now that these rivals had been eliminated, the agitators had lost their rallying point, and the Convention was determined to act with a firm hand. The matter had nothing to do with the Constitution of 1793, and it was pure intimidation. Still, the president invited the petitioners to attend the remainder of the session.

Then Chasles, the Friend of the People, intervened in the debate: he too called for the Constitution of 1793. Tallien responded that the Constitution of 1793 was indeed necessary, but along with organic laws that would "present a barrier to the revolutionary movement," he said. Chasles, Goujon, and Taillefer shook their fists at Tallien, who ended by saying, amid a general clamour, "It is the duty of all good, upright citizens to voice as energetically as possible their opposition to the rogues who want to continue to oppress us."

Next, Thibaudeau spoke out against the Constitution, asserting that if it were suddenly put into effect it would inevitably lead to the resurrection of the Commune and the Jacobins. "By democratic constitution, do you mean a government where the people themselves exercise all the rights?" he asked. "No, no!" was the reply from all quarters. A motion closing the debate was then carried.

Outside, the riot was beginning.

Rather than remain in the Convention to attend the proceedings, the petitioners from the faubourg had gone to the terrace of the Jardin National to tell the workers gathered there what an ungracious welcome they had received. Angered by the news, the workers had more or less concluded that "the members of the Convention were all rogues who deserved to be shot," when the jeunes gens arrived, shouting "Long live the Convention!" and subjected them "to one of their haranguings." When summoned to shout "Long live the Republic!" the jeunes gens refused (a significant point), and a row started. It soon degenerated into a scuffle and then into an out-and-out brawl and the jeunes gens were given a good thrashing.

At the Jardin National, at the Palais Égalité, and on the boulevards, the sans-culottes (the police referred to them as "citizens dressed up as workers" and insisted that they were "citizens who had disguised themselves to stir up trouble") tore into the jeunes gens, calling them muscadins and Fréronist youth, beating them with sticks, dragging them by their hair, throwing them into ponds, tearing out their combs, ripping their clothes, and breaking their canes. There were plenty of witnesses: a merchant named Cornu, whom a man with a wooden leg punched in the face while asking him if he was happy; the carpenter Caron, who was grabbed by the collar and, ironic as it may seem, arrested as a buveur de sang; the hatter Doucet, who had not made any uncivil remarks, naturally, but had merely said, "Down with the Jacobins! Long live the Convention!" and "as he had his hair fastened up, his comb was yanked out"; and there were also the perfumer Aubiniay, the employee Chailly, the merchant Garnier, the pedlar Grobois, the porter Rosier, the civil servant Thouin, and the "indigent family head" Bucaille, who would reappear on the side of the police on 1 Prairial – all of them poor victims of the terrorists.

An observer dispatched to the Palais Égalité by the Butte des Moulins civil committee reported that he had seen "several groups of workers shouting 'Down with the muscadins!,' and whenever they encountered a fellow with his hair held in place with a comb, they made him remove the comb and let his hair hang freely." He added that this was all the workers wanted and that they were not even carrying sticks. However, his account appears to fall well short of reality. Indeed, many youths begged the military patrols to put them under arrest to save them from the sans-culottes: a hatter by the name of Gibon was knocked about "so badly that he would have been murdered had it not been for the military"; the student Godard was "arrested for his own safety"; the employee Raoul was chased by some thirty or so workers who "would have given him a good thrashing had the military not been there"; and the bookseller Laurès was rescued by an armed patrol from the clutches of a pedlar who, seeing that Laurès was carrying a club, had concluded "that he intended to murder his fellow citizens."

For the first time the workers had the upper hand, and they revelled with naïve delight in the exhilaration of finally teaching the jeunesse dorée a good lesson. "It's our turn today!" yelled the locksmith Velter as his gang of ruffians, armed with iron rods, charged at the jeunes gens in the Jardin des Tuileries. He must have enjoyed tearing into a young Polytechnique student like Jean-Baptiste Ricard, or one of the many "friends of the Convention" like Emery Delaigle, or a pillar of the Café de Chartres and infamous "slitter of patriot throats" like Pierre Clergeault. The silk worker Bruyasse, a member of the Gravilliers Section's old revolutionary committee, shouted "that the jeunes gens were all rogues who had been pushing citizens around for a long time, and now it was their turn to be pushed around." And he was not one to fear them: "Twenty good working lads could send two hundred of them packing," he asserted. A certain Leclerc, who had a furnished room in the rue du Muséum, said that he was "going to wade in because the time had come to have done with them once and for all." The commissioner Bottié, of Butte des Moulins, talked of mowing them all down because they were muscadins. "If a cannon were fired from over there," he joked, "think how many would be flattened!" On the Boulevard Montmartre the carter Béguin set upon a young man with his hair done up who was sitting in a carriage: "You're no more made to ride in a cabriolet than I am!" The mason Mulot, of the Gravilliers Section, said "that three or four thousand workers would be enough to wipe out all these jeunes gens with their hitched-up hair." The carpenter Leiris, of the Bondy Section, shouted, "amid a group of women and workers easy to lead astray," that the jeunesse dorée were all rogues. A woman named Lefebvre claimed "that she would eat the heart of a muscadin if she could get her hands on one." The Bodson brothers, at the head of a group of forty workers, stormed into Krabbe's jewellery at the Palais Égalité and tore off the proprietor's plaited wig, claiming that it was a rallying point! Tissot, the brother-in-law of the people's representative Goujon, egged on the workers to throw the jeunes gens into the ponds in the Tuileries. The gunner Véri mounted a platform in the Cité Section and, showing the scars on his stomach from the Vendée, called for the people to rise up in revolt, declaring that he was the one who had fired the Thermes guns on May 31 and that at the first sign he would do as much again. His anger and exasperation were symptomatic of the worsening social climate and heralded the clashes of Germinal and Prairial.

The jeunes gens were equally angry. They arrested the saddler Cochery, the petitioners' spokesman; the sergeant Teissier, who had accused them of being "merchants' informers"; the locksmith Lievin, who had taken exception to the way they fastened their hair; the gendarme Guénet, who had heard them shout "Long live Lafayette! Down with the Convention!"; the silversmith Volant, who had thrown some of them into the ponds; and the citizens Desforges and Solier, who rebuked them for having mistreated a disabled soldier the day before. They also set upon anyone who opposed their "civic action," such as the shoemaker Couvreux and the hatter Godard, who had objected to the arrest of a Jacobin. So blinded were they by their hatred that they did not hesitate to attack onlookers, like the innkeeper Orceyre and the coiffeur Thibault, who remarked, "It would appear that Fréron's army is not having its way today," and even passers-by and other innocent people who apparently had nothing to do with the conflict, such as the police inspector Bayard, who was there on duty "to find out what the trouble was"; the bootmaker Plastereau, apprehended for having said, "It seems that a lot of people are being arrested"; the gendarme Morin, who complained, "Will there never be peace and quiet?"; the shoemaker Destaudan, seized by men who said, "You must belong to some party!"; the vinegar dealer Beauvais, arrested because some men "wanted to know what his intentions were"; the locksmith Fraine, taken away because "he was doing nothing"; and scores of others, among them Aubry, Beaujean, the Genevois brothers, Lamy, Maigne, Gilbert, and Deboufeuille – the latter arrested by order of Merlin de Thionville, "who doubtless would not have given such an order if this citizen had not disturbed the peace."

All this agitation seemed rather formidable to the police, who feared for a time that the day's clashes might end in serious bloodshed. Some shopkeepers closed lest they be looted. The Committee of General Security, in a letter to the Police Comission, expressed fear that the disturbances might spread to the faubourgs: "Certain elements are attempting to incite the inhabitants of the Faubourg Antoine to revolt, telling them that whenever they see a young man with his hair done up in plaits and wearing a hat, they should fire at him as if he were a Swiss guard, since he must be a soldier in Fréron's counter-revolutionary army."

As the riot was beginning, Sieyès tabled a special police law in the Assembly to "ensure the protection of the national representatives." "The filthy pack of brigands and hired killers that swarms everywhere in the large towns and cities during times of revolutionary upheaval" had to be crushed, he said. Chasles remarked that citizens also needed protection, and that it was essential to ensure that "peaceful citizens [are] not slaughtered and then forced to shout 'Long live the Convention!'" As he spoke, there was a great stir at the far left of the hall. A voice in the galleries cried: "The royalists are slaughtering the patriots!"

Turmoil descended on the Assembly. The people's representatives called en masse for the decree to be put to a vote immediately, and in the blink of an eye it was passed. The Left had abstained. Overcome with indignation, Duhem shouted, "The law that has just been passed is a trap. The Convention has been duped!"

But Clauzel reassured his fellow members: some furies of the guillotine and fellows yelling "Down with the Convention!" had managed to slip into the crowds, but the good citizens had driven them away and had vowed to shield the nation's representatives with their own bodies.

The rapporteur then submitted to the Assembly the first article of the decree, under which anyone caught uttering seditious cries would be deported or, under extenuating circumstances, clapped in irons.

"I would rather be deported than put in irons," exclaimed Ruamps.

"Because anyone put in irons," added Duhem, "would have his throat cut by Fréron's youths!" There were loud murmurings; many members rose, shouting "Order, order!"

The first article was passed, but the Montagnards succeeded in having shouts against the Constitution of 1793 included in the definition of "seditious." Articles 2 and 3 were also passed, and members were debating Article 4 when Merlin de Thionville interrupted the deliberations to announce that an address had just been submitted to the president. He then read it out. It was from the jeunes gens, and was signed by Louis Jullian. They had come to express their devotion to the National Convention and to condemn the audacity and the ambition of these terrorists, who thought only of murder and flight. The Convention was at present considering measures important to the Republic, and the young men respected its proceedings. Then came the following pretentious peroration: "If your wisdom is united with our strength, the Republic will be saved. You are at your post; we are at ours. Long live the Republic, one, indivisible and democratic!"

Some members applauded, but the people's representative Gaston was bold enough to defy them. He had just come from the Tuileries, he said. There he had seen stick-swinging citizens who called themselves "group regulators" set upon others and disperse them to shouts of "Long live the Convention! Down with the Jacobins! Down with the bloodthirsty cutthroats!" He explained, "I cannot accept that citizens should police other citizens in this manner`... We cannot allow citizens to take the law into their own hands. Citizens of one party would soon be taking those of the opposing party to the Committee of General Security, and vice versa."

This was indeed what was happening, save that Gaston had neglected to mention the Committee of General Security's bias in favour of the jeunes gens, who as soon as they were arrested were set free again. Thus, when Pierre Clergeault was apprehended by the locksmith Velter and his gang, it was suggested that he be taken to the guardhouse, to which it was replied that there was no point, since the authorities simply let them all go again.

After Gaston had spoken, Rovère remarked that the situation was beginning to calm down but that the country had been in real danger. The Committees were going to submit a report: "The origin of the unrest is known, and you will finally hear the sad truth about it. Some people wanted to save Collot, Billaud, and Barère." Then Chateauneuf-Randon revealed the measures that the Committees had taken to put down the disturbances: they had called in the military to occupy the Égalité and Tuileries gardens and asked three neighbouring sections for assistance,

… but since written orders travel very slowly, we had the drummers beat a call to arms, and a huge crowd quickly gathered at the place of your deliberations [applause]. In serried ranks, these citizens restored law and order and dispersed the groups that were causing disturbances. Certainly some of these citizens were jeunes gens, but I kept a close eye on them, and I can assure you that I witnessed only the purest of sentiments and the greatest devotion to the National Convention.

This is a revealing statement. It shows that to deal with the "agitators," the Committee of General Security had had to rally the routed troops of the jeunesse dorée and provide them with leadership. There was thus no denying that the youths were acting as the Committee's private militia.

Then Louis Jullian, who had written the address read out just a few minutes before, mounted the rostrum: "Citizen representatives, I can say with pride that I assisted my brothers in chasing from the vicinity of this building those who were instigating revolt and pillage. I have been sent to report to you on the day's outcome, to apprise you that the friends of our national representative body remain in full control of the situation, and to assure you that we have vowed to defend this body to the last drop of our blood."

The president of the Convention responded by urging them to continue to arrest those who pressed for civil war, who were the same breed of men that their brave comrades were fighting at the front. This comment was as laughable as it was pitiful – as if the deserters among the jeunesse dorée and the veteran troops of the front line were facing the same enemy. The president's concluding remarks were of a piece: "Enter this august chamber, and then go and fulfil your noble mission of restoring law and order." The government had no proper police force, and so the jeunesse dorée was acting in its stead.

Alexandre Méchin, representing the "young citizens of Paris," was then admitted to the speaker's platform. Méchin had been a close friend of Girey-Dupré, the Girondin whose mother had appeared before the Assembly at the start of the session. He explained that "insane agitators, despicable royalists" had dared to raise their heads and threaten liberty, but that good citizens, numbering over forty thousand, had forced them to scatter. "The Jacobins have returned to the filth of the gutter, and we swear they shall remain there."

The jeunesse dorée's sole aim in all of this was to confuse the issue and hide the truth. Its members could cry victory over the terrorists as much as they wanted; it was nothing but bluff and rhetoric. The police reports attest quite clearly that the two sides had waged "a battle in which the jeunes gens had got the worst of it." The sans-culottes had finally punished the jeunesse dorée for their ridiculous fashions, their frivolous conduct in the theatres, their beardless chins which recalled the first conscription, their meetings in the cafés, and their acts of provocation. For the sans-culottes, this was still the surest form of justice.

FRUITLESS ATTEMPTS AT FRATERNIZATION

The unrest of late Ventôse and the skirmishes of early Germinal turned public opinion against the jeunesse dorée, which saw itself becoming increasingly isolated. The bourgeoisie no longer followed its lead, and dreaded a confrontation with the populace. Fréron wrote, "Peaceful citizens found it difficult to conceal their impatience when they saw the future of the Republic, the future of the Convention, being entrusted to mere youths. People were secretly upset to know that children were now in charge of maintaining law and order and ensuring the triumph of justice."

Among the lower classes, too, there were signs of exasperation. According to a police agent, "It seems that the general public is beginning to tire of the behaviour of the jeunes gens at the Jardin National. The public regards it as a tactic to incite the people, and is astonished that the government appears to condone such actions."

The jeunes gens were the vanguard of the bourgeoisie, just as the "Jacobins" were the vanguard of the lower classes. Until now, whenever the two vanguards had clashed, the jeunes gens had had the upper hand, chiefly because their opponents had never joined forces in a common front. However, with the food shortage pushing the populace back toward Jacobinism and reuniting the bonds of sans-culotte solidarity, the jeunes gens were in danger of finding themselves alone against the toiling masses, which were beginning to agitate again. The events of 1 Germinal had shown that the jeunesse dorée was no match for the sans-culottes when they were fully mobilized. Having come to this conclusion, the bourgeois strat-

egists of the class struggle decided that a switch in tactics from provocation to appeasement was in order.

A counterweight had to be found to the Jacobins, who behind the
scenes were inciting the common people to revolt and rallying them
– with a certain degree of success, if *Le Messager du Soir* is to be believed – against the jeunesse dorée.

They scour lofts, taverns, and workshops in their efforts to stir up the credulous working class against what they refer to as the gilded million, the
muscadins, the shopkeepers, and Fréron's youth ... Simple, hard-working
men who rarely leave their workshops have the weakness of believing this
abominable slander. Our society is already torn by hatred and political factions. These criminals hope to rid themselves of the irksome vigilance of the
young men who hound them by setting them against estimable, hard-
working men whom they hope to dupe again, so as to reign anew under
their name.

In its attempts at appeasement, the bourgeoisie seems to have
adopted a three-pronged strategy: fraternal dinners held for workers at the Palais Égalité, deputations sent by the jeunes gens to fraternize in the workshops, and posters and pamphlets advocating
reconciliation of the two parties. On 2 Germinal, workers from the
Faubourg Antoine were invited to dine at the Café de Chartres. At
the Théâtre de la République, the performance was interrupted to
invite the jeunes gens to attend the dinner, and the invitation met
with warm applause. It seems that a large number of guests were expected, for tables were set up in the garden. The dinner was held in
the evening, but there is no record of how many workers turned up,
nor of who they were. However, we do know that there was considerable opposition to the dinner, particularly from the women of the
faubourgs. "The sans-culottes are fools to let themselves be pestered
by these swine," the women said, adding that the muscadins were
constantly calling them rabble and useless idlers. Others remarked
wryly, "The fellows who were assaulted are paying the fine! From
now on, whenever the sans-culottes want the muscadins to treat
them to good wine, they just have to force them to drink pond water
first! The national baptism must make them human!" Apparently
the event was not a complete failure, however, if we are to judge by
the crowing of *Le Messager du Soir*: "So, *messieurs les terroristes*, it is
time to wrack your brains for new plots! That of arming old against
young, poor against rich, worker against merchant, faubourg
against city has failed miserably."

A dinner had also been scheduled for the next day, 3 Germinal,
but it had to be postponed. A rumour circulated that the jeunes gens

were trying to lead the workers on and trick them. On the fourth, a deputation of twelve habitués of the Café de Chartres was awaited in the faubourg, but only six showed up; the others must have got cold feet at the last minute. According to an observer, both sides acknowledged that they had been infiltrated by agitators seeking to sow discord. They vowed to wage war on royalists and anarchists alike, and agreed that a new deputation of jeunes gens, twelve this time, would be received in the faubourg to strengthen the fraternal ties that had been established. The talks must have been very perfunctory indeed. It is easy to imagine jeunes gens and workers coming to blows, but one wonders what they could ever have found to discuss and agree on.

The jeunes gens' visit to the faubourg actually stirred up trouble. Guilhem, one of Babeuf's lieutenants and a former letter-post courier, was arrested the same day, along with the citizens Pierre-Marie Gonore, Antoine Guillemel, François Grégoire, and a fellow named Guinon, and "charged with causing disturbances in the Faubourg Antoine." The dyer and cleaner Jean-Claude Ortion explained to the Montreuil Section police commissioner that at the café run by the citizen Vernier, at the Porte Dauphine, eight individuals singing Le Réveil du Peuple had offered him a drink and asked him if he would go and sign a letter at the Jardin Égalité. He had refused, pointing out to them that they could not draw up a petition in the name of the faubourg without the participation of its citizens. Pierre-Marie Gonore, of the Théâtre Français Section, said that a furious row had ensued during which he, for his part, had asserted that it was a great shame that youths should molest citizens who had served the Republic and that the men who shouted "Long live the Convention!" so loudly were perhaps the ones who actually wanted a king. Gonore then went to a tavern near the Quinze Vingts guardhouse. There he got into a discussion with two men who said that they were deputies from Lyon who had come to fraternize with the workers of the faubourg. They too invited him to join them at their table, but he declined, remarking that the Convention was in session and that that was the place to fraternize.

Another tactic tried by the jeunes gens was the deputations they sent round the Paris workshops on 3 Germinal to fraternize. We know little about how they were received, save that at the Arsenal workshop women called them muscadins and threatened to give them a good dunking. In the evening, however, a deputation of workers was welcomed at the Café de Chartres; again, their names are not known. What we do know is that efforts were made to fraternize, that it was decided that the Barrière du Trône would no longer be regarded as the demarcation line between the city and the faubourgs, and that the two sides would henceforth avoid insulting each other – as if denying the existence of the class struggle were enough to eliminate it.

Lastly there were the written exhortations. The day after the clash of 1 Germinal, *Le Messager du Soir* proposed the drafting of a "fraternal address from the young men to the patriotic, industrious workers whose hands make commerce and the arts prosper" – rather unusual expressions to use at a time of food shortages and unemployment. The aim was to "make the people realize" who their real enemies were: "either the monsters who have devastated and depopulated the Republic, destroyed workshops, burnt down houses, and set alight flourishing towns, or the men who want the workshops and trade to regain their earlier activity and splendour."

The text was written the next day by the regulars at the Café de Chartres. Titled *Adresse des jeunes citoyens à leurs frères, les ouvriers de tous les âges* (Address of the Young Citizens to Their Brothers, Workers of All Ages), it was posted in the faubourgs and was read out in a number of sections.

The jeunes gens begin their address by saying they first wish to explain themselves. They feel that this is necessary because the veterans of the Revolution have not been told the truth about them. What is the meaning of these calls to the workers to rise up against the muscadins? Are the muscadins the same people as the jeunes gens? But some of them are workers. So they are being stirred up against their families, against themselves. Are the muscadins the rich? But that would mean attacking those who buy, and if that starts, all commerce will cease, and the workers will no longer have any means of subsistence. Some people have said that the muscadins want a king and that they wage war on the sans-culottes. There is not a grain of truth to it. They are for the Republic, and if they wage war, it is not on the sans-culottes but on crime, and the sans-culottes surely cannot defend crime. "Ah, comrades! Our cause is one and the same!" the publicist proclaims. Everyone is threatened by the Jacobins, who will not waste time selecting their victims in future. Let us forget these "insignificant labels" muscadin and sans-culotte, which were thought up by scheming traitors, and stand together to form an impregnable fortress around liberty! The address concludes, "Long live all good citizens, regardless of their means or their profession."

This is an interesting document because of the very weakness of the argumentation: the bourgeois publicist really has nothing to offer the workers other than a common front against the Jacobins – nothing particularly exciting for people who were utterly destitute.

Soon afterward, a pamphlet appeared which claimed to be the workers' reply: *Réponse des ouvriers à l'adresse des jeunes citoyens* (Response of the Workers to the Address of the Young Citizens). It answered the address of the jeunes gens point by point.

They have not been misled about the jeunes gens, they say. They have eyes. They have seen the way the youths abuse liberty in public places; their ridiculous, affected manner of dress; the dangerous weapons they carry; the seditious shouts they utter; the way they offer their arm to those beings, "whom we dare not name." They have seen them again and again exhorting the common people to resign themselves to getting by on reduced provisions – thus "leaving the very strong suspicion" that they themselves do not go without anything.

And then there are the "battues" at the Palais Égalité to flush out supposed buveurs de sang; the disturbances in the theatres, where only *Le Réveil du Peuple* is allowed to be performed – a blatant incitement to civil war; the way they order good, honest citizens not to assemble in the streets and squares – have the workers ever left their workshops to do the like? Moreover, was it the workers, the unarmed workers, who attacked them on 1 Germinal?

Then the workers' advocate waxes sarcastic. This term muscadin, which is used to refer to the youths, certainly cannot have originated among the workers, for they do not even know what it means. It must be a term of abuse, though, because the youths are complaining about it. In any case, if used to refer to an enemy of equality and concord, it obviously does not suit them, he adds, "since you have shown such a desire to strengthen our fraternal ties." As for the accusation that they want a king, it is nothing but an "atrocious piece of slander" thought up by their common enemies in an effort to divide them. But this effort will fail!

The youths say that they wage war on crime. This is all very fine, but if unpowdered hair, common frock coats, and dirty shoes are signs of crime, then there are plenty of criminals, and the jeunes gens have a terrific job ahead of them! Perhaps it would be preferable not to distinguish between "those who wear boots" and "those who wear clogs." Citizens are obviously dependent on one another for their happiness, the workers' spokesman concedes. So why do the jeunes gens – whose relatives "most likely run large businesses and thriving companies," since they do not require them to work from morning till night – why do they not urge their relatives to lower the prices of basic necessities and put their confidence in the assignat? How could citizens get by with everything costing so much?

You suggest that we rise up against the rogues, the author continues. They are most certainly guilty, "but we can rise up only against men assembled together, against armed men who call for insurrection and stir up trouble. Where are these insurgents? ... We cannot see any ... Would it be you, by chance?"

The workers' pamphlet ends with the following threat: You can rely on the wisdom and energy of the people. They are quite capable of taking revenge on the little runts who dare to attack them.

This piece is much better argued. The lines exude irony and sarcasm. Whenever the workers' spokesman addresses the young men, he calls them his "brothers." We can only conclude that the *Adresse des jeunes gens* was taken for what it was: a clumsy ploy, gilded with disingenuous overtures of fraternity, whose ultimate aim was to sap the populace's spirit of revolt.

Unrest continued from 1 to 12 Germinal as the sans-culottes, who wanted the Convention to give the people bread, fought for influence against the honnêtes gens, who, less affected by the food shortage, were more motivated by the political question, and called for the indictment of the "four ringleaders." Torn by the two opposing sides, the Assembly became timorous and disoriented, and considered disbanding. Anarchy was not far off.

The "dunkings" of 1 Germinal had dealt a severe blow to muscadin vanity. "The youths appear to be furious over the treatment some of their comrades were subjected to yesterday," wrote *Le Courrier républicain*. "They remember how their fathers were slaughtered." In a similar vein, *Le Messager du Soir* appealed, "Why assault men who were neither dirty nor despicable? Why drown them à la Carrier in the ponds while invoking the names of the fiends who worked under this butcher? Who were the aggressors? The young men were quietly passing by. When a fury caught sight of them, they were dragged off by the ruffians."

The following day, 2 Germinal, the jeunes gens wanted revenge, and there were further rows and brawls in public places. At the Porte Denis a mob of six hundred jeunes gens attacked a handful of workers who were just heading home for the day. Louis-Simon Lair, a journeyman carpenter from the Amis de la Patrie Section, was seized "by a pack of youths armed with sticks and various other weapons who were shouting 'Long live the Convention! Down with the Jacobins and the buveurs de sang!'" They grabbed him by the collar and started to drag him off, along with a few others, but, Lair went on, "when they saw the huge crowd that had gathered, they let us go." Wielding their sabres and sticks, the jeunes gens then stopped a coach in the rue Bourbon Villeneuve. A "young man" who had been arrested in Germinal, Year II, for illegal currency dealings and who was now working as a garçon at the Café de l'Europe in the Palais Égalité, Louis-Joseph Laplanche, was led off to the Committee of General Security by a detachment of the guard for "elbowing and shoving other citizens." In the Jardin des Tuileries, an office employee of the Department of Paris, Pierre d'Hardivilliers, was arrested in the midst of a large number of youths who had linked arms and were brandishing sticks. Also at the Tuileries, a pupil seeking admission to the École centrale, Étienne Delmas, and a printing-shop manager, Pierre Patry, were put under arrest during a scuffle with a gang of malicious characters who were shouting, "Down with Fréron's youth! Down with the muscadins!"

The workers were responsible for their own share of provocations which degenerated into fights with the jeunes gens. On the Pont Neuf the paperhanger Devoyez declared, "The rich are all rogues. Paris has a million of them who need punishing!" The blacksmith Cornesse, of the Invalides workshop, wandered about the Palais Égalité armed with a stick, asking, "Why don't we lay into these muscadins? They're all blackguards, the lot of them!" At the Tuileries, the citizens Guait and Leract, as they passed within earshot of a group of jeunes gens, were imprudent enough to call them muscadins. This angered the youths, who wanted to give them a good thrashing; they hurled abuse at them, roughed them up, and, since they easily outnumbered them, put them under arrest. In a café in the Place de l'Estrapade, a certain Michelot taunted a group of youths from the École normale, calling them muscadins and declaring loudly that he was a Jacobin, adding, derisively, that it had certainly been quite a day and that the muscadins' turn would come. The armourer Delmotte said that the Café des Invalides was more than a match for the Café de Chartres and that the blacksmiths would not put up with any harassment from the muscadins. In the rue Honoré the citizens Bique, Baudot, and Féraud rattled their sabres at the jeunes gens. The jeweller Jean-Auguste Souque, a returned émigré, testified before the Committee of General Security

that he had been at the Tuileries an hour before and had seen several young men walking about shouting, "Long live the Republic! Long live the Convention!" when a citizen belonging to a patrol from the Chalier Section had suddenly darted out from his column to yell "Down with the royalists! Down with the muscadins!" The term muscadin seemed to offend the young men, who shouted "Down with the Jacobins!" and called on the citizen to shout it too. But he persisted in yelling "Down with the muscadins!" and a brawl would have ensued had the military not dispersed the crowd.

All in all, however, the events of 2 Germinal were much less turbulent than those of the previous day, chiefly because of the large
security force deployed by the Committees. The Military Committee
was instructed to call out whatever armed force was thought necessary to maintain the peace, and the general staff of the National
Guard was ordered to beat the call to arms in the forty-eight sections
of the capital. But these measures were excessive and foolhardy. A
general call to arms in all of the sections meant that the terrorists
would make up the majority of the security force. And so the
Committee went back on its decision. Only the National Guard from
what were considered to be the three most reliable sections –
Fontaine Grenelle, Invalides, and Champs Elysées – was called up.
The twelve arrondissement watch committees were instructed to
keep "very close watch" and to provide the Committee of General
Security with "swift, detailed intelligence reports." Citizens were
prohibited "from walking about or assembling with arms of any
kind." Bells that could be used to sound the tocsin were hurriedly
taken down, that of the Pavillon de l'Unité being the only one allowed to remain up. The Committee of General Security ordered
one hundred rifles to be distributed in each section to "good citizens
who have no weapons and who ask for them." This measure was
designed to create a core of reliable men within each National Guard
battalion who would keep troublemakers in line. Such an impres-
sive show of strength did not, however, prevent a flare-up of agitation in the Gravilliers Section on 7 Germinal, nor a mass revolt of the
faubourgs on the twelfth.

In the meantime, the debates at the Convention were dominated
by the question of the "four ringleaders." The jeunes gens had
driven the terrorists from the public galleries, which they now controlled as a conspiratorial clique. On 2 Germinal, they were there at
eight o'clock in the morning. "The galleries are full of murderers!"
asserted Duroy. "They're not being paid today!" someone replied.

The following day they were back again in great numbers, singing
Le Réveil du Peuple. They had to be silenced before the session could
begin. The Assembly was deliberating under the threat of the jeunesse dorée's cudgels!

Over the next few days the jeunes gens significantly curtailed
their agitation in the streets. On 6 Germinal, Thuriot again denounced them in the Assembly for assuming "the right to impose
law and order and assault other citizens, form patrols, and march
abreast with the National Guard." Yet from 2 to 12 Germinal it
seems that only four street incidents were reported. On the sixth,
the citizen Marillac was set upon at the Jardin National: "I was col-

lared, shoved, and knocked over by seven or eight youths." The leader of the group was the president of the Brutus Section, Pierre Eigasse, an adventurer of sorts who had previously been compromised in an affair involving counterfeit assignats and had had a chequered career as soldier, shop assistant, secretary at the Convention archives, and secretary to the Committee of General Security. On the seventh, André Doderay, of the Gardes Françaises Section, was led away to the Palais Égalité guardhouse by six young men for having denounced the honnêtes gens. On the eighth, the carpenter Lapanne, of the Quinze Vingts Section, was arrested after getting into a quarrel with "a citizen who had plaited hair held up with a comb." And on the eleventh, a certain Magloire Brune was taken to the Committee of General Security for having said in the Tuileries "that the jeunes gens were acting in a high-handed manner."

Meanwhile, however, the jeunes gens were increasing their presence in the sections. On 30 Ventôse they had gone as a body to the general assembly of the Piques Section, and on 3 Germinal they were instrumental in bringing about the arrest of fifteen or so of the most unruly terrorists: Charriot, on the charge of trying to prevent the youths from singing *Le Réveil du Peuple*; Lemoine, on the charge of being an agent of intrigue; Beloeil, for being an agitator; Clavière, for being an extremely bloodthirsty character; Moussard, a Jacobin of 9 Thermidor; Morin, accused of being a mad terrorist; Maugin, a section rabble-rouser; Térasson, because he muttered at motions favourable to the Convention; Montallier, because he had established a sort of "mountain" in the section; Maugein, because he encouraged his children to shout seditious slogans; Morel, because he was known as "an exceedingly brazen and outrageous embezzler"; Rimbaud, Marotte, Damilot, Lavocat, and others were also detained. The section's terrorist leaders were thus neutralized in very short order. On 10 Germinal the jeunes gens took control of the general assemblies in the Tuileries, Butte des Moulins, Champs Elysées, Halle au Blé, Guillaume Tell, and Unité sections, and succeeded in having the assemblies adopt virulent antiterrorist addresses to the Convention. The address from the Tuileries Section, prepared by Louis Jullian on behalf of property owners and honest citizens, threatened the Assembly with reprisals if it refused to indict Barère, Billaud, Collot, and Vadier: "Accuse the criminals who slaughtered the people," it ordered the Assembly, "lest the people rise up and accuse all of you." *L'Orateur du Peuple* that appeared on the same day was no less menacing: "Think carefully! If you abandon your post without having judged them, you will be brought before the tribunal of the nation. And it will judge you."

Under attack from all quarters, the Assembly now considered disbanding. On 3 Germinal, rumours spread that the deputies had horses at the ready and were preparing to leave for Châlons. The following day, only half the Convention was supposedly going to flee. These rumours, coupled with the motions presented in the Assembly on 8 Germinal to summon the primary assemblies and defer indictment of the "four ringleaders," created an uproar at the Café de Chartres. "If we do not keep a close watch on the rogues, we are lost," the jeunes gens said. At the Théâtre Martin, the deputies were called "cowards and fools." But the Assembly remained at its station – doubtless under pressure from the honnêtes gens – and by the eleventh people were demanding explanations. Commissioners from the Quinze Vingts Section went to the Convention and, defying repression, harangued members with a threatening address which summed up the bitter feelings of the populace. Imagine this handful of poor, starving, humiliated men, standing in their filthy rags amidst the sea of indecisive and corrupt Convention deputies. Imagine their spokesman, a man of the people, obscure and forgotten by history, lashing out in an impassioned indictment of Thermidorian policies: Why was the Law of the Maximum suppressed? Why were the popular societies closed? Why the continuing food shortage? Why were patriots still in prison? Why had the Constitution of 1793 never been implemented? Furthermore, why were only fanatics and the jeunesse dorée of the Palais Royal permitted to gather together? And finally, a warning which, in its ominous conciseness, portended the uprising that was to ensue the next day: "We stand to defend the Republic and liberty."

THE FIRST HUNGER RIOT

On the evening of 11 Germinal, the Committee of General Security was warned – how is not clear – that an insurrection was afoot, and sent word to the jeunesse dorée to report to the courtyard of the Louvre at six o'clock the following morning. According to Duval, two or three representatives went round the groups at the Jardin Égalité, advising the young men to bring muskets with them. Those who had none would be provided with them. Isidore Langlois, who was there, suggested that anyone who did not turn up the next day ought to be banished forever from the ranks of the jeunesse dorée and be forbidden to show his face at the Jardin Égalité. Souriguère took umbrage at the insulting suggestion that some of the jeunes gens might be cowards, and in a burst of enthusiasm they all swore they would be there. This version of the incident, describing it essentially as a question of honour, was Duval's; however, in the Assembly the next day, Ruamps accused the Committee of General Security of having handed out thirty thousand livres to the youths. The upholding of honour would no doubt have seemed more attractive under these circumstances.

So, between six and seven o'clock on the morning of 12 Germinal, the Committee's minions gathered in the courtyard of the Louvre. From there they were led by some deputies, among them Tallien and André Dumont, to the Cour Royale, where they took up their posts. It seems that the Committees, underestimating the strength of the uprising, imagined that the jeunesse dorée alone would suffice to defend the entrances to the Convention. In the lower-class areas of the city, it was rumoured that the jeunes gens had gathered at the Bois de Boulogne. In the Assembly, Ruamps said that he had seen them there with his own eyes. The Committee of General Security instructed Auguis to go and see for himself, but he found no one there. The rumour was false, but it gave the workers yet another reason to go into action.

Early in the afternoon, a crowd of women appeared in the Place du Carrousel – "in truth, women of the most contemptible class of the populace," remarked Duval. The people's representative Merlin de Thionville saw them approaching and, perhaps out of some sort of Machiavellian complicity, had the jeunes gens let them through to the Cour Royale, whence they rushed to the Assembly, demanding bread. "For shame!" de Thionville cried. "All they send us are women!" ·

But this was merely the mob's vanguard. A stream of workers followed in their wake. The jeunes gens attempted to stop them, but were knocked to the ground or thrown against the walls, and the crowd poured into the chamber, shouting "We want bread! We want bread!" They had arrived just at the right moment: Boissy d'Anglas, known as Boissy Famine, was reporting on the state of food supplies in Paris and congratulating himself on having had farmers released from prison. Turmoil descended upon the Assembly. A young man who claimed to be a regular visitor to the Convention's galleries and said that he had "closely followed" its debates since 1 Germinal sought, along with his comrades, to reassure the representatives of the people: "Be firm! We shall die with you, for you, and in your defence!" But the crowd soon filled the hall, and as it was vital, he said, not to let all the seats be taken, he and his comrades rushed to the right side. Thereafter, for over an hour, nothing more but shouts and cries of rage were heard. Moments later, de Thionville was in the Assembly, mingling with the crowd and embracing the workers. From the left came shouts for him to take his place. "My place is with the people," he retorted. "The citizens have told me that they were not acting with evil intentions." "Only the muscadins have evil intentions," replied Ruamps.

But de Thionville's actions roused suspicions. What was he up to? And why the sham fraternization with the workers? To Barère it was all too obvious that the Thermidorians had paid five francs a head to "persuade" the demonstrators to march on the Convention, and an anonymous "democrat" asserted that they had organized the riot themselves so as to have a pretext for crushing the Montagnards. This is obviously overstating the case, but it does seem that the government's Committees did not do all they could to prevent the riot. Whether this was a ruse or a stratagem on their part remains an open question, especially since in this particular case all the roles were reversed: the Montagnards, who the day before had been planning to join the uprising if it gained any real strength, were now calling for the hall to be cleared!

"Mr. President!" called out the deputy Gaston. "Please ask the citizens to leave. It is stifling in here." To the citizens he added, "Friends, you want bread and you want the patriots who have been imprisoned to be freed, do you not? Well, we agree with you on both counts. You shall have satisfaction. But please clear the hall. It is stifling in here."

Choudieu then demanded that the chamber be cleared; one of the insurgents shot back, "This is our chamber!" Duhem apparently enjoined the carpenter Ponpont, of the Temple Section, who had come to the Convention "with the intention of cutting the throats of all the members of the Plain," to leave the hall. In the opinion of Bourdon de l'Oise, Duhem was clearly behind the riot, since the bewildered citizens immediately followed his orders and withdrew, although they had refused to do so when asked by the president. However, the Left was not of one mind in this instance, since an unidentified deputy urged the petitioners to remain where they were and not to cede their places to the jeunes gens: "Comrade," he said to a rebel, "stay with us. If you all leave, the muscadins will take your places to put pressure on us. Until now, because of them, we have been unable to do anything for you or for the people." According to the artist Jean-Baptiste Rogniat, Duhem too apparently urged a citizen to go and fetch his comrades and bring them all into the Convention.

So the demonstrators had poured into the Assembly, creating chaos and shouting curses against the jeunes gens: "We want bread and action against the muscadins! Down with Fréron's youth! Down with the Café de Chartres royalists!" Deputies were refused the floor. "No bread, no floor!" exclaimed the worker Rivière, of the Arsenal Section. Eventually there was silence for a moment, and Commander Van Heck, at the head of the Cité battalion, took the floor on behalf of the insurgents. They were the men of 14 July, 10 August, and 31 May, he said. They had sworn to live free or to die. They were tired of spending their nights in queues outside the bakeries; they wanted bread. What had become of last year's harvest? They also wanted the patriots to be set free. They wanted the Constitution of 1793. And furthermore, said Van Heck, "we are asking you to mete out justice and punish Fréron's army, punish these *messieurs à bâton!*"

Next to take the floor was the Fidelité Section, which, among other things, called for the young men of the first conscription to be sent back to the front; it was followed by the Fraternité, Bonnet de la Liberté, and Bonne Nouvelle sections. The president of the Assembly stared at the insurgents: "They are forgetting that the thunderbolt will crash down on their heads ..." "The thunderbolt is your Palais Royal army!" retorted Ruamps.

The jeunesse dorée was indeed preparing to intervene. The forces loyal to the Convention had been slow to rally; Salverte, one of the young men who was to take part in clearing the Assembly, explained that "the citizens who work in businesses and offices had not finished eating." Evidently it was out of the question to disturb *nos petits messieurs* while they were at table! But the general turmoil that reigned in the streets was doubtless a contributing factor in their procrastination. "Anyone with plaited hair who tried to cross the streets or squares was assaulted," wrote *Le Messager du Soir*. Thus, one Jean-Baptiste Verdier, a military-transport employee who approached a group of men on the boulevards talking about provisions and asked them to disperse, was attacked for being a muscadin and was "struck several times in the face." A colleague of his at the Military Provisions Commission, Charles-Nicolas Viraux, corroborated his story. In the Place du Cloître, where the Bon Conseil battalion was posted, the saddler Pierre Caillaud showed the people standing around him a packet of cartridges, saying, "The merchants, the muscadins, and all those other rogues will not be our masters forever." According to Boissy, the man who denounced him, he had said, "If the members of the Convention think I have come here to defend them, then they are wrong. Those rogues have put all the best sans-culottes behind bars. Only Fréron's army enjoys their protection." A certain Prodhomme, of the Lombards Section, vowed "that the current reign would not last forever, and that the muscadins would get the boot." Even in the prisons there was great agitation. At the Plessis prison, the inmates sang and created a ruckus despite the notices forbidding any manifestation of joy that might have been "heard round about." At the Orties jail, where the prisoners were "all dressed as though they were getting out that day," the sole topic of conversation was "freedom given by the people"; Dulac, the source of this information, concluded, "It was obvious that the prisoners were in contact with the conspirators." This general climate of unrest could well have hampered the mobilization of the jeunes gens. Finally, at around six o'clock, the forces loyal to the Convention were ready. All the patriotic young men known under the derogatory name of muscadin were supposed to be slaughtered, declared Salverte. But that did not daunt us, he declared passionately; we were ready to die at our posts. Merlin de Thionville had sent messengers to rally the Piques, Le Peletier, and Butte des Moulins sections. Jullian had gone in person to the Faubourg Montmartre, Champs Élysées, and Tuileries sections. All would have been lost, Salverte said, had it not been for the courage of a handful of men who rallied the honest citizens in their sections.

But to what degree were the jeunes gens actually involved in clearing the Convention? Beaulieu is very vague on this point; in his *Essais*, he says nothing about what the jeunesse dorée did on 12 Germinal, save that Pichegru had agreed to lead the sectional forces loyal to the Assembly and that "all the bourgeoisie, all the young men outlawed by the crowds, were only too happy to carry out his orders." Lacretelle asserts that some three hundred of them, led by Legendre and flanked by a handful of soldiers under the command of Pichegru, burst into the Assembly at about seven o'clock, singing *Le Réveil du Peuple*, and drove out the petitioners. They had dispersed the crowd around the Assembly beforehand, isolating the petitioners inside. This version of events is corroborated by Jullian. Choudieu, on the other hand, says that only after the insurgents had complied with his request to withdraw did the jeunes gens, led by Jullian and Méchin, enter the chamber. Lastly, Levasseur states that the jeunes gens, led by Legendre, Kervelégan, and Tallien, used their bayonets to clear the corridors, but did not enter the actual hall of the Assembly. Which of these five accounts are we to believe?

Contrary to Tønnesson, there is no reason to dismiss the hypothesis that the jeunes gens entered the actual debating chamber, particularly since it is bolstered by the manuscript testimony of two eyewitnesses who are not suspect in any way. The first, the dragoon officer Monbarisson, whose account was substantiated by the policeman Froidure, had quarrelled in the Convention with a certain Michel-Antoine Legagneur, a labourer from the Gardes Françaises

Section, who asserted "that the people had been right to force their way through the guards and that they were entitled to enter wherever they wished." Monbarisson rejoined that he was wrong, that there were galleries for the people, whereupon Legagneur began to lose his temper. "Fortunately, just at that moment, scores of youths surged into the chamber," Monbarisson explained, "and so he said nothing more." Thus, it appears that the jeunes gens not only went up to the galleries, but also entered the actual debating hall of the Assembly. The second witness is Ignace Eck, a merchant and currency dealer from the Le Peletier Section (who later, on 1 Prairial, Year III, acted as a messenger between the Committee of General Security and the Thermidorians, under siege by the mob). In a statement made on 25 Prairial, he claimed that at about seven o'clock on the evening of 12 Germinal he had helped Merlin de Thionville clear "the furies" out of the Convention; he had then returned to his seat next to Prieur de la Marne, in the Assembly chamber. The testimony of these two witnesses is supported by Duplessis-Bertaux, who remarks, in his *Tableaux historiques*, that "the armed youths rushed to the Thermidorians' rescue and helped them to drive out the insurgents."

Once the Assembly had been cleared, the *"peuple des honnêtes gens*," as Baron Fain put it, filled the galleries again. At the entrance to the Convention, in the Place du Carrousel, young men sang *Le Réveil du Peuple*. Now free to act as they pleased, the Thermidorians passed a decree, without debate, ordering the immediate deportation of Barère, Billaud-Varennes, Collot-d'Herbois, and Vadier. André Dumont presided over the session. "Ah, what a great service he has rendered to France on this day of glory for all good citizens!" one of the youths who was there wrote enthusiastically. Then Tallien took the president's chair and urged the honnêtes gens in the galleries "to support the Convention with all their energy" – an appeal which elicited lengthy applause. Choudieu, Chasles, Léonard Bourdon, Duhem, Amar, Foussedoire, Huguet, and Ruamps, who had inveighed so vehemently against the jeunes gens during the sitting, were put under arrest. "How beautiful, how magnificent, how calm it all was!" remarked the little muscadin who had praised André Dumont. His assessment of the day's events was most accurate: "The riot was the determining factor in a decision which otherwise would not have been made." Thus, the demonstration of 12 Germinal had the effect of quickening, rather than slowing or reversing, the reactionary course of Thermidorian politics.

Unrest continued throughout the evening in some sections: Panthéon, Quinze Vingts, Cité, Popincourt, and perhaps Thermes and Bon Conseil. There is no evidence of any activity on the part of the jeunesse dorée, save in the Popincourt Section, where the shoe-maker Jean-Victor Dubée burst into the offices of the civil committee with an armed band, hoping to pick a quarrel with a certain Tabouin, a regular at the Palais Égalité: Was he wearing his comb? What about his black pin? Why did he go about insulting the work-ers? But the civil committee managed to break up the altercation before it went any further.

The next day was quieter. Crowds formed here and there; though the jeunes gens did not go and disperse them, they made sure to re-port them to the Committee of General Security. Thus we learn that in the Place de Grève, workers gathered in groups and talked about making the rounds of the workshops, beating the call to arms in the sections, and going to "rouse the Faubourg Antoine so as to march together to the Convention." On the Pont au Change, too, there was talk of rallying the Faubourg Antoine and the Faubourg Marceau. Stonemasons and other workers who were angry at receiving only half a pound of bread gathered in the rue Feydeau. "They force their comrades who disagree with them to accompany them anyhow," noted an observer. At the Palais Égalité, the citizens Collin, Noël, and Buirette arrested a fancy-goods maker by the name of Thomas who, in the midst of a large crowd, had been complaining about the price of food. In the rue du Bacq, the mason Léger Vigeon, armed with a stick, was saying things that drew a crowd of at least 150 peo-ple. Below the Pont National, the gendarme François Chavanne was whipping up a group against the merchants. Near the Pont Neuf, a man was making seditious speeches; the citizen Binet, who pro-tested when the fellow was arrested, was himself seized by two young men, the merchant Claude Girard and a legal clerk from the Marchés Section, Louis Christlich, who had earned a reputation in May of 1793 as a staunch opponent of the recruitment campaign.

Meanwhile, a detachment of three hundred young men under the command of Pichegru – a "highly irregular" detachment, according to Lacretelle – had been assigned the task of transferring out of Paris the deputies who had been arrested by decree. Serving under Pichegru's orders were Commander Nicolas Raffet, Brigadier-General Saint-Cricq, General Officers Haintrailles and Lapallière, Major Roques, and Police Inspector André Sadous, dispatched by the Paris Police Administrative Commission. But the operation was not all smooth sailing. With the passage of the Law of 1 Germinal, which stipulated that in the event of an emergency the Convention would leave Paris and meet at Châlons sur Marne, it was feared that the people's representatives might abandon ship, leaving no one at the helm of public affairs. Thus, on 12 Germinal, agents of the 6th arrondissement reported, "Several groups of women have been taking it upon themselves to arrest citizens, alleging that they are either deputies trying to escape or else muscadins." Some of the common people objected to seeing "the good deputies" being deported, deeming that the Convention did not have the authority to decide their fate.

Léonard Bourdon was the first to be arrested. The coach that was taking him to the Château de Ham in Picardy was stopped at about ten o'clock in the morning; he was seized and taken to the watch committee of the 6th arrondissement, and from there to the Committee of General Security. At around seven o'clock that evening, the gunners of the Faubourg Montmartre wanted to roll out their guns, shouting that the best patriots were being murdered and that Léonard Bourdon had been jailed. The section's standard-bearer said "that it was senseless not to react while our brothers were getting their throats cut."

At about half past six, the carriages transporting Barère and Billaud-Varennes were stopped in the Place de la Révolution by the République and Invalides battalions. Barbat, the commander of the Invalides battalion, reported that there were shouts "to stop the carriages and the deputies who were being spirited away." An officer of the gendarmerie wanted to bring in the guns to "mow down the rabble," but the gunners became indignant at the use of the term *rabble* and refused. The painter Patrice Champagnat stated that he had seen several citizens leave the ranks of the battalion and chase after the carriages, saying that deputies were trying to escape. The citizen Antoine-Marie-Nicolas Hertaud, head clerk of the Public Relief Commission, noted that the coaches were stopped by people who were worried by this departure, some saying that the members of the Convention were making off one by one and leaving them in a fine mess, others that if these men were accused, they should be tried and sentenced to death. The citizen Derugy, a legal official from the République Section, said to various groups that the Convention had committed an arbitrary act the day before by ordering the arrest of the people's representatives. The dock labourer Cadet Duvivier complained that the Convention had just had the best patriots arrested and deported. The locksmith Henri, of the Arcis Section, came out of a café to stop Billaud-Varennes's carriage and lead it back to the Committee of General Security with the intention of seeing that he was either punished if guilty or acquitted if not. Shortly thereafter, Henri was apprehended by some thirty jeunes gens at the Tuileries, where he had said to one group "that two worthy chaps like himself, armed with sabres, would make short work of the muscadins." The pharmacist Auguste Nicolas, of the Halle au Blé Section, maintained that the Convention was not competent to judge the deputies who had been put under arrest. The restaurant owner Roubeau, of the Temple Section, opposed the departure of the Montagnards because "the sovereign people should not leave home without knowing where they are headed."

Meanwhile, the three carriages bearing Amar, Duhem, Choudieu, Foussedoire, Chasles, and Léonard Bourdon were stopped by a huge crowd at the Neuilly customs post. The fan painter Gaspard Mourette, of the Gravilliers Section, ran after the coaches waving a pistol. Also in the crowd were the upholsterer Dufour and the gunner Catté, both from the République Section, as well as the second lieutenant Corniquet, also from République, who said to his company, "You must be real cowards to let our good deputies leave without doing your utmost to keep them in Paris." In Butte des Moulins, the linen merchant Jean Dreys went from group to group and seemed very perturbed by the departure of the accused representatives. Resistance here was stronger, and Commander Raffet was wounded by a pistol shot fired by the locksmith Étienne Cornille. It was far from a direct hit, however, and he removed the bullet himself, put it in his pocket, and carried on with his "assignment." Toward midnight the carriages set out again, taking the Pont Royal, accompanied by an escort from Butte des Moulins. This time they were able to leave the city unimpeded.

The purge was over, but it was as if a basin of blood had been let from a failing patient. The Assembly's repeated acts of self-emasculation were progressively reducing its membership to a band of eunuchs, whereas it took men to forge a republic.

TOWARD THE DECISIVE CONFRONTATION

The uprising of 12 Germinal was a warning. However, the Thermidorians regarded it merely as a great victory over the terrorists. According to *Le Messager du Soir*, the failure of the insurrection had left the sans-culottes completely dumbfounded, so much so that some of them had even started to plait their hair. On 14 Germinal, *Le Réveil du Peuple* was applauded in all the theatres, and at the Théâtre Feydeau the last couplet about the representatives was given a six-minute ovation. On the morrow the jeunes gens went to the Théâtre de la Cité to cheer *Les Jacobins du 9 Thermidor*, a play that parodied a session of the Jacobin Club, with each character highlighting his various titles – murderer, butcher, bankrupt, poisoner – while the others sang the chorus:

Bon! Bon! C'est un coquin!
C'est un excellent Jacobin!

(Hear! Hear! What a villain!
What an excellent Jacobin!)

Yet the festivities were short-lived indeed. From Germinal to Floréal, the food scarcity in Paris degenerated into genuine famine, and social unrest once again reared its menacing head.

An idea of the horrendous misery of the lower classes in the spring of the Year III can be had from reading the day-to-day news briefs in the press and the chilling notes of the police reports. On 4 Pluviôse, a woman is found dead in her room in the rue des Filles Dieu. The same day, another gives birth on a mattress on the floor because her husband has burnt the wood of the bedstead to heat the room. On 19 Ventôse, the inmates of the Madelonnettes prison stage a revolt because they have not been given any bread. On 9 Germinal, a woman who has nothing to feed her three children kills two of them. On 23 Germinal, the police commissioner of the Arsenal Section reports, "Many people are falling ill for want of food, and there are a considerable number of burials." Three days later, a woman breast-feeding a child faints from weakness on the Boulevard du Temple. Exhausted workers leave their workshops, saying they cannot go on any more. At the Marché Martin, in the Place Maubert, long-dead, half-rotten fish are being sold. On 28 Germinal, on the boulevards, the police arrest a fellow who, they say, can no longer stand, he has had so little to eat. In the evenings, the sentries' "Who goes there?" is answered with "Empty belly!" or "No bread!" On 2 Floréal, bakery assistants leave the capital owing to lack of work. The prices of basic foodstuffs rise hourly. Finally, people begin to crack: on 5 Floréal, the rumour spreads that the drum has been sounded in several sections, urging citizens who have a few crusts left to take them to Hôtel Dieu hospital. The same day a baker in the rue Denis is arrested after boasting that "he sh-- in his bread," and an inspection of his goods shows that he isn't joking. Women who complain of hunger are told by a supplies commissioner, as he points to a carpenter, that they can always eat planks. On 7 Floréal, a man jumps from a fifth-floor window in the rue de la Petite Truanderie. The city squares are teeming with thimbleriggers, open-air singers, mountebanks, and strolling players of every kind. Black-humourists claim that the entertainers are paid by the government to put the people to sleep, because they who sleep forget their hunger! Dogs that have not yet been eaten drag their translucent carcasses along the banks of the Seine. On 21 Floréal the police note, "Many citizens go for days without bread, and yesterday many put an end to their misery." Such is the fate of a locksmith in the rue des Noyers who is refused bread and answers simply, "I won't need it now," before throwing himself into the street from the fourth floor. "The number of suicides in this unhappy commune is truly alarming," writes *Le Messager du Soir*. At the rate things are going, an observer declares, "we shall soon see nothing but walking corpses busy rendering the last rites to those who precede them into the grave." On 28 Floréal, three days before the decisive confrontation, *La Gazette française* sums up the situation: "Things are still the same. Two ounces of bread per person. Thousands of speculators swarm around the Palais Royal. Muted grumbling can be heard in every part of the city. Corpses are pulled out of the river daily. Yet inexplicable luxury can be found everywhere, even in the faubourgs. Gloomy, painful silence reigns in all the shops."

The lower classes might have resigned themselves to dying of hunger had they not been insulted in their misery by the extravagant luxury that the jeunes gens displayed everywhere quite shamelessly. In the streets, where people dying of starvation struggled to prop themselves up against stone posts, and others who had fallen no longer had the strength to get up, the muscadins strolled along in their powdered wigs – strange phantoms passing in a cloud of musk. They could be seen in the pastry shops, where the confectioners set out their brioches, pies, and cakes although the bakers next door had no flour. They could be seen in restaurants such as the Veau qui tète, the Marmite perpétuelle, the Cadran bleu, or the Grand Méot, whose menu offered some hundred different dishes daily; or in the fifteen restaurants of the Palais Royal, where the chefs of the *ci-devant* had found a new clientele for their culinary talents. The youths revelled in the feast, and thought nothing of paying the hurried waiters as much as fifty livres for a meal. In the theatres, and particularly at concerts in the rue Feydeau, there was the same smiling debauchery, the same brazen flaunting of luxury. The merveilleuses, in their most elegant finery, rode up in smart carriages driven by gold-liveried coachmen. One woman paid one hundred francs for a hat on condition that her milliner reserve her exclusive ownership until after a concert – a concert that was essentially a fashion show: before and after the performance, stylish

young people paraded up and down between two rows of spectators, who gazed critically from behind their spectacles. "We are republicans," the women explained, "but like the Romans under
Augustus." Boudoir dandies holding forth on fine taste and good
manners while, nearby, shivering women were on their knees in the
garbage fighting with dogs over ungnawed bones, half-naked merveilleuses in their absurd apparel, orgiastic feasts in the midst of
widespread famine, the mocking and merrymaking parties *"à la victime"* – it was all too much. The jeunes gens were becoming agents
provocateurs, acting as a catalyst on the despair of the populace and
transforming it into the rage of revolt. Even *Le Journal de Paris*, on
9 Germinal, denounced "these behind-the-scenes schemers" who
were determined at any cost to make everyone well aware of what
fun they were having.

The rising anger of the lower classes – against the jeunes gens because of their provocative behaviour, and against the Convention
because of its improvident neglect – corresponded revealingly with
the declining bread rations. On 20 Germinal, a porcelain painter by
the name of Couturier declared sarcastically that the people's representatives "were villains who did not want bloodshed ... but who
suffocated children in the womb." At the Porte Martin, on the banks
of the Seine, in the Place de Grève, crowds gathered spontaneously.
"See how things have deteriorated since the sans-culottes were
ousted," it was said. "It's the gilded million that reigns now." If a patrol passed through the Tuileries, women would hurl abuse at it: "So
how do you like the bread of the deputies and the muscadins? At
least you must have full stomachs. Just give us bread, and we'll be
off." In the arms workshops on 11 Floréal the clerk Chaudel handed
out copies of a song called *La France vengée* (France Avenged), which
had the following refrain:

Ah! les beaux messieurs vraiment!
Mais le peuple les attend!

(Oh, indeed, such gentlemen!
But the people await them!)

On about the same date the locksmith Mingaud spoke of going to
present a petition to the Convention armed with a pistol: "We'll fire
a volley at the villains, and then you'll see whether we have any
bread in Paris." In a café on 13 Floréal, while talking to a certain
Picard who was complaining that he had no work, the wigmaker
Vitry said that there would soon be plenty of jobs "because all the

plait-heads are going to get a good working-over." On the twenty-fourth, the candlemaker Pierre Juhel ran through the streets shouting that he would wipe his arse (and he showed it) with the entire Convention and all the deputies, and several other vile remarks.

Worried by the unrest, the government Committees sought to strengthen the forces of repression at their disposal. After disarming some 1,600 "terrorists," the Convention set about reorganizing the National Guard on 28 Germinal, with the aim of ensuring bourgeois dominance by excluding sans-culottes in favour of jeunes gens. A decree was adopted establishing crack companies which would wear special uniforms and arm themselves at their own expense. Sans-culotte opposition to this move was fierce. They said that the intention was to re-establish "Lafayette's old army, which [would] now be made up exclusively of Fréron's soldiers," and that no one needed an expensive uniform to defend himself. In several sections, the next day, the officials who proclaimed the new law were insulted, and some were not even allowed to finish their proclamation. In the République Section, a woman by the name of Desmolières advised the police commissioner, Claudot, that he would do more good "on the pot" than he would making the announcement. At the general assembly of the Faubourg Montmartre Section, the reading of the new law caused "an uproar on the left side of the hall." In the Amis de la Patrie Section, the carpenters Ferrand and Saurrand were set upon by some fifty youths, who kicked them and threw stones at them.

Despite all this, the jeunes gens showed little enthusiasm for joining the National Guard, perhaps because of the prohibitive price of the uniform. No one was buying cloth, noted *La Vedette*, and the merchants who had posted their prices, hoping that "smart youths would immediately become fired up about wearing the new uniform," got nothing more out of it than "the shame of having revealed their cupidity." *Le Messager du Soir* deplored the reticence to enrol of young men "who zealously attack the brigands and terrorists, but only in the theatres, where they are sure they can speak their minds safely." Between the hostility of the sans-culottes and the general indifference of the jeunes gens, the reform of the National Guard was a dismal failure.

So the army was called into action. On the pretext of assuring delivery of provisions to the capital, the stationing of regular troops on the outskirts of Paris had been authorized on 28 Germinal. On 7 Floréal, a detachment of chasseurs entered the city; badly clothed and badly fed, they were soon won over to the cause of the populace. They were replaced by a regiment of carabineers who, when they too became unreliable, were evacuated in their turn. In trying to prevent an insurrection, the authorities merely succeeded in corrupting their troops. Finally, two divisions of gendarmes, soon followed by strong reinforcements, were quartered in barracks outside Paris, well away from the insurrectional contagion, yet ready to intervene at short notice. The troops' reliability thus remained uncertain, and their presence simply annoyed the lower classes. The citizen Filliot considered that "the troops brought in to safeguard the supply of provisions were in fact there only to disarm the citizens of the capital." A Mme Gaudichet said that she preferred a king to gingerbread soldiers; at least with a king she would have some real bread. As early as 12 Floréal, Fréron had spoken out against bringing in the troops, feeling that they were hardly fit to foster the "sublime devotion" and "heroic sacrifices" of the people of Paris while at the same time commending the populace's unwavering respect for property, its spirit of peacefulness and resignation, its unshakeable strength, and its steadfast love for the Republic.

The only force that still stood by the Convention was the jeunesse dorée. However, in late Floréal its loyalty also began to waver owing to the prolonged food shortage, the tangible, though timid, revival of royalist sentiment, and the crackdown on speculation.

Either because it too eventually began to suffer from the lack of bread, or because it feared that the inability of the authorities to deal with the food shortage might lead to another round of looting, the jeunesse dorée now refused to allow *Le Réveil du Peuple* – and particularly the last couplet about the representatives – to be sung in the theatres, and responded to it with shouts of "We want bread!"

Emboldened by the reactionary course of the Assembly, and perhaps by the waning of republican convictions among the lower classes as a result of the famine, the jeunesse dorée was hard-pressed to conceal its royalist sympathies. On 21 Floréal, the actor Talma appeared before the Convention, on behalf of the Mont Blanc Section, to ask for the repeal of the law passed the week before against supporters of the monarchy on the grounds of insignificant language and vague wording. In *Un mot pour deux individus auxquels personne ne pense et auxquels il faut penser une fois* (A Word for Two Individuals Whom No One Thinks of and Who Ought to Be Thought of Once), a mathematics student and employee of the archives for émigré papers, Germain Petitain, appealed for better conditions for the children of Louis XVI, detained at the Temple – explaining in all earnestness to the police that this was necessary "for the greater glory of the Republic." Further, a certain Sirejean, of the Bonne Nouvelle Section, was not afraid to denounce the surgeon Lagarde on 25 Germinal for having said a year earlier at the Café de Chartres "that rather than kick all the *ci-devant* out of Paris, it would make more sense to cut their throats because they were bloody rogues" – remarks that were apparently supposed to attest to his terrorist convictions!

The Committees, which had hitherto turned a blind eye to the rampant speculation carried on by the jeunes gens in full public view, now changed their minds – no doubt under pressure from the populace – and decided to stamp it out. On 25 Germinal, a group of brokers and currency dealers – Keller, Liébaud, Couturier, Uliac, Chirat, and Ferrand – were arrested on charges of speculation at the Palais Égalité. Keller categorically denied having traded in currency. He explained that there was such a food shortage that he was forced to use all possible means to procure supplies abroad for the Republic, that payment could be made only in real assets, and that he therefore had no choice but to obtain currency. The police understood: it was nothing but pure speculation. But the deputy Goureau interceded on behalf of his friend Ferrand, explaining, "They are good fellows, whose greatest offence is to have been zealous supporters of the healthy part of the Convention." Then an anonymous party recommended to the Committee of General Security that it exercise caution "when it comes to jailing men who are useful to their country." Even the notorious speculator Louis Delpech intervened. The matter went no further, and the six were released a few days later.

In the last week of Floréal, however, the Committees took harsher measures. On the twenty-third, at the Palais Égalité, the jeunes gens arrested a deputy who had been denouncing speculation and took him to the Committee of General Security. The following day, the Committee retaliated with a raid, and several speculators were put under arrest, including no less a figure than Jean-François Legrand, the secretary-general of the National Accounting Office. However, the groups of traders gathered again immediately afterward. According to *La Gazette française*, this showed "that force is of no use if there is no government." On the twenty-fifth, patrols were organized to disperse the speculators at the Palais Égalité. But the effort proved futile: on the twenty-eighth the police counted over a thousand of them! The credit the Committees sought to gain with the lower classes by cracking down on speculation was credit they lost with the jeunes gens.

Thus, on the eve of the Prairial insurrection, the Assembly appeared to be in a desperate situation. Public opinion was very much against the deputies. The National Guard was in disarray. The loyalty of the jeunes gens was beginning to waver: it was even feared that if the use of armed force became necessary, the jeunesse dorée and the military might well fight against each other rather than against the insurgents, thus leaving the government with no force for maintaining law and order. Such a turn of events was the one most dreaded by *L'Orateur du Peuple*. In the 22 Prairial and 30 Prairial issues, Fréron cautioned the soldiers who had begun their military careers before the jeunes gens not to heed the slanderous claims of the Jacobins, who he said wanted people to believe that the young men were destroying from within the sacred cause that the soldiers were defending at the front. It was all lies, he said. These men who were known "by the silly name of muscadin" were in fact "an invaluable class of citizens" who had saved the Republic on 12 Germinal as they sang the "sublime couplets" of *Le Réveil du Peuple*. The term muscadin had been dreamed up by "seditious criminals seeking to organize massacres."

On 30 Floréal, the rumour spread that an insurrection was imminent. At the Théâtre de la Gaîté, someone cast a note onto the stage and fled. The message was an ominous threat:

Réveille-toi peuple de frères,
Et frappe ces affreux tyrans,
Qui, sans pitié de ta misère,
Te font languir toi, tes enfants.
Réveille-toi, je le répète,
De la foudre arme ton bras.
Elle gronde déjà sur leurs têtes
Et bientôt elle les écrasera.

(Awake, fraternal people,
Strike out at these hideous tyrants,
Who, without pity for your misery,
Let you and your children perish.
Awake, I say,
Arm yourselves with the thunderbolt.
Already it rumbles over their heads
And will soon crash down upon them.)

The decisive moment had come in which the forces of the bourgeoisie and those of the populace would clash, forces hitherto allied in their efforts to destroy the ancien régime and defend the gains of the Revolution of 1789 against a united Europe. In this historic confrontation, the jeunesse dorée would stifle its rancour and temporarily shelve its royalist aspirations. It would first deal with the "vile rabble" and then, in Vendémiaire, Year IV, have it out with the Convention.

CHAPTER FOUR

The Defeat of the Sans-Culottes

1 PRAIRIAL, YEAR III, TO 15 PRAIRIAL, YEAR III

The jeunesse dorée's role in the insurrection of Prairial, Year III, was a complex one. In the first place, it seems that the populace's hatred of the muscadins was a contributing factor – minor, but significant nevertheless – in the mobilization of the masses. Witness the women who wanted to see how muscadin heads would look on the ends of their pikes, and the cries of joy prompted by the false news of the death of Fréron, *"le général des cadenettes."* At the same time, paradoxically, the jeunes gens were successful in hampering the very mobilization for which they were in part to blame. This they achieved on the one hand by trying to persuade the insurgents to march under the command of the regular officers, and on the other by insisting on marching in the rebel ranks – where they would have plenty of opportunity to sabotage the revolt. These actions sparked rows among the insurgents and caused delays, thus draining the insurrectional energy of the masses.

With the rebels' first assault on the Convention, the jeunesse dorée, its praetorian guard, was driven violently back into the hall. The result of this clash patently refuted Duval's claim that, without the jeunesse dorée, the Assembly would have been crushed by the Jacobins, "the two dreaded faubourgs, St Antoine and St Marceau, and the dregs of the populace." Once the Convention had been overrun, the jeunes gens found themselves outside – without a leader, without orders, and without a rallying point. To be sure, there was a small detachment around the Committees' headquarters at the Hôtel de Brionne, and there were the two spies, Margouet and Ignace Eck, who carried messages back and forth between the Committees and the Thermidorian "prisoners" in the Assembly, but all in all, after the initial attack on the Convention, the jeunesse dorée was not used on the first day of the insurrection until eleven o'clock at night, when they helped to clear the hall. It was late by then, and most of the sans-culottes had already gone home to bed. Doubtless the authorities could have managed perfectly well without the jeunes gens, depending solely on the regular troops to do the job.

The following day, 2 Prairial, the muscadins were put to work more systematically. They informed the Committees that crowds had begun to form
in the faubourg, and were dispatched to disperse groups in the Place du
Carrousel; once there, they proceeded to make arrests. As on the previous
day, they were also stationed around the Hôtel de Brionne. This time the
Committees organized the youths into a reserve battalion of some 150 men
and posted them in a concealed spot not far from the Assembly. There was
also great agitation in the sections, where the jeunes gens opposed the insurgents' plan to write seditious slogans on their hats, notably "Bread and
the Constitution of '93": this agitation reached such a height that there was
fear of "a serious clash between several battalions." The rebels finally set out
for the Convention at about half past three. Once there, they soon found
themselves directly in front of the Assembly, following a mistaken manoeuvre by the Butte des Moulins Section. A cannon was immediately trained on
the Convention, and its fuse set alight. But the time was not yet right for the
people's revolution. The people's representatives proposed to fraternize
and, taken in by their honeyed words, the insurgents trooped back to their
sections.

The people's revolution was not for the morrow either. Early in the morning, the jeunes gens gathered at the Committee of General Security, which
organized them into a battalion and gave them weapons. However, one
madcap could not resist swaggering about, boasting to the soldiers of the
22nd Regiment of the Line that he had pull with the Committee of General
Security and would see that they were fed, while at the same time condemning them at the top of his voice for being in Paris when they ought to
be at the front. It was unspeakably humiliating for these men, many of them
brave volunteers from the Army of the East, to see their fate in the hands of
such an impudent ass! Worse yet, this troublemaker's misplaced zeal came
close to sparking a fight between the muscadins and the soldiers, and thus
close to wiping out the Assembly's already fragile, somewhat paradoxical
defence force. From then on, it was one or the other, the army or the muscadins, and the Committees, having seen that their praetorian guard was no
real match for the populace when it rose up in revolt, opted for the army.
So the youths who had been given weapons early in the morning had to
hand them back. In the meantime, the news had spread that Tinel, Féraud's
alleged murderer, had escaped; this roused the indignation of the honnêtes
gens, who were advised by word of mouth to assemble. The muscadins had
hastened to the Tuileries, where the Committees rearmed them and organized them into a battalion, this time under the command of the military.

On the morning of 4 Prairial, the jeunes gens set off on what was to be a
rather ignominious expedition to the Faubourg Antoine. Dispatched to arrest Cambon and Thuriot, who were believed to be directing the uprising
from the house of the brewer Santerre, they left at dawn full of enthusiasm,
imagining that there were honours to be won, and returned toward mid-

day, humiliated and outraged by the hail of gibes and blows they had suffered at the hands of the sans-culottes. Then the National Guard, the rabble
purged from its ranks, advanced from five different directions to surround
the faubourg. There was a repeat of the dramatic showdown of 2 Prairial:
the little muscadins, well fed and perfumed in their stylish clothes, face to
face with the men of the faubourg, clustered together, drunk, standing in
rags around their guns. Guillaume Delorme, the captain of the Popincourt
gunners, attempted to fire one of the cannons, as on 2 Prairial, but someone
threw himself on the fuse to put it out, unaware that this gesture, as it had
on 2 Prairial, would change the course of history. In the final analysis, the
jeunes gens' foray had been nothing but an act of folly; the real outcome of
the uprising had been decided by the army.

The role played by the jeunesse dorée in the ensuing repression is much
easier to discern. They compelled the arrest and imprisonment of a host of
terrorists at sectional general assemblies, took their revenge for the conscription of May, 1793, and, by their vociferous interference at the Military
Tribunal, succeeded in securing the conviction of the Prairial martyrs.

THE PRAIRIAL UPRISING

At five o'clock on the morning of 5 Prairial, the peal of the tocsin
sounded in the faubourgs, calling on the people to mobilize.
Women began combing the streets, scouring the houses and the
workshops to gather up more women. The citizen Gonthier, an artist at the Opéra Comique who lived in the Faubourg Montmartre,
was at home when she suddenly found herself surrounded by a
group of women: "Come, Gonthier. Come on. You'll come with us
if you're a good citizen." "Oh, look!", one of them said. "My baby
isn't getting milk from my breasts any more, just blood."

At ten o'clock, a crowd of four hundred women marched briskly
toward the Convention. Led by the citizen Barbot, whom the jeunes
gens had whipped at the closure of the Jacobin Club and whose
brother had been president of the Société du Vertbois, in the
Gravilliers Section, they were off to demand bread from the deputies, but did not intend to stop at that. "The muscadins' cravats will
be dirt-cheap tonight," they said. "We'll get our hands on some nice
shirts. We'll see what kind of bodies they've got. Their heads will
look just fine on the ends of our pikes."

The Assembly began its session at eleven o'clock, with Vernier in
the chair. After the *Insurrection du Peuple* (Insurrection of the People)
had been read and a decree outlawing the leaders of mobs had been
passed, representatives were sent to the various sections "to enlighten the people." Henri Larivière, who went through Butte des
Moulins, was mistaken for Fréron. He was attacked in the rue de

Chartres, and escaped with his skin only because a group of jeunes gens came to his rescue. Meanwhile, the women had arrived at the Convention and burst into the debating chamber. One of them, a Mme Huret, shouted, "There they are, the blackguards, the rogues who are starving us to death! I've seen them going to their fancy restaurants. I know all about them. Come on, let's give them what for!"

Then Mélanie Voisin yelled that in her opinion they were all scheming villains. A brigadier-general by the name of Fox happened to be on the speaker's rostrum. The representative André Dumont called out to him, "Citizen, I appoint you acting commander of the armed forces!" and urged him to have the galleries cleared. Fox went out and returned immediately with four soldiers and two jeunes gens, armed with postboys' whips. One of the young men was Adjutant-General Vial. That morning he had been working in one of the offices of the Committee of Public Safety when he was warned of the gathering storm. He had gone home to put on his uniform, and had returned to take a seat in the public galleries of the Assembly. Three times, he said, he had had the galleries cleared by the gendarmes and the soldiers "who had joined us." Then the president gave him a note for Fox, which instructed the latter to arrest "some of the worst insurgents." At that moment, however, Fox was busy clearing the main corridor of the Convention. "I had to make my way through the crowd to reach him," Vial recounted. "Several times I was stopped by men and women who asked me where I thought I was going with my embroidered collar. They grabbed my clothes and shook me, shouting abuse at me." He was able to deliver the note, nevertheless, and returned to the chamber of the Convention. A period of calm followed, but then the cleaner Dorisse broke down the door, and the crowd surged forward. Whereupon, said Vial, "gendarmes and many good citizens – I don't know from which section – whom I had fetched from the lobby to the right of the president, came and formed a solid block in front of the insurgents. They just had to stand their ground, and this succeeded for a while."

But, outnumbered, the jeunes gens were soon forced back into the chamber, and a flood of angry men and women streamed in. "These are the people I love," shouted the people's representative Sergent, clapping his hands in enthusiasm. "Not a muscadin among them ..." Indeed, the sans-culottes had come down from the faubourgs. It was half past three, and they would remain until almost midnight – approximately eight hours.

Much valuable time had been wasted before they finally set out from the faubourgs. The authors of *L'Insurrection du Peuple*, counting on the revolutionary spontaneity of the masses, had imagined that the insurgents would march "in brotherly disorderliness." The labourer Marchand, of the Indivisibilité Section, shouted, "Down with the epaulettes! We must march to the Convention with our cannons if we are to have bread. There is no longer any authority. The people are in revolt. There is no longer any need for order. Only the people command." A number of sections still wished to march under the orders of the regular commander, however. This sparked quarrels and caused delays. It was not until about two o'clock that the marchers set off, leaving behind them the commanders and officers who had refused to lead the mob.

The insurgent sans-culottes harboured a deep-seated hatred of the Assembly. "We'll cut the blackguards' throats," said the carpenter Olivier, of the Quinze Vingts Section. "Let's strike while the iron is hot. Now is our chance to give them what they've got coming, so let's see that they get it."

They also hated the muscadins. One insurgent spoke of sparing only the married men, and only the older ones. The citizen Vierrey, who had been out on business, said that he encountered a crowd of people who had "The Constitution of '93" written on their hats. They had struck him with their pikes and sabres, and someone had put a pistol to his ear, because he had his hair held up with a comb. He managed to escape, and ran to the Committee of General Security, where he was advised to remain until nightfall.

Another source of conflict and cause of delay was the sans-culottes' refusal to allow jeunes gens into their ranks. In the République Section, as the battalion was assembling in the rue Ville l'Évêque, some members of the 5th and 6th companies took issue with the citizen Jean-Baptiste Gabet, a military hospital inspector, because he "suggested milder methods." The mechanic Guillot said that next décadi [last day of the ten-day week], at the general assembly, they would see how the citizen Gabet and all the muscadins would be dragged through the mud. The citizen Adam, second lieutenant of the 14th Company, was accused in the general assembly of 5 Prairial of having cast slurs, while under arms, against the men he referred to as muscadins; of having arrested people on grounds that they were too well dressed to be patriots; of having said that he didn't give a damn about the Convention; and of having threatened citizens who showed respect for principles. Previously, on 13 Germinal – according to the men who denounced him, Second Lieutenant Lamothe of the 10th Company and the same Jean-Baptiste Gabet mentioned above – Adam had insulted "decently dressed citizens" on the Pont Tournant and called for them to be arrested.

Reactionary elements remained scattered throughout the insurgents' ranks despite these efforts to weed them out. Jullian corroborates this in his *Souvenirs*: "Although we were not legally allowed to assemble, we encountered one another everywhere, even in the midst of the mob." So does Lacretelle: "The battalions that came to attack the Convention and those that came to defend it mixed together and seemed to form a single army." During the four days that the insurrection lasted, jeunes gens were thus present in the sansculotte ranks, seeking to foil the revolutionary uprising. The gunner Fontaine, of the Arcis Section, who urged his comrades on 2 and 4 Prairial to "avenge the sans-culottes, lay into the muscadins, and give them what they deserved," was deemed by the fellow who denounced him, a certain Laval from the same section, to be "highly dangerous." "All the men in the guard who appeared to him to be better dressed than the others were muscadins, in his view," said Laval. This reactionary presence in the rebel ranks is certainly remarkable, and it may explain the insurgents' indecisiveness at strategic moments during the revolt.

We have seen that, for a few minutes at least, the muscadins managed to stand their ground against the insurgents who were trying to force their way into the chamber. At one point, Brigade Leader Landrieux had had to come to General Fox's rescue when he was surrounded on the main staircase of the Palais National. In the scuffle he lost his sabre, his belt, his watch, his pocketbook, his handkerchief, and his snuffbox. A young man who had recently returned from the front, and who happened to be the son of the people's representative Mailly, was shot twice when he tried to grab an insurgent's hat. The people's representative Féraud, who rushed with General Doraison to the rescue of Adjutant-General Liebaux, was shot and killed. His head was stuck on the end of a pike and paraded around the Place du Carrousel. In the turmoil of the insurrection it was believed for a moment that Fréron, and not Féraud, had been killed, and the news prompted remarks that revealed the hatred he inspired as the supposed leader of the jeunesse dorée. On 5 Prairial, at the République Section's general assembly, the younger Chaussay-Stainville denounced the citizen Bocard, of the Faubourg du Roule, for having said, "Bravo! At last the muscadins' general has got his comeuppance!" At the same meeting, a woman by the name of Raimbaud was denounced by a certain Perret for having said that they had just assassinated a representative of the people, that there was more to come, that they would soon be showing off the heads of the cowards who fastened up their hair, and that by that she meant the citizens whom the terrorists called muscadins.

The musician Jean-Michel Perrin, of the Droits de l'Homme Section, was denounced at the section's general assembly of 17 Prairial by Gougard, a legal official who had heard Perrin say at around half past eleven on the evening of the first, "Now the muscadins have had it! Fréron's been killed! They're parading his head around on the end of a pike. What a victory for the patriots!" The wallet-maker Bousquet, "believing that it was Fréron, and not Féraud, who had been assassinated, rejoiced over his death." Isidore Langlois said that people began dancing outside bakeries, convinced that "the general of the *cadenettes* and the gilded battalion" had been killed. As for Fréron himself, he cynically feigned regret that he had not been killed instead of Féraud in *L'Orateur du Peuple* of 17 Prairial: "Oh, Féraud! For a moment the similarity in our names associated me, so to speak, with your distinguished demise; the cannibals thought they had taken my head when they actually had yours. Thus I shared in your glory, yet my heart will long bear the traces: why did they not get me! At least they would have spared me the bitterness of knowing that I was the indirect cause of your death!"

The insurgents thus found themselves in complete control of the chamber. The Montagnards wanted to take advantage of their support to impose on the Assembly a legislative program that would halt the reactionary course of Thermidorian politics. In response to an invitation from the president, Vernier, who was only too happy to see them compromise themselves with the "villains," they compelled the eighty deputies who had not fled to pass the following measures: the release of the patriots, the establishment of the sections on a permanent basis, an inventory of grain and flour supplies, an obligation for bakers to make only one kind of bread, abolition of the death penalty, and replacement of the Committee of General Security by a four-member executive commission. "It is *Le Réveil du Peuple!*" (the awakening of the people) Goujon remarked triumphantly, while Bourbotte proposed that the journalists who had misled public opinion "with their poisoned papers" should be arrested – a move which testified to the pervading influence of the Thermidorian press. "See those rogues up there?" said Duquesnoy in the Convention, pointing out the press gallery to an insurgent. "They have all taken up arms against the people, but we shall ensure that they never again return to their lair." Afterward, Duquesnoy noted that the journalists had fled the press gallery. We shall soon see who these journalists were and where they had gone.

What was the jeunesse dorée doing during this time? According to Duval, messengers had gone round telling the youths to prepare for action. Jullian says that he visited the various sections in an effort to rally the young men, as he had done on 12 Germinal. They assembled at about two o'clock; at the behest of Fréron, Barras, and Legendre, some of them took up positions on the terraces in the Tuileries and along the Seine, and in the courtyards of the Tuileries and the Manège. They were left there without a leader, without orders, and without a rallying point. Meanwhile, the sectional battalions, more disposed to side with the rebels than to repulse them, were not meeting with any resistance as they approached the Convention. The insurgents' "savage cries" could be heard from the garden. According to Hyde de Neuville, Lacretelle, and Louvet, other groups of youths had formed a ring around the Hôtel de Brionne to protect the Committees, which expected to be attacked. It seems that their numbers were limited, however, for Louvet acknowledged to the Assembly on 14 Prairial that if just a third of the "unholy mob" had come to disband the Committees, resistance would have been futile. Among the youths was a former ship's captain by the name of Margouet, who noted that at about two o'clock he had been assigned to defend the small door of the Committee of General Security, which the rebels were threatening to break down. That morning, Margouet had escorted the people's representative Blad "to various places where his presence might be necessary," and at about one o'clock he had been given the task of relaying the orders of the three Committees to the Arms and Powder Commission. After midnight, he was sent to the Gravilliers Section to announce the news of the Committees' victory, and when he returned, at about three in the morning, he was instructed to escort to the Château du Taureau the Montagnards who had been arrested by decree.

But let us return to the government Committees. The insurgents had committed a serious error in judgment by leaving them to deliberate quietly, and they were now preparing their counterattack. They risked being cut off from the Assembly for a time, but then they dispatched the informer Ignace Eck, who was to report back to them regularly on how things were developing. Eck had turned up at about two o'clock on 1 Prairial, in the first group of jeunesse dorée volunteers. He was the one who went to tell Auguis and Legendre at around eleven o'clock that the Committee of General Security had just been relieved of its duties and replaced by an executive commission, news which cleared the way for the counterattack against the insurgents.

Meanwhile, the jeunes gens were champing at the bit, "asking boisterously when they would be sent into combat," said Lacretelle. At around eight o'clock, Martainville, who was not privy to the

Committees' deliberations, asked the commander of the Butte des Moulins battalion, Raffet, to intervene. But Raffet replied that he had no orders. "The situation was becoming more and more dangerous by the minute," remarked Duval, "but they left us standing there, God knows why, weapons in hand." In the Le Peletier battalion, Lecourt-Villière's men were growing annoyed at not being sent into action, and years later Cassanyès still found it amazing. "Did they need ten hours," he wrote, "to deck themselves out in their uniforms and take command of a detachment? After all, as we saw, a mere detachment sufficed to disperse a gang of villains that thirty well-armed men could have held at bay."

It is clear that by eight o'clock the Committee of General Security had assembled sufficient armed force to crush the insurrection; it delayed going into action because it wanted to give the Montagnards enough time to ally themselves with the insurgents – in other words, enough time for them to prepare their own condemnation by the military commission that would carry out the subsequent repression. When Ignace Eck informed the Committee that the members of the provisional executive commission were about to take up their duties, it judged that the time had come to intervene.

At this point it seemed that the insurgents had triumphed, and in public the sans-culottes began to taunt the jeunes gens, as they had done on 1 Germinal. At the general assembly of 5 Prairial, four young men of the Mont Blanc Section denounced the citizen Lavaquerie for having said to one of them, on 1 Prairial, "that the plait in his hair was a rallying sign and that it was obviously a sign of Fréron's youth." This had occurred at around eleven at night, the young men said, "at the time the rebels passed their disastrous decree which dismayed us all, save this citizen, who appeared delighted." Seizing one of the gilded runts by the collar, Lavaquerie had said to him, "If I had you eyeball to eyeball in the rue St Honoré, among the women, you'd see!" "Huh! What would you do?" "I wouldn't knock you up, but I might knock you about! If I don't like a man's face, I fix it for him!" But for Lavaquerie and his fellow sans-culottes, as for the chair-maker Chardin, who said that he would die happy if Fréron, Tallien, and Legendre were killed, and who may have been fooled by the death of Féraud, victory was to be short-lived.

At about eleven o'clock, according to Lacretelle, Legendre left the Committees leading a troop of jeunes gens armed with sabres. Together with Fréron and Tallien, he assembled the scattered battalions of the three sections that remained loyal: Butte des Moulins, Le Peletier, and Fontaine Grenelle. In the gardens, Duval and the young men with him were waiting "in mortal agony." A deputy came up to them: "Friends, all is lost. The rebels have carried the day ... The Convention no longer exists. Think of your own safety ... Be off, unless you want to die at the hands of these blackguards!"

They had already begun to disperse when Fréron, Tallien, and Legendre marched by, on their way to the Convention, and managed to rally them. What followed is recounted in Féraud's funeral oration, read by Louvet in the Assembly on 14 Prairial. On the heels of the people's representatives Auguis, Legendre, Fréron, Bergoein, and Kervélégan, "a few brave men dashed forward": the federalist Malo, Albert Diétrich, the son of the mayor of Strasbourg who had died on the scaffold, General Fox and a small group of soldiers flanked by Charles His, Jullian and Martainville, "and several others whose names I forget, all of them polemical writers. They have shown by their actions that when France is in danger, the man of letters also knows how to handle a sword."

These are the journalists whose absence from the Convention's press gallery had been noticed by Duquesnoy a few hours earlier. With them were the three battalions of the loyal sections. After a short fight, they forced "the henchmen of crime" to flee, and the Convention was able to resume its deliberations; it began by decreeing the arrest of the fourteen representatives who had allegedly sided with the mob.

Just as the motion to put Duroy and Prieur de la Marne under arrest was being proposed, a father of five from the Bonne Nouvelle Section, Antoine Lafollie, yelled from the public gallery, "Down with the rogues! Down with the villains! Down with the blackguards and their phoney debates!" A group of citizens immediately pounced on him and took him away to the Committee of General Security. The group consisted of five men, all of whom were unknown except for the *ci-devant* Count Daureville, or Dorville, who was a regular at the St Amarante gambling dens. A recently returned émigré of twenty-eight, he had been a page, a member of the king's guard, and a captain of the retinue in the Noailles Regiment, and was suspected of complicity in an affair of forged assignats. He was to be arrested in this connection a few days later, on 6 Prairial, but would be released on 24 Vendémiaire, Year IV, for lack of evidence. The man who denounced him, Ruelle, a former French chargé d'affaires to the Netherlands, described him as a man "who, by virtue of his birth, must be suspect, and whom I still suspect because of his constant presence in the National Convention. I have never been there without seeing him, and he is always in the company of people whose bearing and elegant style of dress bespeak

men more faithful to the ancien régime than to the Republic."
Former émigrés who whiled away their time in gambling dens –
such were the men the Convention recruited for its defence!

By now it was midnight. Thinking that the insurrection had been
successful, many sans-culotte rebels had gone home by the time the
jeunesse dorée arrived at the Convention. They had been up since
dawn, and had had nothing to eat. News that Legendre and the
muscadins from Butte des Moulins were cutting patriot throats fell
on deaf ears at the Pont au Change guardhouse; the sans-culottes
were already fast asleep.

RECOURSE TO THE MUSCADINS

The insurgents gathered again the next day, 2 Prairial. "Today's uprising seems even more violent than yesterday's," wrote Thibault,
second-in-command of the Popincourt battalion, to the Committee
of General Security. But the Committee had already been warned.
Young men "full of zeal and good will" had reported that in the
Faubourg Antoine, notably in the Montreuil, Popincourt, and
Quinze Vingts sections, one of "those crowds that become a cause
for real concern" was forming and, as on the previous day, women
were flocking to the Tuileries. The Committee of General Security
immediately ordered the Military Committee to disperse the crowds
as quickly as possible; it was "the young men full of zeal and good
will" who delivered the decree. The jeunes gens thus served as informers and emissaries alike – and the inhabitants of the faubourgs
were well aware of it. That same day, an observer reported that at a
workers' rally in the Place de Grève, where the tocsin was being
sounded, "any jeunes gens seen in the square were chased for being
spies of the Convention; one of them was disarmed and led off to
the Arcis Section. There were grumblings about Raffet ..."

It seems, at least if we are to judge by the arrests that were made,
that the jeunesse dorée was also given the task of dispersing similar
crowds at the Carrousel. For instance, the painter Sambat, of the
Guillaume Tell Section, was at the Carrousel at around eleven
o'clock, talking about provisions with five cavalrymen. They told
him that they had not eaten since the day before, and that "if anything came up" they would refuse to march. Four young men, one
of whom was Louis Delpech, who had witnessed this conversation,
said that they recognized Sambat as a former juror on the Revolutionary Tribunal; they therefore seized him and dragged him off
to the Committee of General Security.

But Delpech knew so little about the "terrorist" he had just arrested that before the Committee he identified him several times as

Topino-Lebrun, another former juror on the Revolutionary Tribunal. This error was of little consequence in the eyes of the Committee, it seems, for when Sambat stated who he was, Delpech corrected himself immediately – "Yes! That's the man I mean!" – and Sambat remained under arrest. What is more – and this reveals either the complicity that existed between the jeunesse dorée and the Committee of General Security or the chaotic state the Committee's offices were in – Delpech took it upon himself to do whatever paperwork was required for jailing Sambat. Then he and his gang took Sambat to the Orties prison, together with another erstwhile juror on the Revolutionary Tribunal, Auvrest, "who had likewise just been arrested by similar characters who did not know him." Sambat reported,

During the trip, the fellow who had denounced me and the others who were leading us tried their best to incite bewildered citizens to cut our throats. "They're jurors! They're bloodthirsty terrorists!" they screamed. "They deserve to be slaughtered!" (These are their own words.) Fortunately, the trip did not take long; otherwise we would not have escaped the wrath of the furious mob, which was already poking its weapons into our breasts.

There was similar confusion over Auvrest's identity, and his arrest was just as arbitrary: he was accused of having talked to cavalrymen about provisions. This denunciation was so trivial in itself, he said, that he was about to be set free when a stranger advised the people's representative Gauthier that another denunciation had been made against him the day before. Auvrest protested that it was untrue, but the stranger retorted, "If you have not yet been denounced, then you will be tomorrow." And indeed, the denunciation was made the next day. But there was a problem: the denunciation had been made against Auvray, the commander of the Mont Blanc Section who had been languishing in the Plessis jail for the last two months and who therefore could not possibly have been seen where he was alleged to have been seen! Once again the Committee of General Security treated this as an insignificant detail; Auvrest was not released until three and a half months later, on 16 Fructidor.

Likewise in the Place du Carrousel, a soldier who had returned wounded from the front, Pierre-Martin Berney, of the Marchés Section, was apprehended by two young men who called him a buveur de sang and accused him of having said, "My sabre serves to cut down the muscadins!" Throughout the day, the jeunes gens policed the streets and squares, arresting whichever militant sans-culottes struck them as being too active: the citizens Blamont and Diette, who dared to "cast slurs" on the Convention; the citizen Pierre-Symphorien Bouillon, "a fanatical terrorist"; the caster Philibert Deflacelière, who shouted "To h---- with the Convention!"; the citizen Jean-Baptiste Girolle, who yelled "Down with the muscadins and their hitched-up hair!"; the citizen Laflotte, "a henchman of the decemvirs"; and the citizen Maurice Remont, for "having participated in the excesses committed by the Jacobins."

While the Carrousel was being cleared by the jeunesse dorée, the forces of the insurrection were rallying in the sections. The Committee of General Security had the drum sounded everywhere. Since there was no way to prevent the sans-culottes from marching on the Convention, it made more sense to keep the initiative by summoning them. They would thus march under the command of the regular officers rather than under the leaders of the mob, and the honnêtes gens would be there to keep an eye on them. In contrast with the day before, however, the security force took up its position in good time. By eleven o'clock, the Le Peletier Section battalion had drawn up in battle formation before the walls of the Palais National, backed up by a cavalry detachment under the command of General Dubois. They were joined by the battalions of the Butte des Moulins, Brutus, Mont Blanc, Théâtre Français, Fontaine Grenelle, Piques, Temple, and Halle au Blé sections and by regular troops. At the Palais Égalité, the police inspector Lefebvre saw "sixty well-dressed men go by with their sabres drawn." It is not known what proportion of the total force defending the Palais National was made up of jeunes gens. However, to judge by the observations of a police inspector, the youths were certainly present "around the Convention. The forces defending the building appear to be motivated by the right principles. Plenty of shouts of 'Long live the Convention! Long live the Republic! Down with the Jacobins and the buveurs de sang!' can be heard."

As on the previous day, the jeunes gens also gathered in groups around the Hôtel de Brionne, where the Committees were sitting. Brigade Leader Landrieux, who had come to offer his services as a soldier, recounts that General Fox, whom he had rescued from the wrath of the mob the day before, took him in to see the Committee of General Security, while the war commissioner, d'Hillerin, was present, and introduced him as a liberator. He was then shown into a room to wait with other officers who had no duties (no doubt because they were deserters!). He knew none of them. "An hour later," Landrieux wrote, "we were told that the Committee had decided to organize us into a battalion and that we would be under the command of General Lapoype. This was done immediately, and an hour later we were given muskets."

The Committee of General Security had commanded Lapoype to assemble patrols of reliable men and to disperse the crowds at the Place du Carrousel and elsewhere; the Committee of Public Safety instructed a secretary, Chabeuf, to supply him with 150 service muskets "to arm the companies of volunteers he had organized in accordance with the Committee's orders." The troop of jeunes gens then went to take up a position in the garden, under the trees, to the right of the main avenue. This appears to have been a concealed spot; it was as though the Committees did not want people to known who their defenders were! Landrieux continued:

Several representatives visited us during the day. The representative Fréron came to tell us that the Convention was counting on us as its crack troops, and that it was correct in its judgment because we were steadfastly resolved, in the event of a rout, to escort the remaining deputies to Châlons at the risk of our lives. I must pay tribute to my fellow combatants. It seemed to me that every last one of them was willing to risk his life for this cause.

Landrieux's wording "in the event of a rout" indicates just how precarious the Convention's situation was.

As the battalions were forming, the citizens who had been disarmed – and who were excluded from joining the battalions because they had lost their civic rights – were opening the general assemblies. In the Popincourt assembly, the gunner Dubé rebuked Legendre for having driven the patriots from the Convention the day before. In the Arcis Section, the general assembly decided to move to the Maison Commune and declare itself to be the National Convention. Cambon was to be mayor of Paris, and Thuriot prosecutor of the Commune. This development sparked an indignant outburst at the "real" National Convention. The Arcis assembly was outlawed, and the Le Peletier battalion and General Dubois's cavalry were ordered to march against it. But by the time they arrived, it had already dispersed. As late as 4 Prairial, the authorites, still convinced that Cambon and Thuriot were directing the insurrection, had General Kilmaine lead a battalion of jeunes gens into the faubourgs to flush them out.

As on the previous day, the insurgents had written on their hats the slogan "Bread and the Constitution of '93!" The questions of whether people should be forced to erase the slogan and of whether those caught displaying it should be arrested then arose. This was a delicate problem, for in each battalion there was quite likely to be a large number of undecided men who were ready, at the first provocation, to go over to the insurrection. The jeunes gens understood nothing of these subtleties. To them, the slogan was seditious, and therefore had to disappear – and that was that! Thus, the citizens Gigan and Duval, who were displaying the slogan, were apprehended and dragged off to the Committee of General Security. Likewise the café owner Grosnon, whose hat also bore the inscription. A certain Durand, of the Lombards Section, was arrested because he did not want the slogan to be erased. The gauze-worker Claude Lallemand, of the Quinze Vingts Section, was taken away for objecting to the arrest of a citizen who was displaying it. No doubt, many others came in for the same treatment. These altercations grew so numerous, according to Salverte, that a serious clash between several battalions was feared, and the Committee of General Security was forced to intervene to forbid the good citizens from carrying on "this civic act" and to urge them generally to avoid picking quarrels. By its excessive reactionary zeal, the jeunesse dorée was compromising the very cause it claimed to serve!

It was already about half past three by the time the sans-culottes set out for the Convention. At the Pont au Change, General Dubois, who was heading toward the Maison Commune, thought it wise to let them pass. Around the Assembly, a hitherto unseen concentration of armed forces had taken up positions, forming a veritable rampart. However, as a result of an ill-timed manoeuvre by the Butte des Moulins battalion, which allowed the insurgents to rush into the vacuum it had left, the sans-culottes were able to deploy themselves directly in front of the Convention. The two sides suddenly found themselves face to face. The sans-culotte Louis Duclos said of the deputies that it was "time to finish with this bunch of crooks once and for all." They were nothing but "rogues whose only supporters were the criminals from Butte des Moulins!" A woman by the name of Quitte said "that she knew what cowards the Butte des Moulins representatives were and that they might just as well fill their breeches as they had yesterday."

Then came the moment of truth. Set on edge by a manoeuvre of the Butte des Moulins battalion, the sans-culottes trained their cannons on the Convention. Guillaume Delorme, the black commander of the Popincourt gunners, strode up to one of the guns and lit the fuse. It was a quarter past seven. Would the Revolution have lost much with the death of Fréron, Legendre, Tallien, and company? We shall never know, for a fellow by the name of Vovin put out the fuse by throwing himself on the cannon, and so saved the Thermidorians. But the gunners from the bourgeois sections – Halle au Blé, Fontaine Grenelle, Observatoire, Théâtre Français, and Piques – immediately defected to the insurgent side. Their cannons, which had until now been trained on the sans-culotte rebels, were turned around and aimed at the Assembly. There was nothing for the deputies to do but await death on their benches; whether now or later matters not a scrap, said Legendre. Nevertheless, negotiations were initiated. The Committees well understood the sans-culotte mentality – violence tempered by naïveté. They thought that by fraternizing, they would be able to regain control of the situation. A ten-member deputation from the Convention went to parley with the rebels. Legendre was excluded from the group at the last minute – and with good reason. Had the gunner Delorme seen this general of the *cadenettes* approaching, he would surely have reloaded his gun! A spokesman for the insurgents, Ligier, was received on the Assembly rostrum, and Vernier gave him the fraternal embrace. Won over by old, spent promises, the people returned to their sections. They had once again been taken in by noble words.

That evening, Porte, the printer of *Le Messager du Soir*, came home in a triumphant mood and said to the health officer Prieur, who lived in the same house, that the sans-culottes were done for. "Away with you, you blackguard!" Prieur shot back. "The royalists will never triumph over the sans-culottes!"

At this point, nothing was certain.

THE JEUNES GENS IN TEMPORARY DISGRACE

Brigade Leader Landrieux was at the door of the Committee of Public Safety at seven o'clock on the morning of 3 Prairial. This was where he and the troop of jeunes gens to which he belonged had been told to report when they had separated the night before, after spending the entire day waiting in the woods for orders that never came.

Curiously, however, Landrieux noticed that few of the men from the day before had turned up, but that there were many new faces. Seven in the morning was indeed early for night people who devoted much of their time to revelry. In any case, what was the point of rushing to take up arms if, as on the previous day, they were not going to do anything with them? Especially when the weapons could easily have been used to mow down the "rabble" that, to quote a police agent, "had sworn to wage a merciless war on the young men known as muscadins, who were regarded as the supporters of the national representatives."

At ten o'clock, in a surprise move, the Committee of General Security had the youths hand back their muskets, on the grounds that all was quiet. However, Landrieux made the following shrewd observation: "I tend to think that the mistakes made by a few numskulls who had just joined our ranks gave the troop a bad name in the eyes of the authorities. I also think that we were disarmed because of grumbling from some of the men. After having occupied a post of honour the day before, these men were disgruntled to find themselves flanked by fresh faces." After they had given in their weapons, the young men were dismissed, but told to report back to the Committee of Public Safety at the first call to arms ... "and we went our separate ways," said Landrieux.

Thus the Committee of General Security discharged its praetorian guard. So what had happened? The explanation lies in the file of one of these young "numskulls," Alexandre Dargeavelle, who claimed to be an adjutant-general and colonel in the service of Poland who had been living in Paris since late 1788, in the Le Peletier Section.

Like Landrieux, Dargeavelle had gone to the offices of the Committee of Public Safety that morning. Among the other youths who had turned up were the citizen Michel, who was armed with a musket that the Committee of Public Safety had given him when he joined the battalion of young men the day before, and the citizen d'Alichamp, who had likewise been armed by the Committee of Public Safety. Passing by the Place du Carrousel, Dargeavelle saw some soldiers of the 22nd Regiment "in a very sorry state who were complaining they had not eaten for thirty hours." Not to worry! Dargeavelle would soon take care of that. If they had not eaten, it was because the Convention had been under siege the day before and had not been able to see to their needs, but the situation would be dealt with immediately; he said that he would go in person to the War Office to urge the deputy Delmas "to give special attention to their representations." He had no card? No matter! The citizen Tridon, the section police chief – "who has known me for a long time," he added – would take him to the people's representative Gauthier, who would give him a pass to see Delmas. No sooner said than done, and Dargeavelle was able to come back and announce to the regiment "that everything had been taken care of and that the cavalrymen would soon be content."

But could these soldiers who had not eaten for thirty hours – and who may well have been intrepid volunteers of the Rhine or the Sambre and Meuse armies, which for years had been holding in check the regular troops of a hostile, united Europe – be "content" at seeing their fate in the hands of such an insolent scoundrel? What followed would make it seem doubtful.

After dining at a restaurant called Chez Sibille, "with almost all of the young men who had been armed by the Committee of Public Safety," Dargeavelle went back to the garden of the Palais National, where he got into a fierce dispute with some soldiers. The people's representative Auguis, who observed what happened, said,

I heard a citizen who was walking in the Tuileries, acting like a man who had pretensions to being important, and who had gone up to a cavalry brigade leader and a carabineer officer, say to the two officers before a regiment of dragoons drawn up in battle formation, "Why are they here? The proper place for brave soldiers like these is with the army at the front, not here!"

One of the officers replied that he was sure of his men, but Dargeavelle persisted, saying that "they were brave soldiers who had fought well, but that fighting here and fighting at the front were two different things." (No one could argue with that: the jeunesse dorée and the regular troops were hardly defending the same cause!) The officer pointed out that his carabineers had no boots, and the quarrel would have degenerated into a scuffle had not Auguis intervened to have Dargeavelle arrested. He later confessed, "I may not have shown sufficient restraint and composure in dealing with the representative who accused me."

It is not difficult to imagine what disastrous consequences the rash, tactless zeal of a troublemaker like Dargeavelle, who all alone managed to create a disturbance in the Assembly's defence force by his reckless, untimely agitation, might have had on the loyalty of the troops guarding the Palais National. The same conclusion was reached by the people's representative Courtois de l'Aube, who had recommended Dargeavelle to Barras and Aubry as a good patriot: "Better informed," he explained, "I went back on everything I had done for him. I believe him to be a dangerous man, not because of his moral disposition, but because of his audacity."

Dargeavelle was indeed audacious, and this is quite evident from the way he spent his time during the first days of Prairial. His activities also reveal the wide network of connections he must have had in government administration and in the Convention. On the afternoon of the first, he was seen with the citizens d'Alichamp and Ruotte outside the Feuillant Club where, he said, "I was surrounded by a host of men and women who took me for a representative of the people." On the second, he was at Tallien's with General Barbassan, and he then went to see Fréron, "who was just stepping out to go to his printer's to have a plate redone." Afterwards he arrested two men who had rallying signs on their hats; he and the citizens Marqué, the former comptroller of the Prince of Conti, and Meaux, the owner of a restaurant in the Mont Blanc Section, took them away to the Orties prison, but when they got there they were attacked by the prison guards, "who called us Fréron and Tallien's soldiers."

But Delmas sized up the situation accurately. As well as constituting an unnecessary provocation of the military, the jeunes gens' futile, wanton agitation risked hampering the effectiveness of government action. Concerned by the jeunesse dorée's devil-may-care conduct, and well aware that the popular uprising was gaining such strength that the youths would be crushed by the force of it, the Committees had decided to depend henceforth on the regular army units for their protection. Already, the day before, they had simplified the structure of the supreme command, entrusting it to three people's representatives: Delmas, Gillet, and Aubry. Three thousand cavalry entered the city, the regular troops stationed in the outskirts were called up, and instructions were given to make sure "that all troops stationed in Paris [were] paid with scrupulous punctuality." The decision to rely upon the regular army explains the Committees' sudden about-face with regard to the jeunes gens and the youths' sudden disgrace, which spared no one: even General Fox, who had been in charge of clearing the Assembly on 1 Prairial, was put under arrest. He was released a few days later, the Committee acknowledging that he had been detained "purely for political reasons, since a change in generals had been deemed necessary."

But the disgrace was only temporary, lasting no more than a few hours, and was forgotten in the flurry of events. It seems that the jeunes gens did not even bother to curb their activity in the meantime: a certain Noël Davenne who had said the people's representatives were all "rogues" was dragged off to the Committee of General Security by five young men, including Jean-Baptiste Gomel, one of the scoundrels who had picked a row with Armonville over his red cap in Ventôse.

At around eight o'clock in the evening, the assistant locksmith Jean Tinel, of the Popincourt Section, who had been arrested on 1 Prairial while bearing Féraud's head on the end of a pike, was plucked from the tumbrel taking him to the scaffold in the Place de Grève and escorted triumphantly to his home in the rue de Lappe by his comrades from the faubourgs. The Committees, which had been informed of the plot ahead of time, had done nothing to prevent it. There was even a rumour that they had staged the skirmish to provide themselves with a pretext for attacking the faubourg. "I asked a number of people who should have known about it whether it was true," wrote Beaulieu naïvely, "and they all said that it was not." Naturally, an honnête homme such as Rovère could never have acted in such a Machiavellian fashion!

Whatever the case, the news of Tinel's escape caused a tremendous stir among Paris's honnêtes gens. "Immediately the cry 'To arms!' was heard in several quarters," reported Le Moniteur. "All true patriots, all enemies of the buveurs de sang, were overcome with indignation," added Le Messager du Soir. And a police agent noted that when the news was announced at the Opéra Comique, "the performance was interrupted and everyone left the theatre shouting 'To arms!'" Tønnesson rightly points out that Tinel's getaway facilitated the mobilization of the honnêtes gens, who were not always eager to take up arms. Groups gathered at the Tuileries and the Jardin Égalité, and at around eleven o'clock "a considerable crowd of good citizens was demanding to march against the rebels who had helped a guilty man escape the punishment meted out by the law." In the force sent to crush the faubourg, the jeunesse dorée proper must be distinguished from the mass of honnêtes gens.

From the Correspondance intime du conventionnel Rovère avec Goupilleau de Montaigu (Private Correspondence of Rovère, Member of the Convention, with Goupilleau de Montaigu), we know that, contrary to the preceding days, when troops in the sections had been levied en masse by a general call to arms, this time the good citizens were called to arms in person, the aim being to form homogeneous battalions from which the rabble had been pruned. This switch in tactics is corroborated in a letter from the people's representative David to Merlin de Thionville. As a result, wrote Rovère, the Convention found that by four o'clock the next day it had an army of twenty thousand men, all of them "upright citizens … who had wealth to preserve," resolute volunteers who had miraculously been assembled, organized, and armed in a single day, and who now stood ready to march against the faubourg.

The jeunesse dorée had been busy for some time already, having finally found an outlet for its zealous energy. Upon hearing of Tinel's escape, the youths had rushed to the Tuileries to put themselves at the disposal of the Committee of General Security, which had enlisted them once again. In his *Histoire du bataillon des jeunes citoyens à l'attaque du faubourg Antoine, le 4 prairial an III* (History of the Attack of the Young Citizens' Battalion against the Faubourg Antoine, 4 Prairial, Year III), the mathematics professor Louis Costaz, later to become Baron d'Empire, gives the following account:

I was out walking at the Jardin Égalité between eight and nine o'clock on the evening of 3 Prairial. In the galleries it was rumoured that the fellow who had assassinated the deputy Féraud had just been snatched from the hands of the law. I dashed off to the Tuileries with the intention of joining the citizens whom I imagined would volunteer to assist in crushing the rebels. The main door, which stands to the side of the Committee of General Security and which had been closed all day, was open. A voice could be heard urging the citizens present to enter the building to receive orders from the Convention's Committees. I hastened toward the door. I found that the voice belonged to the citizen Liebble, who had been my sergeant-major when I was living in the Halle au Blé Section. Together we went outside onto the large terrace: there we found many more citizens who had come for the same reasons as we had. Many others followed us. Soon we were four to five hundred strong.

According to Vasselin, another member of the battalion of jeunes gens, the Committee of General Security was likewise recruiting around nine o'clock in the Le Peletier, Butte des Moulins, Brutus, Gardes Françaises, and Fontaine Grenelle sections. This is corroborated in the account given by the people's representative Lamothe-Langon.

From Costaz we know that arms were handed out at the Feuillant depot, and that Bergoein was in charge, as attested to by a Committee of Public Safety decree ordering the Arms and Powder Commission to distribute 260 cartridges. Costaz hesitated momentarily about whether to take a musket because the munitions storekeepers were noting down the names and addresses of those who were given arms, and he feared that in the event of defeat the lists might be used as "proscription tables." In other words, at this point the bourgeoisie still thought that the sans-culottes might carry the day.

Some 1,200 men spent the night of 3 to 4 Prairial before the door of the Committee of General Security, vociferously demanding that an attack be launched to disarm the Faubourg Antoine. But the Committee was faced with the same dilemma: which force should it send to subdue the faubourg? The jeunesse dorée right away, or the regular army later on? The muscadins pressured the Committee to let them take care of the whole operation, insisting that their own battalions would suffice to bring the faubourg to its knees. The Committee eventually gave in. This was a mistake; Kilmaine, the commander of the expedition, himself admitted that by launching an early attack with obviously inferior forces, they were taking the risk of compromising the major expedition planned for the evening. But the Committee, believing that Cambon and Thuriot were directing the uprising from the house of the brewer Santerre, no doubt wanted to take advantage of the wee hours, when the faubourg was still asleep, to seize the two principals and leave the insurrection leaderless. The jeunes gens spoke of enforcing the law, restoring morality, and winning honour. In reality, however, they were driven above all by a thirst for revenge – by the desire to crush the faubourg, of whose inhabitants they said, quoting Mithridates, "May they in turn tremble for their own homes!" The Committee of General Security must have found this edifying, for it let them have their way.

But alone against the Faubourg Antoine, the jeunesse dorée itself risked being crushed and swallowed up. We shall now see how the youths fared.

THE JEUNESSE DORÉE AGAINST THE FAUBOURGS

On the night of the third to the fourth, Delmas, Gillet, and Aubry, the people's representatives who had been put in charge of the armed forces of Paris, instructed General Kilmaine to assemble in the Place du Palais National a division made up of the battalion of jeunes gens, which was quickly given the overblown title of vanguard, and the detachments from the Butte des Moulins, Le Peletier, and Champs Élysées sections, bolstered by two hundred dragoons: in all, 1,200 men and two cannons. Costaz estimated that some five hundred young men had shown up to enlist on the evening of the third, and from his account it seems that the jeunesse dorée made up about half of the force under Kilmaine's command, not counting any jeunes gens who may have joined the three sectional detachments already mentioned. His instructions, Kilmaine explained, were to march into the Faubourg Antoine, surround the house of the brewer Santerre, and apprehend the deputies Cambon and Thuriot, who were thought to be hiding there, using the house as a base for directing the insurrection. Some 1,500 or 2,000 reinforcements were to follow later.

The column set out from the Place du Carrousel at around three in the morning, a detachment of light cavalry leading the way and the dragoons bringing up the rear. The jeunes gens were in high spirits, and though many of them had never met before, they were already acting as if they were old acquaintances, so strong was bourgeois solidarity in these times of social unrest. Costaz recalled, "We felt as if we all came from the same region, as if we had been raised together, raised to respect law and order, to love justice, and to hate violence. We formed a sort of sacred battalion, firmly resolved, like the young Thebans, to defend one another to the death."

There was a definite social homogeneity to the vanguard battalion, which was composed entirely of "good citizens." The clockmaker Ignace Roy, of the Théâtre Français Section, could certainly have testified to this. On the morning of the fourth he had gone to his section, thence to the Tuileries, where he had been enlisted into a hundred-man detachment "for an expedition," he said. But just as the detachment was about to set off, two men stepped out of the ranks and went to tell Adjutant-General David, and General Menou himself, that they found it "repugnant" to have to march with Roy. He was immediately ordered to surrender his weapons to Captain Jouhannot – and was then led off to jail! Thus was the "rabble" pruned.

The troops marched along the banks of the Seine, as wild-eyed sans-culottes looked on – "men and women with hideous faces, gnashing their teeth," remarked Costaz. When the column reached the Place de Grève, it avoided the arcade, took a street facing the Seine, and followed side streets to the rue St Antoine, at St Gervais. Then it entered the faubourg. The sun was just coming up. It was five o'clock.

The division advanced in total silence. It was crucial not to wake the sleeping inhabitants of the faubourg, and so "the glorious expedition," as Clarétie said, "bore a vague resemblance to a police raid." Yet already men and women, pressed against the walls on each side of the street, were staring at the invading troops. While a few grisettes, swept off their feet, exclaimed, "Oh, what handsome young men!" or "Look how wonderfully they march!," the sans-culottes, who had only their pikes, and who saw all the muskets swinging rythmically, recalled the massacre of the Champs de Mars, and muttered under their breath, "Lafayette's grenadiers!" In the Popincourt Section, a certain Vigoureux shouted that the sans-culottes had to take up arms "to fight against the jeunes gens who had come to disarm the section." The shoemaker Chesson, of the Poissonnière Section, wanted to rouse the construction workers in the rue d'Hauteville and the rue de l'Échiquier and lead them to the faubourg. All over Paris, people were saying that they had to "support [their] brothers of the Faubourg Antoine, teach the representatives a lesson, and show no mercy to the merchants and the muscadins."

The column reached the Barrière du Trône at half past five and halted. The jeunes gens were hungry. "A fellow next to me bought a basket of small turnips," said Costaz. "The woman asked for one hundred sous; he gave her twenty francs." All the way along the line, the youths purchased provisions, paying more than the asking price. Costaz lauded their generosity, which supposedly won over many of the women, "who said that we were worth more than the cursed Jacobins." Like Clarétie, however, we can draw quite another conclusion from Costaz' account: all that this rather suspect generosity proves is that while the lower classes were starving, the bourgeoisie had more than enough of everything.

While the young men were assuaging their hunger, Kilmaine had his soldiers surround Santerre's house, which was nearby. There was talk of looting it, of drowning "General Suds" in his own brew. They searched for an hour and a half, but turned up no one. In the meantime, Kilmaine, who was clearly becoming worried, sent out reconnaissance patrols to see whether the expected reinforcements were on their way. But there was no point: the two thousand support troops who were supposed to join up with his – half of which he had been planning to post at the entrance to the faubourg, and the other half at a point midway between the boulevard and Santerre's house, so as to cover his retreat – would never arrive. At the last minute they had been dispatched to the Pont Marie to prevent the Antoine and Marceau faubourgs from joining forces. To replace these troops, three hundred dragoons under General Montchoisy and four pieces of artillery had been mobilized. But they left too late, and in any case Kilmaine knew nothing of these developments, as his reconnaissance patrols had been captured by the insurgents.

Since the search had turned up nothing, it was suddenly realized that the expedition had been pointless. To make matters worse, a messenger from the Committee of General Security arrived just at that moment with orders for Kilmaine not to enter the faubourg, but instead to guard the exits until the main force caught up with him. The orders were a little late – he had already been in the faubourg for two hours! The only thing left to do was to go back, or, more precisely, to get out. Rather than leave by the Barrière du Trône and return to the city centre by skirting the faubourg, Kilmaine chose to retrace his steps along the rue Antoine, no doubt hoping to meet up with the reinforcements he was still expecting.

So the troops did an about-face and started back. On the way, Kilmaine learnt that the sans-culottes were barricading the streets. When he passed by the civil committee of the Quinze Vingts Section, he called over two of its members and ordered them to accompany him to ensure his safety. "They begged me, in the name of France," he said with mock humaneness, "to use force only as a last resort." When the jeunes gens reached the first barricade, at the rue de la Roquette, they were "greeted with yells and vulgar abuse from a mob of armed men and an even greater number of women, or rather furies, who swore they would cut our throats." The two members of the civil committee went to negotiate, while Kilmaine uttered threats and the gunners unlimbered their cannon. Eventually the barricade opened, and the column continued on its way. It soon reached the second barricade, at the rue Charonne. Again there were yells and threats; after a quarter of an hour of parleying, this barricade opened and the troops proceeded. But they had barely gone a few paces when word spread that the rearguard, in passing by the Montreuil Section guardhouse, had seized its guns. The rumour caused a great tumult, and the sans-culottes quickly closed the barricade again. Never had the jeunes gens been in a more perilous position. Caught between the two barricades, as though in a vice with cobblestone jaws, they could be shot at from the front, the rear, and the sides, as well as from the windows and rooftops. Kilmaine could conceivably have stormed the barricade with a bayonet charge or demolished it with cannon fire, but the jeunes gens were beginning to lose their nerve: "rage, and thus a certain amount of confusion, swept through our ranks," wrote Costaz. From the description given by Lacretelle, one can well understand why:

Whichever way they turned, guns and a forest of pikes barred the route. In the windows overhead, women and children appeared ready to cast down on them anything they could lay their hands on in their frenzy. The inhabitants of the faubourg had it in their power to stain their hands with the blood of the most distinguished young men of Paris. The youths would doubtless have put up a fierce fight, but most would have perished in a position that even regular soldiers considered hopeless.

This account is corroborated by Duval: "We were completely surrounded, and about to be attacked ... We would inevitably have been crushed by force of numbers." Seeing themselves trapped, they considered surrendering. But they had lost none of their swagger, and displayed what Hyde de Neuville called "that arrogance which, for some inexplicable reason, will always overawe the masses and prevent them from seeing things as they really are."

The people's representatives Vernier and Courtois were accompanying the expedition incognito. Because of the imminent danger, they urged Kilmaine to order the rearguard to return the guns; this he did, not really having any choice. He was clearly ashamed of this episode, however, and later sought to explain himself in his report: it would have been difficult to take the guns without causing bloodshed; it was important not to endanger the two representatives, who might have been recognized; the soldiers had neither rope nor horses with which to haul the guns. He even went so far as to say that when the rearguard had abandoned them, "it had done so with good grace and had not in any way been forced by the rebels." Naturally, we are not obliged to believe him.

Now without the guns, the jeunes gens proceeded to the third barricade, on the border between the city and the faubourg. Kilmaine had only to cross it and he would be on the boulevard, where he could deploy his troops. He saw himself in a better position than in the narrow streets from which he had just escaped, and was able to show more resolve. But the sans-culottes were growing more determined in their resistance. Men from the Indivisibilité Section who had rushed to the scene were vehemently opposed to letting Kilmaine and his troops through. Only after the two Quinze Vingts committeemen and "a number of good citizens who had mingled in the crowd" had intervened did they yield, and even then only very reluctantly. After surrendering the pikes they had vainly taken as trophies, the jeunes gens were subjected to the humiliation of having to edge their way through a narrow opening in the cobblestones, under a hail of jeers from the mob. "Goodbye, white hands!" the women shouted. "Good riddance, black collars!" As Baron Hyde de Neuville, who was commanding a detachment of the vanguard, stepped across the barricade, someone yelled, "There's a head that will do well to stay firmly on its shoulders! Ah, they're good sorts, all the same!"

Once out of the faubourg, the column could breathe more easily again, especially with the arrival soon afterward, by the rue Antoine, of the three hundred dragoons under General Montchoisy. Fréron, who was with them, saw his jeunes gens returning "with their faces downcast in humiliation, their stomachs empty, and their hearts swollen with rage," and rushed to the Committee of Public Safety to hasten the arrival of the main body of troops.

No sooner had the youths escaped than the insurgents regretted having let them go. Jamolet, a shoemaker from the Thermes Julien Section, vociferously accused his fellow rebels of having committed a crime. Police inspectors who entered the faubourg noted, "Some people are sorry they did not cut off the hair of the young men who came to disarm them. Others say they ought to have been shot." The citizen Gilles, a Montreuil Section police commissioner who had intervened on behalf of the jeunes gens – and who a few days later was to question a girl by the name of Vignot, asking her "whether she had been one of the women who had egged on the men not to allow the troops to leave the faubourg" – was heckled by some character in the rue de Lappe: "So you're the one who betrayed your brothers by letting pass men who came to disarm us."

One wonders how the inhabitants of the faubourg could have let slip such a golden opportunity to have done with the jeunesse dorée once and for all. Considering the hatred they harboured against the youths, Tønnesson's hypothesis – that they were easily daunted by the sight of the regular troops in Kilmaine's column and that the jeunesse dorée would have been slaughtered had it been alone – seems to be the only explanation for their indecisiveness. Thus, ironically, it was the military that saved a ragbag of deserters from being massacred!

The column then marched back – or, rather, beat a retreat – up the boulevard. At the rue de la Loi, it was joined by a detachment of cavalry and infantry under General Stengel, and the march continued. Opposite the rue St Gilles the troops disarmed a group of men who were contemplating an attack. At the Porte St Martin they drove back "a huge mob of women in a state of convulsive rage" who were demanding bread. Could anything else be expected of a regiment of rosy-cheeked sixteen- and seventeen-year-olds? Yet Costaz boasted of having "terrified" the faubourg! "We knew we could bring it to its knees when we wanted to," he added. Such was not the general feeling. Hyde de Neuville, somewhat more perceptive, counted himself lucky to have escaped with his life.

The column halted at the corner of the rue Montmartre and the boulevard Poissonnière. The cavalry dismounted and the infantry was allowed to rest. It was ten o'clock, and the great military leaders felt that it was time to drink to their exploits. There were numerous cafés on the boulevards, but they served only beer and Bavarian creams and were virtually out of bread. So the youths went off to Chez Rose, a restaurant where Danton, Hérault de Séchelles, and

Camille Desmoulins used to dine. The entire battalion burst in, singing "Le Réveil du Peuple." Each of the youths was allocated half a
bottle of wine – "excellent wine," claimed Costaz, who split a bottle
with a teacher by the name of Patris, of the Observatoire Section.
Constaz continues his account with his usual ingenuousness: "It
was hard to dine in better company than that of these young men;
they sparkled with wit, were brimming with positive ideas, and
were as decent as virgins." Obviously these were just the men to
crush the blood-thirsty terrorists!

While the boudoir soldiers were satisfiying their hunger, the regular troops waited under the trees, their arms at the ready. Women
from the faubourg approached to try and persuade them to go over
to the insurgents. One of the women, indignant at not getting a
reply, said mockingly, "What's this? Young and French, and you refuse to speak to a woman?" "When I'm on duty, I speak only with
my sabre!"

Apparently there was a certain degree of danger involved in chasing away these women or in arresting them, since Kilmaine refrained. However, the officers were concerned about the dragoons
of the 3rd Regiment, whom the women "wooed" more persistently,
but Kilmaine reported that he was sure of their loyalty, and quoted
remarks supposedly made to him by a dragoon:

General, when the royal despot attempted to use us to oppress the people,
it was our duty as citizens to side with the people against despotism. But
now things are quite different. A horde of criminals and murderers is trying
to rebel against the sovereignty of the people of France. This sovereignty is
delegated exclusively to the National Convention, which is the sole depository. Whoever rebels against the Convention rebels against the French
people.

That such subtleties of constitutional law should be explained by a
dragoon, no matter how refined, is of course highly implausible. As
Tarlé points out, Kilmaine probably cited the "remarks" simply for
propaganda purposes, since the soldiers had to be made aware of
the official justification for the expedition. In any event, the regular
troops resisted the advances of the sans-culotte women and remained loyal to the Committees.

At about ten o'clock, when the jeunes gens were emerging from
the faubourg, the Convention passed a decree formally summoning
the inhabitants of the Faubourg Antoine to hand over Féraud's assassins forthwith, as well as the cannons belonging to the faubourg's three sections. If they refused, the faubourg would be

declared in a state of rebellion, food supplies would be cut off immediately, and the National Guard would reduce it by force. This intimidating decree, the prospect of seeing already ridiculously
insufficient bread supplies cut off entirely, the inhabitants' impression that they had no support on the outside, and the pressure ex-
erted on them by the "good citizens" within the faubourg were all
factors that withered the resolve of the insurgents; some, growing
timid and cautious, began to lose heart. How could an effective defence be organized under these circumstances?

Police agents reported that the inhabitants of the faubourg's three
sections had calmed down since the jeunesse dorée had withdrawn,
that defensive measures were being taken, and that it was being rumoured that the cavalry had refused to obey orders. A merchant
called Christon, commander of the Quinze Vingts battalion, who up
to this point had devoted all his energy to restraining the insurgents, suddenly changed his attitude and declared that he was
"firmly resolved to match strength with strength." His determina-
tion, he added, was a reaction to the tyrannical conduct of the
armed forces who that morning, on the pretext of fraternizing, had
been cowardly enough to seize the Montreuil Section's guns.

An hour later, at about eleven o'clock, the watch committee of the
6th arrondissement received the following report from two of its
members:

An armed force from the Faubourg Antoine has drawn up in battle formation on the boulevard Popincourt, around guns loaded with grapeshot. The
force is commanded by a coloured man wielding a pair of pistols who calls
everyone who is not from the faubourg a muscadin or an aristocrat. He has
already had several citizens snared and dragged off into the faubourg.

So, despite the insurgents' lack of resolution, a violent clash was
imminent. Sensing what was coming, the Committees instructed
some thirty young men under the command of the people's representative Dentzel to transfer the munitions of the Arsenal to a safer
armoury in the rue Honoré. At about three o'clock, the news spread
through the faubourg.

They [the sans-culottes] heard that the muscadins were removing the powder from the Arsenal, and they decided that they should go and stop them.
So they went and prevented the wagons from leaving. They were told that
they were for army service, but they did not believe a word of it. Some had
already left. They sent to the Faubourg Antoine for reinforcements, and
now they are waiting for them to arrive.

A mob of six to eight hundred people from the faubourg marched on the Arsenal to prevent the munitions from being taken away, perhaps with an eye to plundering it to arm the insurgents. While they were initially successful, they failed to exploit their position, and Dentzel and his jeunes gens managed to hold them off until more soldiers arrived. However, one of the youths, an instructor named Robert who had been called up in the first conscription, was captured by the rebels and dragged off to the Faubourg Antoine, where he was kept prisoner until the capitulation.

At about four o'clock, the National Guard, rallied under the command of Menou, was ordered to advance on the faubourg. "The guard," said Lacretelle, "was fired up by the speeches of the jeunes gens, who were itching to take revenge for the humiliating treatment they had suffered that morning." From five different directions, five columns converged on the faubourg to encircle it. Once Kilmaine's troops had finished eating, his column reformed and resumed its march along the boulevards. At the Porte Martin it again encountered the starving mob it had confronted earlier in the morning. At the corner of the rue Vieille du Temple, "many young, affluently dressed citizens" watched the column go by. "What are you doing?" Kilmaine shouted to them. "Do you think you are spectators at the Opéra? Begone with you, or I'll put you in uniform and force you to march with us."

When the column reached the rue St Gilles, it turned off the boulevards into the rue des Tournelles and came out at the Place de l'Indivisibilité, facing the rue Antoine. There, Kilmaine had his troops draw up in battle formation opposite Beaumarchais's house and trained his guns on a barricade. An adjutant-general happened to have in his pocket the Convention's decree ordering the faubourg to surrender. On Vernier's advice, Kilmaine sent him, with four hussars and a troop of cavalry, to read it out in front of the barricade. The insurgents replied by asking for more time. Kilmaine responded with an old cliché: If the faubourg did not surrender within the allotted time, it would be reduced to rubble, and people would search in vain for the place where it had stood. The minutes ticked by without any reaction from the insurgents, so Kilmaine ordered his men to dismantle the barricade, thus leaving the faubourg unprotected. With the barricade gone, the two sides – the company of jeunes gens armed by Bergoein, and the rebels crowded around their cannons – found themselves face to face in a dramatic confrontation.

The commander of the Popincourt Section gunners, Guillaume Delorme, was a black man whom Fournier l'Américain had brought back from Santo Domingo. A powerful fellow with "a large face and face and a considerable girth," he led the entire quarter of the Cul-de-Sac Sébastien at the mere wave of a hand. Bourgeois historians have bequeathed us a terrifying image of the man: "A monster belched up by the African coast," wrote Duval, who sketched Delorme's "hideous portrait" in his *Souvenirs thermidoriens,* and naïvely attributed to him all responsibility for organizing and galvanizing the Prairial insurrection at the instigation of the Montagnards. "The symbol of murder and the avenger of his race," wrote Lamartine in his *Histoire des Girondins,* in which he limned Delorme as one of the principal perpetrators of the September massacres, a deranged killer who never tired of murder, slaughtering his victims with peals of savage laughter. These caricatures simply testify to the nineteenth-century bourgeoisie's great fear of popular uprisings, which stemmed from the Revolution. More accurate, in my view, is the description given by Jules Clarétie: "He was a Herculean figure of thirty-eight. A wheelwright-locksmith by trade, he could bend an iron bar over his knee. On the fourth, half naked, he commanded his guns in his shirt sleeves, with pistols hanging from the red belt slung about his hips. He could be seen on the barricade, his bronze face lit up by a savage smile, with his frizzy hair, white teeth, and bare legs."

Was a man like this going to surrender without a fight? Not on your life! Instead he ordered his men to fire on the muscadins. When they refused, he struggled in a drunken rage to light the fuses himself. But, in a scene similar to that two days earlier, the locksmith Dubé and another gunner threw themselves on the cannons to prevent him. He found himself standing alone before the company of jeunes gens. A fellow by the name of Séguin approached one of the batteries

"If you go any further, I'll run you through with my sabre!" menaced Delorme.

So General Menou himself went up to him: "Are you a republican?"

"Have you any b-b-bread you c-c-can give me?" asked Delorme, who had a stutter.

"Give me your sabre."

"Here you are," he said, after much hesitation. "Don't worry, it will never be in better hands than mine!"

Then, pointing to the gunners who, though with "a rebellious look about them," were already filing past in front of the jeunes gens, he shouted, "There go the cowards who refused to give you a drubbing this morning! They're surrendering the guns!" He was arrested immediately, the battalion of jeunes gens following him as he hauled away his gun. He was beheaded the next day.

In the end, the jeunesse dorée's foray into the faubourg had simply been a reckless escapade. Duval described it as "an act of young fools that accomplished nothing whatsoever." About ten arrests were made in all. Christophe-Louis Rivière, of the Mont Blanc Section, who had stood across the street from the civil committee in the rue Honoré and made innuendoes "against people who ate brioche and cake and spent a hundred livres a day," was put under arrest by five youths armed with pistols, who "had neither orders nor character, but sported earlocks and green cravats." A wood seller from the Quinze Vingts Section, named Gallois, who on the morning of the fourth had taken aim at one of the young men in the vanguard battalion returning from the faubourg, was arrested by a certain Gaillard. A woman by the name of Chozami was led off to the Committee of General Security by Henri-Joseph Martincourt, who claimed that she was nothing but a "bitch in the pay of the Jacobins." The mathematician François Denot, who on 14 July 1789 had paraded the head of the commander of the Bastille, Delaunay, on the end of a pike, was denounced at the Lombards Section general assembly on 11 Prairial by the citizens Porte the younger and Lefebvre for having been arrested on the boulevards by the battalion of jeunes gens which had just returned from the Faubourg Antoine. The hussar Louis-Nicolas Chantrot, of the Popincourt Section, was apprehended in the rue du Chemin Vert on Fréron's orders. The citizen Lorry, of Droits de l'Homme, was denounced by the youngest Grandjean, whom he had called a muscadin, and to whom, on the evening of 4 Prairial, he had announced the disarmament of 150 soldiers by the rebels of the faubourg as "good news." Also put under arrest was the carpenter Jean Muzeret, who, on the morning of the fourth, had spread the false rumour that the muscadin battalion had been hit by a volley from twenty-four cannons, "that he had been unable to see how many had fallen because of the smoke, and that at that very moment the muscadins and the insurgents were exchanging musket fire." The clockmaker Barrack was arrested by five youths for having said "that it would not be long before the damned muscadins got the bum's rush." And that was the lot. It was a rather poor showing for a supposed crack corps which was forever bragging that it had saved France and the Republic. In reality, everything had been decided by the regular troops.

Yet once again it was the jeunesse dorée who reaped the glory. In *L'Orateur du Peuple*, Fréron praised "the unswerving courage displayed by the youth of Paris"; Goupilleau de Fontenay, in a harangue in which he called upon the heavens as his witness, honoured the jeunes gens by proclaiming them heroes. Louvet paid them a tribute in Féraud's funeral oration; certificates were even printed up and presented to the young men, attesting that they had marched in the vanguard against the faubourg and had conducted themselves with the valour and prudence of true republicans.

It would have been somewhat paradoxical to glorify the part played by the regular troops in the events of 4 Prairial, for, as the Marquis de Frenilly so aptly put it, the outcome represented "the death of the popular revolution and the dawn of royalist hopes." Moreover, this was how the outcome was interpreted by the reactionary bourgeoisie, and on the evening of 4 Prairial it was celebrating its victory. "With all the merrymaking, the evening seemed like some special holiday," noted one observer. "In some places, the casement windows of entire façades were lit up." Indeed, the spectacular victory was so complete that it marked the definitive ousting of the sans-culottes from the political arena, and henceforth political affairs would interest only those who spent their time in the cafés. As one Marin wrote to his friend Goupilleau de Montaigu on 5 Prairial,

What a day it was yesterday! What a difference between morning and evening! In the morning the Faubourg Antoine was laying down the law. In the evening it was made to obey it. In the morning it had given some deputies a very rude welcome. It had forced troops who had gone to fraternize [sic] to put down their arms. It had forced the return of its guns, which had been seized. It had taken up the cobblestones in the streets, blocked all the exits with carts and beams ...

... and in the evening it had surrendered the arms that had enabled it to triumph on 6 October, 10 August, and 31 May, and that, even the day before, could have let it still hope for victory if some determined leader had put himself at the head of the rebellion. The next day, 5 Prairial, the Committee of Public Safety ordered all citizens who owned pikes to hand them over immediately to their civil committee, claiming that they were of no real use as defensive weapons and could be used only to kill! The government had already had a large number of muskets distributed, by the Committee's own admission, "to the true friends of France," and was planning to have yet more distributed. The pikes were handed over without any resistance. "The men watch, the women remain silent," noted the police. This disarmament of the lower classes was to have far-reaching consequences. "This is a revolution which wrests the force of arms from the proletarians by transferring it from the working-class areas of the city to the richer areas," remarked Baron Fain.

But was the reactionary bourgeoisie that thus regained the arms it had lost in the Year II going to let them rust in their storage racks? Did it not have a score to settle with the oligarchy in the Convention that had done nothing to defend its economic interests during the Reign of Terror? At the time of the transfer of arms from the lower classes to the honnêtes gens, the bourgeois insurrection of Vendémiaire was already a foreseeable consequence of the social and political situation. When a woman by the name of Bousquet handed in her weapon to the civil committee, she remarked sarcastically, "Go ahead! Disarm us! Soon it'll be your turn! And then *you'll* be guarded by the green coats."

THE REPRESSION

Even before the insurrection had been put down, the Convention and the government Committees were organizing the repression that was to follow. On 3 Prairial, the Committee of General Security instructed the twelve arrondissement watch committees to draw up a list of the "agents of anarchy." On the fourth, the Convention authorized the holding of permanent assemblies in the sections for the purpose of disarming and arresting "bad citizens." All of these assemblies, which continued until 13 Prairial, were dominated by the honnêtes gens, with the sans-culottes appearing only as the accused. In a parallel move, on the morning of 4 Prairial, the Convention passed a decree setting up a military commission, a special ad hoc tribunal responsible for judging offences connected with "the conspiracy of the first few days of Prairial." Repression was thus conducted simultaneously on two levels, sectional and judicial, and the jeunesse dorée had a role to play at each level.

The repression in the sections affected not only the Prairial insurgents themselves but also, and perhaps to a greater degree, all the cadres of the popular movement. This can be seen from the systematic arrest of the members of the revolutionary institutions of the Year II: those of the old watch committees, the Revolutionary Army, the companies of National Guard gunners, the Jacobin Club, and in a general way the pre-Thermidor sectional officers. Many of these people had not taken part in the insurrection; however, had it been successful, they would have been its most obvious beneficiaries, and this marked them for condemnation by the bourgeoisie.

Even the most orthodox revolutionary practices were grounds for proscription. The citizen Herbert the younger, of the Marchés Section, who was arrested by the sectional general assembly for being a "revolutionary extremist, terrorist, and henchman of the revolutionary committee," wrote in his own defence:

I may well be a terrorist, but the only time I showed it was before the châ-teau of the tyrant Capet, on 10 August 1792, where my terrorism cost me my left arm. My wounds were so severe that I shall never be able to use my arm again. I am an *homme de sang* [man who sheds blood], but I am unsparing only of my own, which flowed on 10 August. I regretted the loss solely because it prevented me from going to fight alongside my brothers at the front. The revolutionary committee, knowing that my wounds made it impossible for me to work, chose me to guard the seals, and if I was not available, others were. Thus was I its henchman.

Mere aspiration to climb the social ladder was sufficient grounds for arrest. This was the fate of the citizen Adrien-Georges Cassemiche, who was arrested by the Lombards Section general assembly because "he was without virtue, and wanted to be something so that he might impress people." Indulging in revolutionary fraternity was likewise a reason for arrest, since in some cases it was considered evidence of disloyalty to one's class. The vice-president of the Criminal Court of the Department of Paris, Pierre Henri Blandin, was arrested by the Lombards Section general assembly because "in his speeches he was always praising the class he referred to as the sans-culottes by making insulting parallels between them and the well-to-do."

Tønnesson has focused attention on the massive scale of the repression in the sections. While in absolute terms it affected only a limited number of individuals, some three thousand perhaps, it was still extremely harsh, especially considering that the militant revolutionaries represented only a tiny fraction of the total population. The Committees apparently did not foresee the scope of repression in the sections; they looked on anxiously as it developed, and from 1 Prairial stepped in to curb it by revising the sections' decrees for arrest and disarmament, in most cases by quashing them.

It seems that the jeunesse dorée was, to a large extent, the driving force behind the repression. The Convention, recorded Lacretelle, "harboured little anger against the party it had just crushed, but it was forced to yield significantly to the resentment of the auxiliaries it had called on for its defence." The jeunesse dorée vehemently demanded vengeance. In *Le Moniteur* of 6 Prairial, Trouvé expressed his regret, in the name of humanity [*sic*], that the traitors had not been wiped out on the evening of the insurrection, exclaiming,

Death to the rebels! Give the inhabitants of this city who shielded you with their own bodies, and the soldiers who rushed to your defence, this display of strength ... It will be the recompense for their courage and loyalty ... You will do justice by giving the writers who dedicate themselves to truth and to the principles of humanity, justice, and liberty the consideration warranted by the valuable and honourable authority they exercise over public opinion. This leniency toward criminals must stop!

There being no historical study of the sections during the Thermidorian period, it is impossible to determine precisely what role the jeunes gens played in the repression. One can venture no further than to report what actions they took in some fifteen sections, including the following:

Arcis: The citizen Antoine Brugère was arrested because he appeared to seethe with rage whenever he heard someone shout "Long live the Convention!"

Le Peletier: The citizen Bouée was apprehended for having said that she would disembowel the muscadins; also arrested was the artist Menier, of the Opéra Comique, accused of having sung in public a song in favour of the guillotine.

Mont Blanc: An ex-member of the civil committee, Jean-Baptiste-Félix Tronc, was arrested for saying that the Section was run by the muscadins and for having shouted, on 12 Germinal, when the assembly was overrun, "Forward, right through the muscadins!" Far from denying it, Tronc repeated his allegations in his request to be released, declaring "that the Mont Blanc Section general assembly was indeed made up of muscadins who had had themselves requisitioned for government service so as to escape being conscripted into the army fighting at the front. It was a well-known fact."

Fraternité: The fruit vendor Bastien Vidot was denounced by Jean-Baptiste Magin, wine merchant and port inspector, for having said of the latter, "There's a little muscadin who'll find my bayonet in his stomach if we have the whip hand tomorrow."

Réunion: The porter Étienne Deveaux was put under arrest after being denounced by the former Customs and Excise inspector Phélippe, called Duclos-Lange, who accused him of having said that he could not die happy if he had not killed three or four muscadins.

Contrat Social: The citizen Barbe Sergent, who ran a brothel in the rue Bourbon Villeneuve, was denounced by a certain Bacon for being "president of the Jacobin Club, at a salary of twenty-one livres per day," and for causing disturbances in queues. "Today she was insulting the jeunes gens," he said; whereupon, she was immediately arraigned before the Criminal Court.

Indivisibilité: In denouncing the widow Barbaut, the postal employee Jean-Louis Fontaine couched his accusations in typically muscadin terms: she was "one of the furies of the guillotine spewed out by hell to destroy the human race"; she had spent her days knitting at the Jacobin Club, where she never tired of calling for blood; and "whenever a supposed muscadin or anyone else who was decently dressed passed near her, she shouted, 'Look! There's another b---- fit for the guillotine!'"

In many sections, the jeunes gens had arrests made in retaliation for the way they had been treated during the recruitment unrest in early May, 1793, and particularly at their gathering at the Champs Élysées on 4 and 5 May. In the Amis de la Patrie Section, the fancy-goods maker Louis Roman was decreed to be under arrest following a denunciation by the clock-maker Crevier, who accused him of having written to the section's general assembly "that Duval had just been arrested at the jeunes gens' gathering at the Champs Élysées, armed with pistols," contrary to what was stated in the police report on his arrest. In Bon Conseil, the general assembly passed a decree for the arrest of the upholsterer Jean-Noël Dumoulin, who was accused of having taken the floor at the general assembly of 5 May 1793 "to say that the jeunes gens should leave, that the muscadins had to be forced out, that there were ways of controlling them." In Homme Armé the public-health officer Bernard Naury was arrested because, on the day when the jeunes gens had gathered at the Champs Élysées to draw up a petition, he had sought to have the citizen Creton sent to city hall on the trifling pretext that he had a tricolour cockade attached to his ribbon. Such arrests testify to the jeunesse dorée's Girondin origins, its recruitment of members among the absentee conscripts, and the links between the events of Prairial, Year III, and those of May, 1793.

The Military Tribunal sat concurrently with the sectional assemblies, and the influence of the jeunes gens on its proceedings is easier to discern. The task of drawing up the list of judges was assigned to Rovère, the organizer of the parallel police force. The sessions were dominated by jeunesse dorée spectators, who greeted the deputies as they entered the hall with calls for their execution, and decided many convictions by their catcalls and clamour. A typical example was that of Nicolas-Étienne Chebrier, a member of the Arsenal Section's former revolutionary committee, who was convicted on a series of charges, including shouting "Muscadin" at a citizen in the street, and was executed on 11 Prairial.

In the trial of Romme, Goujon, Bourbotte, Soubrany, Duquesnoy, and Duroy – the martyrs of Prairial – the chief witnesses for the prosecution were Jourdan and Martainville, editors of *Le Moniteur*, and Louis Jullian, Fréron's right-hand man. Their depositions covered every possible angle: they had seen everything, heard everything, and been everywhere. The bill of indictment had been drafted using the report in *Le Moniteur*, a copy of which was submitted as an exhibit. Fréron's army had already heard the case in advance, and the tribunal was there simply to validate its decision. And so the last Montagnards mounted the steps of the scaffold – steps that, despite the jeunesse dorée, also raised them to immortality.

CHAPTER FIVE

The Failure of the Bourgeois Reaction

15 PRAIRIAL, YEAR III, TO 30 FRIMAIRE, YEAR IV

Although victory in the Prairial insurrection – in which the armed rebellion of the Jacobins must be distinguished from the revolt of the starving populace – had been won by only a narrow margin, it was nevertheless an unequivocal victory which saw "the mob" definitively deposed. Thus, not only was the outcome cause for the honnêtes gens to rejoice, in their eyes it also marked the end of "anarchy" and appeared to usher in a period of political and social stability in France. Now that the workers had taken up their tools again and the women, "having ceased to comment on political events," had gone back to their housekeeping, the bourgeoisie was finally assured that people and property would be respected. In this light, 4 Prairial appeared to correspond to 9 Thermidor, and, to judge by "the utter bewilderment of those who favoured disorder and looting," it seemed that the "working class" would henceforth abandon all involvement in the political arena. It was Costaz's view that the real founding of the Republic had taken place that day. All that remained now, as L'Orateur du Peuple had written in early Nivôse, was to educate "the multitude" about its true interests and to draw for "the common herd" a clear line showing where liberty ended and abuse of liberty began. And educating the multitude would be easy since, according to one police agent, people in the lower classes already realized that a victory for them would have "resulted in dire calamity." Whence it was just a small step for them to acknowledge that the Revolution had for too long been a war between rich and poor, wise and foolish, educated and ignorant, and that it was only reasonable for "all classes of citizens" to return to their natural places in the social hierarchy.

But there are two sides to every coin, and as early as 5 Prairial the view began to spread that the Convention, which had just instructed the sections to purge bad elements from their ranks, should likewise move quickly to weed out those of its members "whose principles are the cause of all our troubles." It was a view which contained the seeds of the bourgeois insurrection of Vendémiaire, Year IV.

Once the sans-culottes had been crushed, the Thermidorians had to confront the jeunes gens, who had developed from useful auxiliaries into awkward protectors and finally into reckless, domineering hooligans. The youths had become superfluous to the policy of equilibrium, since they no longer served to offset a rival force. Having been rescued from the mob, the Convention was now set on ridding itself of the burdensome tutelage of its irksome, anarchic militia.

If, during the turmoil of Prairial, the Assembly had called on the military, it was in part because the jeunesse dorée could no longer hold the masses in check. But it was also, and perhaps above all, because it feared that a victory by the jeunesse dorée alone over the sans-culottes would make the government entirely dependent upon the jeunes gens and carry it much further than it wished to go – that is, toward the Restoration. Indeed, according to Mallet du Pan, several National Guard battalions consisted solely of monarchists. Thus, as soon as the Prairial insurrection had been put down, the Thermidorians began to feel increasingly mistrustful of the jeunes gens, some of whom, such as Martainville, publicly declared their support for the monarchy. In the opinion of the younger Lacretelle, the Convention was much too lenient in its punishment of a party it thought still enjoyed popular support because it had no faith in the young men it had called upon to defend it; because it feared being dominated, it was afraid of too crushing a victory. Whence the "ingratitude" of a Thermidorian such as Legendre. When the Quinze Vingts Section went to the Convention on 6 Prairial to present the gunner who, on 2 Prairial, had thrown himself on the fuse of a Montreuil Section cannon to prevent it from firing, he praised the young man's zealous action, but opposed his receiving the fraternal embrace from the president, saying that the Committees would be preparing a detailed report citing the names of all those who had shown themselves worthy of their country.

The jeunesse dorée, for its part, harboured similar resentment against the Convention, which it had not forgiven for having let Kilmaine's battalion march deep into the faubourgs without reinforcements on the morning of 4 Prairial. Only at the last minute, when faced with the imminent threat of the mob, had the young men made their peace with the Thermidorians. But once this peril had been dealt with, they soon went back to the view that the Convention was merely a docile instrument of their hooligan rule.

Yet "public opinion," as Lebois had written a short time before, was not the opinion of the people. The time had come for the jeunes gens to realize that their bluster impressed no one and that without the aegis of the Thermidorians they were nothing but a "horde of spineless madcaps." Thus, at the Café Valois on 15 Prairial, prisoners from Robespierre's time refused to let themselves be called "citizen," remarking wryly, "I don't deserve that honour!" At the same café, on the eighteenth, it was noted that the habitués affected "an exaggerated admiration for the National Convention." The "admirers" were young men with green or black collars who spoke "more like obvious aristocrats than conspirators" – young men like Louis-Germain Lacharpagne, a regular at the Café de Chartres, who had been denounced by an agent of the Committee of General Security on the tenth for being an "inveterate gambler, schemer, money dealer, apostle of the counter-Revolution, muscadin, forger of assignats ..."

Annoyed by the Convention's "ingratitude" toward its praetorian guard, Martainville apparently complained to Barras, but was sharply rebuked for his troubles. It would not be long before the latent hostility between the jeunesse dorée and the Convention exploded in open conflict. There was certainly no lack of friction between the two. Would the Committees not move to curb the voracity of the speculators? Would they not send back to the army all the jeunesse dorée in government administration who had pushed up the price of eyeglasses? Would they not react to the stream of abuse that the reactionary press was preparing to hurl at the elected national assembly? Would the thousands of sans-culottes who had been languishing in Paris's forty prisons since early Prairial be left there to rot forever? Would "Le Réveil du Peuple," whose couplets amounted to calls for murder, remain the hymn of Thermidor? Finally, and most importantly, would the Convention be allowed to implement the Constitution of the Year III and the famous Decrees of the Two-Thirds which, in manifest violation of the sovereignty of the people, automatically returned to power 500 of the Convention's 750 deputies, who were already being referred to as "Perpetuals"? The Convention and the jeunesse dorée were preparing to cross swords.

THE BREAK WITH THE NATIONAL CONVENTION

Since Thermidor, speculation had become an economic plague in the French capital. Jullian says as much in his *Souvenirs*:

A rather strange phenomenon had arisen in Paris. It involved a considerable number of jeunes gens who, though often with no name but the one they usurped and with no known resources but gambling, managed to spend some two hundred to three hundred thousand francs a year. In the ranks of these adventurers were several distinguished but disgraced persons who, finding the profession quite to their liking, indulged in the same type of trade.

These were the jeunesse dorée – the men from whom the Assembly now sought to free itself. Crooks such as Jean-Denis Perrot, an erstwhile broker who had amassed a fortune so quickly through illicit currency trading at the Palais Égalité that in two years he had ac quired an estate worth two million livres in Clichy, a house in the Marais, and another "very sizeable" one in the Faubourg Montmartre; on 2 Fructidor, Year III, he was negotiating the purchase of an estate on the outskirts of Paris worth three hundred thousand livres. Or swindlers such as the citizens Pyot and Conceil, both of whom had been called up in the first conscription; they were so successful at speculating that in the space of eighteen months they were able to buy two houses in Paris, one hundred arpents of land in Courbevoie, a house in Passy, a sumptuous residence worth more than seven million livres in the Faubourg du Roule, and grocer's shops in Bordeaux and Marseille.

Speculators could be found all over Paris, but they congregated chiefly at the Palais Égalité, at the Perron (the rickety stairway leading to the rue Vivienne), in the square next to the Bourse known as the Forêt Noire, and in the Place du Louvre. They were generally thought to be responsible for the currency depreciation and the rise in the price of foodstuffs. The police repeatedly denounced "these indestructible vermin," "this odious rabble," and pressured the government "to move quickly to erect a strong dike against this destructive torrent." The sight of such huge fortunes being made with such little effort prompted all idlers in Paris to tap the same source of wealth, so that within the French Republic, wrote *Le Courrier français*, a sort of "speculative republic" sprang up in which a wigmaker set himself up as a sugar or coffee merchant, a shoemaker sold flour, a doorkeeper oil, and a tailor candles. On 18 Thermidor, even workers left their workshops to speculate. "We had no choice," they explained the next day at a large gathering at the Porte Martin. "How can we buy bread at fifteen livres a pound when we earn only twelve francs a day?"

On 8 Messidor, a brand-new form of roguery surfaced at the Jardin Égalité. The speculators there suddenly shouted that the area was being surrounded and took to their heels, carrying off the things people had been offering them.

Speculation had become a social plague which provoked profound annoyance. The public ardently wished to see it stamped out, and so the Committees finally decided to crack down. In the early evening of 18 Prairial the Palais Égalité was surrounded by the National Guard, and the speculators caught there were arrested.

But the crackdown met with resistance. The head of the Supplies Office, Jean-Daniel Bourlet, tried to pick a quarrel with a Lieutenant Laflotte, demanding that he show the orders he had been given. The lieutenant refused, "seeing that there were another two hundred men I would have had to show them to," whereupon Bourlet called him a "jackass" and declared that if he had thrown off one tyranny, it had not been with the intention of falling under another.

The jeunes gens were beside themselves with anger the next day at the Café de Chartres. "Government is just as arbitrary as ever. It has simply changed hands," they said. "I was detained until two in the morning," one of them complained. It was suggested that they go to the Convention to demand the arrest of the Committee members responsible for the operation, which had not been carried out gently. The commanding officer had apparently instructed his men to use their sabres on anyone attempting to escape, and the Butte des Moulins civil committee had later lodged a complaint with the Committee of General Security. Furthermore, it seems that the deputy Delmas, the representative to the armed forces, had only reluctantly passed on the order to have the Palais Égalité surrounded. He remarked to the Committee on 20 Prairial that the measure was badly received by the good citizens; he stressed, "I tell you, the good citizens have been sorely affected, and are still suffering." According to the police reports, the jeunes gens threatened to ignore all calls to arms in the future because they had been so badly treated. But the Committees had already realized that if they ever had to sound the call to arms again, it would certainly not be to rally the jeunesse dorée. On 20 Prairial, the National Guard staged another raid on the Jardin Égalité; from then on, the speculators were hounded constantly by the Committee of General Security. The following day, 21 Prairial, the second-hand dealer Jean-Baptiste Calleteau was arrested at the Palais Égalité for currency trading. On 8 Messidor, one René Vimont, who had come to Paris six weeks earlier putatively to look for work, was arrested for picking pockets at the Palais Égalité; on the twenty-ninth, Delaunay announced to the Convention, on behalf of the Committee of General Security, that in the preceding ten days over four hundred speculators had been jailed: "We are after them everywhere, in the cafés, in the theatres, and in the streets and squares." Also in late Messidor, a certain Saint-Aubin, who claimed to be a mathematics teacher, published a pamphlet in which he asserted that a government which refused to let itself be swayed "by the protests of the mob, whether filthy or gilded" ought to encourage rather than crack down on speculation, which he said was "in no way harmful to the State." It seems somewhat doubtful that he would have convinced many of his readers.

Then there was the problem of the Prairial insurgents, numbering eight to ten thousand by *La Gazette française*'s calculation, who were rotting in prison. According to Bentabolle, Guyomar, and Hardy de la Seine, the jeunesse dorée wanted them to remain there so that it could go and slaughter them when the time was ripe, in a sort of reversal of the September massacres; alternatively, it wanted them brought before the regular courts, which since Thermidor had been dominated by extreme reactionaries who would not have shown them any mercy. Before the Convention on 6 Thermidor, Hardy claimed that the courts in his Department were controlled by the jeunesse dorée and that they were engaged in savage repression of the patriots. "The so-called jeunes gens have a rather remarkable organization in Le Havre," he said. "They are led by a youngster of seventy, and some of their number are fifty, sixty, and even eighty years old. These new-style terrorists refer to themselves as the youth of Le Havre and claim to have the authorities under their thumb."

There were also the *ultras*, who wanted the repression to go much further. On 11 Messidor, the Le Peletier Section, "having learnt that the bloodthirsty villains and murderers were everywhere rearing their ugly heads," went to the Convention to protest against their rearmament. On 3 Thermidor, the section again mounted the rostrum to rail against the terrorists:

The orator: "... It is not enough to bring them before the courts."
Deville: "... Should they have their throats cut?"

Such was not the view of the Committee of General Security, in any event. Regarding the sans-culottes as an effective counterweight to the jeunesse dorée, it had adopted a policy of treating them with clemency. Thus, on 15 Prairial, it asked the sections to provide it with a list of those who had been detained or disarmed, and to give the reasons in each case. But the sections, which had been infiltrated by Moderates, refused to cooperate, either by abstaining, as the Panthéon Section did, or by alleging insufficient documents and instructions, as the Fontaine Grenelle Section did. Some sections even sought to complicate matters by producing complete minutes of their proceedings of early Prairial, which were obviously far too long for the Committee of General Security to go through, or endless lists of names with corresponding derogatory epithets. This prompted the Committee to issue complaints to the sections on 25 Prairial. It could not, it said, "reach a decision on the basis of terms whose use might be subject to dispute." Indeed, how, for instance, could it have decided the fate of the tailor Degris, of the Lombards Section, when the civil committee admitted, "We could not come up with any facts, and consequently we cannot express an opinion," but immediately added, "It is well known that in his neighbourhood Degris has always been regarded as the most abject of beings, a fervent supporter of the Terror, a factious, bloodthirsty, immoral man." The same was true of the journeyman carpenter Alain Chaucogne, of the Lombards Section, about whom the civil committee wrote on 26 Messidor, "... an ill-bred man, he may have thought that in comparison with the mob he was an important figure, since he was paid to deliberate."

In spite of this resistance from the sections, the Committee of General Security pressed ahead with its strategy and began releasing sans-culotte prisoners in late Prairial. There was a tremendous stir in the cafés when men known for their penchant for uttering bloodthirsty slogans were seen to be walking free again. The development caused heated debates on 4 Messidor. On the seventh, the disquieting rumour circulated that the Convention was about to declare a general amnesty for terrorists. On the thirtieth, a riot broke out at the Théâtre des Arts (of that, more later), with people shouting that there were plans to bring back the Terror, that buveurs de sang were being released, and that the Convention should purge the cutthroats from its ranks.

In a new measure of clemency toward the Prairial insurgents, the Convention passed a decree on 6 Thermidor, setting up its own twelve-member commission that would consider prisoners' revolutionary acts in deciding whether to release them. This was too much for the jeunesse dorée; a few days later, on 13 Thermidor, "three citizens of advanced age," delegated by young men of the Observatoire Section, appeared before the Convention to ask for the decree to be repealed. This farce sparked a quarrel in the Assembly:

Dubois-Crancé: "Since you applauded after 9 Thermidor, when the Convention released all the prisoners, you should not be complaining today simply because it intends to decide the fate of those who are in prison now." A petitioner: "We shall always demand justice from the Convention ..." Dubois-Crancé, angrily: "Are we so unjust, damn it? I'll tell you a thing or two about justice! We shall denounce you to all our constituents. You are a bunch of brigands, and you can go to h----!"

The police reported that in late afternoon a large crowd gathered in the rue des Petits Champs and that "the most outrageous abuse" was heaped on the Convention for its harsh treatment of the petitioners. In seven or eight cafés, according to an inspector, Dubois-Crancé's outburst was openly condemned. Discontent seemed so strong that on the same day the Committee of General Security announced publicly, by proclamation, that the releases did not prevent citizens and magistrates from bringing the guilty before the courts. But this was still too little. The following day, 14 Thermidor, "in a good number of cafés ... citizens openly condemned Dubois-Crancé's outburst," and the deputy decided that it would be wise to make a public apology. The right of petition had not been violated, he explained on the fifteenth, since the sitting was already over when the row started. It had been a dispute between two individuals, and nothing more. Then he admitted, "I concede that I was overly aggressive at an inappropriate moment. If I could meet this citizen again, I should be most willing to apologize."

Thus the jeunesse dorée still appeared to be a formidable force, so much so that four days later, on 19 Thermidor, Henri Larivière had the decree of the sixth repealed. The prison releases continued, nevertheless, and the pace picked up after 12 Fructidor, following passage of a decree stipulating that all prisoners had to be brought forthwith before a police officer who would decide whether to release them or send them to be tried by the courts.

But what was the value of freedom if it meant dying of starvation? It is important to keep in mind that a great many Parisians – and, significantly, not just the sans-culottes, but also large segments of the bourgeoisie – were living in conditions of extreme poverty. The first to suffer, of course, were the city's workers and artisans; they faced unemployment because they could no longer find people who had enough money to hire them. But provisions had become so scarce, and thus expensive, that not only was the working class affected, but also some property owners and rentiers, who were reduced to begging after they had sold their furniture and personal effects. As one observer noted, their fortunes virtually melted away when their creditors paid them back in assignats which had plummeted in value. Similarly, salaried civil servants and poorly paid employees found themselves in dire straits. Want was so severe that people were starving to death in the streets. Women could be seen picking through the filthy remains of rotten vegetables for something to eat, or drinking the blood that flowed from the butcher shops where worn-out horses were cut up and sold at an écu a pound. Yet, in the same city, a whole society of idle rich talked about nothing but balls, opera, and new fashions, devoted all its energy to frivolous chatter in the cafés, and never sacrificed even fifteen minutes of pleasure to a serious discussion about affairs of state.

The weakness of the government and mismanagement by the Committees were blamed for the widespread destitution. One observer reported that on 20 Messidor some people were saying "that the wheels of government had ceased to turn, that they had jammed," and that on 11 Thermidor complaints were voiced about a National Convention "that sees everything, allows everything, but stops nothing" – this last remark "being made in particular by the bourgeoisie, with the support of the lower classes." Thus, while the honnêtes gens had been strongly behind the Convention immediately after the Prairial insurrection, their enthusiasm began to wane long before any real political conflict broke out between the two parties. Similarly, well before Vendémiaire, the Assembly, seeing its last remnants of support in the population beginning to crumble, decided that the army was its only chance for survival.

The appalling conditions to which I have referred can be illustrated with a few concrete examples. Many revealing observations are contained in the contemporary police reports, which the officers evidently found unpleasant to write, and in which they apologize for constantly repeating themselves. On 10 Prairial a woman threw herself into a well out of despair, having no bread to give to her children. On the twenty-second the police officer Losset, in making his rounds, came across "many labourers so weak they could barely stand, all life gone out of their faces." In the streets the next day the poor could be seen picking through heaps of refuse for something to eat. On 10 Messidor it was rumoured that so many people were throwing themselves into the Seine that the men working the nets at St Cloud were hard pressed to haul out the bodies. A week later, on 18 Messidor, a large crowd gathered at the corner of the rue Denis and the rue Neuve Égalité, where a man had just died of hunger. *La Gazette française* of 20 Messidor quoted bread at sixteen francs a pound, butter at eighteen francs, wood at three hundred francs a cord, coal at one hundred francs a load, and many other goods, such as cloth and linen, at similarly exorbitant prices. On 29 Messidor, the police reported, "People are dropping in the streets." Nearly a month later, on 25 Thermidor, the situation was unchanged: "Starving people can be seen everywhere." All they had left, said a police agent on 2 Fructidor, was "the hope of death."

According to the police, economic hardship struck at all classes of society indiscriminately. Among the lower classes, it brought, in some cases, disillusionment with politics; in others, renewed Jacobin agitation; and in still others, general ill will against the authorities. Meanwhile, royalist views were making a resurgence. As early as 23 Ventôse, a man by the name of Louis Duval – who had been denounced by Jollivet for having claimed, falsely, to be a habitué of the Café de Chartres – had been arrested for saying that he had been told by some deputies with whom he had just dined that a king would be on the throne within a week. In *Le Moniteur* of 18 Prairial, Trouvé wrote:

People everywhere are entertaining the wildest hopes. The question now is who will throw off his mask the soonest and the most overtly. To judge by what is being published and by what is being said by people who believe they are speaking in confidence, one would conclude that the Republic is on its last legs. Now that the Convention, supported, not to say driven, by the zeal and energy of our good citizens, has won a great victory over the terrorists, over Robespierre's successors, it appears that all it has to do is proclaim the monarchy.

A certain Gaudin Lagrange, in his *Essai sur les moyens d'arriver à un bon gouvernement* (Essay on the Way to Achieve Good Government), even took up Delacroix's argument and called for a referendum to choose between the Republic and the monarchy. A monarchy differs from a republic only in name and in the form taken by authority, says the author, and true royalists are just as strongly in favour of liberty as are republicans! In the 18 Prairial edition of the newspaper *Paris pendant l'année 1795*, Poultier wrote that at the Palais Égalité the jeunes gens greeted one another by asking "What is eight and a half and eight and a half?" or "What is half of thirty-four?" – an allusion to Louis XVII, "the orphan of the Temple." On about the same date the newspaper *Le Ventriloque ou ventre affamé* (The Ventriloquist or Empty Stomach) wrote, "when we had a king, my stomach was never subjected to the dearth it is suffering now, and it has come to the conclusion that better a king than a Convention."

On 25 Prairial, the Marquis de Vitry was arrested and subsequently convicted of having sought to organize a royalist party in Paris. Two days later, on the twenty-seventh, *Le Journal de Perlet* condemned "the Committees' appalling lack of concern and incredibly inept administration." The same day, the police officer Losset noted that the destitute "openly regretted" the Ancien Régime. On 9 Messidor, the Marquise de Tourzel, the royal family's former governess, applied to the Committee of Public Safety for permission to resume her duties to Louis XVI's daughter; a certain Alexandre Raimond was bold enough to publish a *Lettre à madame Chanterel*, asking her to pass on to "the august prisoner" words of love, affection, and consolation. On 12 Messidor, the police agent Rémy reported remarks uttered by troops of the line against the Revolution. On the twentieth, "highly inflammatory, antigovernment statements were made" in the Le Peletier and Place Vendôme sections. On the twenty-fourth, the police spoke of widespread discontent:

the *décadi* (the tenth day of the Republican week) was no longer being observed, and the use of "citizen" as a title was ridiculed. While people in the lower classes did not go so far as to call for a king, noted an observer, they did not seem opposed to the monarchy either. Their overriding sentiment was one of having been tricked. They said that they had taken the oath of loyalty to the Republic in good faith, but that no one had told them then that they would be left to starve.

On 4 Thermidor, *Le Courrier républicain* had the nerve to write "that people would suffer less under one tyrant than under several." On the sixteenth, *La Gazette française* reported that some sort of cryptic print was circulating that at first glance appeared to be a picture of a funeral urn in the shadow of a cypress; upon closer examination, the profiles of Louis xvi, Marie-Antoinette, and their two children could be discerned in the urn. Three days later, a young man of nineteen, the bookseller and print vendor Henri-Furcy Goujon, was arrested for selling copies of the print. On 23 Thermidor, *Le Courrier républicain* hailed the anniversary of 10 August with the comment, "This was the day that saw the birth of the Republic amid mounds of corpses and a torrent of blood." On the twenty-eighth, it was said that the Convention was prolonging economic hardship on purpose "to force the people to call for the monarchy." On 2 Fructidor, Duval observed in jest that "everywhere hollow stomachs were crying out for vengeance, beating the call to arms and sounding the tocsin against the Convention." On the third, people were again saying that they had been happier under the king than under Robespierre. On 10 Fructidor, citizens throughout the city could be heard cursing the Revolution; in conversations, according to the police, people no longer had any qualms about wishing the return of the monarchy. On the fourteenth, an observer noted, "Hope for a monarchical government is spreading."

Yet there was one man who stood up against the erosion of public opinion that had begun shortly after the Prairial insurrection: the representative Louvet du Couvray, the author of the licentious *Aventures du chevalier de Faublas*. He had been outlawed as a Girondin in May, 1793, and, according to the jeunes gens, owed them his reinstatement in the Convention on 18 Ventôse, Year iii.

In Nivôse, when Fréron published his address to the jeunesse dorée, Louvet had taken up the same theme in the preface to his *Quelques notices pour l'histoire et le récit de mes périls depuis le 31 mai* (Some Notes for History and the Story of the Perils I Have Faced since 31 May): "If, emboldened by your generous temporizing, the bloodthirsty terrorists dare to raise their daggers again, then, brave youth, enough deliberation, enough vacillation: To arms, I say! To arms! Let us exterminate these murderers, these cannibals who devoured your fathers and all of your loved ones, and who will not hesitate to devour you too!"

Immediately upon his return to the Assembly he had lashed out at Barère and "his accomplices," called for a retrial of the Nantes revolutionary committee, and demanded that the property of condemned people be restored to their families. Tallien had only just managed to restrain Louvet in his frenzied hatred of the Jacobins, pointing out that they who had once been outlawed should not now condemn others in turn.

On 1 Prairial, Louvet had urged the jeunes gens to defend the Convention's proceedings, and on 24 Prairial he praised them again in Féraud's funeral oration, paying tribute to the Butte des Moulins Section – "a name which cannot be uttered without a strong feeling of gratitude."

But after being elected president of the Assembly on 1 Messidor, and then member of the Committee of General Security on the fifteenth, he suddenly switched sides. On 6 Messidor, at the invitation of the Committee of Public Safety, which provided him with premises and printing presses and paid for two thousand subscriptions, Louvet resumed publication, in quarto, of his newspaper *La Sentinelle*, which he had published as a bill in 1792. In the very first issue, he attacked the regiments of the "Royal Cravat" and castigated "humanity that kills in reactionary zeal."

According to Louvet, the jeunes gens were following in the footsteps of the terrorists of the Year II. Like them, they were "exclusives," since they claimed to represent all Parisian youth. Like them, they set themselves apart by wearing their hair and clothes in a distinctive fashion. Like them, they used hired lampoonists – an allusion to *Le Messager du Soir* – to libel the authorities. Like them, they organized gatherings – in this case, in the theatres – to impose their will upon the people. This was not the youth of 4 Prairial: "They were ten thousand, while these young men number fewer than a hundred." Furthermore, they were guilty of blatant deceit in claiming to be the sons of the victims of the Year II and calling themselves the youth of France, since most of them were either bastards, foreigners, or orphans. The youths of France were not in Paris, but in the fourteen armies of the Republic. Regardless of where they were, in Louvet's estimation they still ranked after older family heads, women, children, and the elderly.

On 26 Messidor, the anniversary of 14 July, the Convention made another provocative move when it decreed, on a motion by Jean de Bry, that "La Marseillaise" would be played by the relief guard every day at the Palais National, as well as by the music corps of the

National Guard and the regular troops of the line. That evening, the supporters of "Le Réveil du Peuple" and those of "La Marseillaise" came to blows at the Jardin Égalité. At the Café de Chartres and the Café de Valois, blame was laid on the Assembly's decree, which, it was said, recalled the massacres of September, 1792. There was a great commotion at the Théâtre des Arts, where "La Marseillaise" was interrupted to play "Le Réveil du Peuple," though, significantly, the couplet about the representatives was omitted.

On the morrow, the twenty-seventh, while Jean de Bry was explaining to the Convention that his decree of the day before had in no way been aimed at re-establishing the Terror but "at sustaining public spirit and rekindling the energy that drove the Revolution," the "youth in the order of the bourgeoisie" gathered at the changing of the guard and, by threatening to break the band's instruments, forced General Menou to have his men play "Le Réveil du Peuple." That evening, chaos reigned in the theatres: at the Vaudeville and the Opéra the spectators insisted on hearing "Le Réveil du Peuple," while at the République six youths leapt onto the stage and seized the actor Dugazon by the collar because he was too "Jacobin" for their liking.

Instead of yielding, as it had done on 20 Pluviôse under similar circumstances, the Committee of General Security decreed the next day, 28 Messidor, that henceforth no tune would be played in the theatres that was not part of the main performance. This meant that neither "La Marseillaise" nor "Le Réveil du Peuple" would be sung. Although there was no disruption of the changing of the guard that day, "Le Réveil du Peuple" was nevertheless sung in all the theatres, notably at the Théâtre des Arts, where Elléviou was "requisitioned" to perform it from a balcony while the audience in the stalls sang the chorus.

The unrest continued the following day, the 29th, at the Palais Égalité and in the theatres, with the jeunes gens calling for "Le Réveil du Peuple" and, wrote an observer, seeming prepared to fight anyone who dared voice any opposition. At the Théâtre des Arts, two actors from the Théâtre Français, Micalef and Gavaudan, and several other young men were arrested for disturbing the peace, while another group, led by the Palais Égalité procurer Charles-Louis Marquis, went to sing "Le Réveil du Peuple" outside Louvet's residence and shout insults at his wife. Louvet wrote in his newspaper,

What manner of country is this that a peaceful citizen can be disturbed in the refuge of his own home? That a representative of the people can have insults heaped on him and be threatened with violence? What manner of country is this? Did the *chouans* triumph? Are the English cohorts at our walls? ... Must one, in order not to be a terrorist, join a gang, frighten peaceful citizens in their homes and in the streets, tear down the placards of our brothers in the armies, and threaten to kill anyone who dares sing a song other than one's own? I must confess that I do not feel I have the strength to carry love of peace and public tranquillity to such extremes.

Despite his professed pacificism, Louvet had a bill posted the next day, 30 Messidor, encouraging soldiers to attack the jeunes gens. The text of the bill was reprinted in *La Sentinelle* on 3 Thermidor. Addressing the young men, Louvet wrote, "Miserable louts, think twice before you act! A hundred thousand republicans can easily be brought back from the armies at the front. Knowing this is so, perhaps you will be more prudent. Obey the law lest ... The Convention has but to utter a word, and you shall be exterminated."

This sparked a general uproar at the Théâtre des Arts that evening. There were still cutthroats in the Convention, clamoured the jeunes gens. Its ranks had to be purged. And the representative Gouly and his wife, who was nine months pregnant, were thrown out of the theatre most unceremoniously. Merlin de Thionville tried to make himself heard: "Do not forget that if you allow the return of the monarchy in Paris, our soldiers – whose opinions and attitudes I know very well – will vie with one another for the honour to come and destroy you, as well as your king."

But no one was listening, and even Adjutant-General Devaux, one of the victors of Charleroi and Fleurus, whom the Committee of General Security had dispatched to the theatre to restore order, was given a thrashing and dragged off to the Café de Chartres. Late in the evening, the young men went en masse to the Committee to call for Micalef and Gavaudan to be set free, and attempted to force their way into the Committee's offices. But the cavalry was standing guard. The jeunes gens were driven back, and eighty of them were detained. The Committee ordered the Café de Chartres closed "until further notice," and Souriguère, the composer of "Le Réveil du Peuple," was put under arrest. These radical measures overjoyed people in republican circles: Louvet scoffed, "Royal Cravat reduced to a strength of twenty," while Charles Germain, one of Babeuf's lieutenants, wrote from Arras, in reply to a letter from Guilhem,

Be sure to send me further news. After receiving your letter this morning, I cannot wait to hear more. Indeed, I am dying to hear more! Send me more, I shall devour it all ... Two hundred muscadins arrested, you say. So be it.

Now your turn has come, gentlemen, and your cafés, your square-cut coats, your hats à la Coburg, and your green collars will not do you any good! What long, livid faces they must have had! I can just imagine, thinking of the three who came to the Plessis while we were staying there. Ah! You thought you could do whatever you liked, gentlemen of the jeunesse dorée! But we must show no mercy. They must be forced to respect equality. No one has the right to raise himself above the common herd!

But to make such a fuss over the rout of the jeunesse dorée, wrote Mallet du Pan, was to overestimate this "youth in the order of the bourgeoisie." It had alienated any popular support it once had by its rowdy, reckless escapades, and even in the eyes of the bourgeoisie it had already lost all credibility as a political force. Otherwise, the Committee of General Security would no doubt have yielded to it, as it had in Pluviôse, Year III. This time, however, Fréron himself took the jeunes gens to task and praised Rouget de Lisle. In response to the Guillaume Tell Section, which had come to the Convention to call for the release of the young men, the president replied that they were letting themselves be led astray "by a handful of agitators, royalists, and émigrés" and that they were being deceived by their own enthusiasm for liberty. The pamphlets and posters that appeared the same day, urging the youths to remain calm, also testified to the bourgeoisie's repudiation of their efforts to stir up trouble.

If, after all of this, any complicity had still existed between the Assembly and the jeunes gens, the arrest of their journalists in the course of the next few days, the clashes between Louvet and Charles His over "Le Réveil du Peuple" and the release of Gavaudan, the establishment of a democratic press funded by the Committees and hostile to the youths, and the slaughter of Quiberon would have given it the quietus. The break between the jeunesse dorée and the Convention was complete and irrevocable.

BATTLE LINES ARE DRAWN

On 10 and 29 Germinal, Year III, a so-called Commission of Eleven had been established in the Assembly. In principle it was responsible for "drawing up the organic laws" needed to implement the Constitution of 1793, but in practice it ended up drafting a new one, different from the "scribbled placard" derided by Fréron. Having triumphed over the masses in Prairial, the bourgeoisie now wanted to see a strong government, "cherished by those who have something to preserve, and feared by the misguided multitude for whom order is disorder." The basic legislation of the new Constitution – all

377 articles – was introduced in the Convention on 5 Messidor and adopted on 30 Thermidor, after two months of debate. The bill provided for two-tier suffrage and divided legislative power between two assemblies, the Council of Ancients and the Council of Five Hundred, with a third of the members in each body coming up for re-election each year; executive power resided in a five-member Directory which was assisted by six ministers. Public opinion proved to be as indifferent to the debates as it was to Chinese jurisprudence, and only the professional speechifiers of the Palais Égalité took any interest in them, though chiefly in jest. Mallet du Pan reported, "This bill is horrific, some said. It provides for two chambers [*chambres*] but no dining room. You can say what you like about it, others replied. It will be accepted freely, under pain of death."

However, the Convention's members had become so unpopular by the end of their term that, dreading that they would be made to answer for their part in the regicide, the September massacres, and the bloody atrocities committed by the proconsuls of the Year II, and fearing that they might be handing over the new regime to the constitutional monarchists, who were counting on gaining power by legal suffrage, they were induced from the outset to rig the electoral system that they themselves had just established: by the decrees of 5 and 13 Fructidor, the so-called Two-Thirds Decrees, they hoped to ensure their own positions as members of the new legislative body, which would thus become a sort of politicians' oligarchy, an old boys' republic. The representatives in the Convention were intensely disliked by a broad spectrum of the public. It was said that the Convention had royalist sympathies, that it was in collusion with the profiteers who were starving the people, that it was orchestrating the famine and prolonging the disastrous economic situation in order to force the populace to call for the monarchy. Moreover, did the representatives of the people not dine sumptuously in restaurants every day? And did they not have wood, candles, and "everything else they needed" distributed to them at low prices? The argument ended with the wry conclusion, "They took a special interest in our prosperity, and now we know why, since we have nothing left!"

Well aware of how unpopular it had become, the Convention passed a decree on 5 Fructidor "on the means to end the Revolution," stipulating that two-thirds of the Convention's members would automatically become members of the new legislative body. A complementary decree was passed on 13 Fructidor specifying that if this proportion was not reached, the re-elected

Convention members would make it up by co-optation. The primary assemblies were scheduled to meet on 20 Fructidor to vote on the constitution and the re-election decrees and to name the electors, who would in turn name the deputies to the new assembly, which was to meet for the first time in the autumn. The Convention's shady schemers were thus arranging behind the scenes to keep themselves in power despite the institutional changes.

Liberal opinion reacted angrily to the decrees of 5 and 13 Fructidor. The enfranchised bourgeoisie, which had seen its social pre-eminence assured with the defeat of the sans-culottes, suddenly realized that a new political feudal system was being erected to bar its way to power. Was this not to deny the sovereignty of the people? This was the message immediately blazoned by the leading voices of the reactionary press: *La Quotidienne, Le Courrier de Paris, Le Messager du Soir, Le Postillon des Armées,* and *Le Courrier républicain.* In their view, the Assembly was nothing but a motley collection of crooked profiteers desperately trying to cling to power lest they be made to account for their heinous crimes. The scribes of this press were the same little clique of writers that had been described by Lacretelle, and mentioned by Mallet du Pan and Benjamin Constant. *Le Moniteur* reported that, following the Prairial uprising,

a campaign was launched to slander and smear the national representatives. A swarm of scurrilous lampoonists, taking advantage of the freedom of the press given to them by the very men they were base enough to insult, joined forces to chip away daily at the public trust that the Convention was doing its utmost to deserve. The youths seemed to regret their actions of early Prairial.

In addition to the newspapers, there were plenty of pamphlets: *Je ne veux ni de la moitié, ni du quart* (I Want Neither a Half Nor a Quarter of It), *Effaçons tout et recommençons* (Let Us Wipe the Slate Clean and Start Over), *J.-J. Dussault aux Assemblées primaires* (J.-J. Dussault to the Primary Assemblies), *Le Salut public* (Public Salvation), *J.-J. Marchéna aux Assemblées primaires* (J.-J. Marchéna to the Primary Assemblies), and so on. If we are to believe these journalists and pamphleteers, the Constituent Assembly was the source of all ills, and the Legislative Assembly, "vile in general and in the particular," had been full of scoundrels. As for the Convention, its membership had been "skimmed from the sewers of France and the cesspits of foreign countries." *Le Messager du Soir* concluded,

Ah! Du moins par pudeur, taureaux insatiables,
Vous êtes engraissés, regagnez vos étables.

(Oh! Out of shame, at least, you insatiable bulls
Who have grown fat, return to your stables.)

But the Convention fought back with its own slander. Its detractors were "a seditious minority" of hypocrites and perverts who
sought everywhere to incite revolt. On 1 Fructidor, Legendre lashed
out at Mme de Staël, recently returned from Switzerland, who invited deputies from all the parties to dine with her. "Even if they
swear they are incorruptible, can they guarantee me they will remain deaf to the seductive charms of these bewitching sirens?" On
3 Fructidor, Tallien did not hesitate to name names, denouncing
Ladevèze, erstwhile editor of *L'Ami du Roi*, the priest Poncelin, the
Spaniard Marchéna, and the editor of *L'Accusateur public*, Richer-
Sérizy, as "political insects" and "seedy hired slanderers." Sarcasm
was the chief weapon used against the jeunesse dorée itself, and
when the jeunes gens suddenly began wearing spectacles, to give
themselves the disability they needed to be exempted from conscription, *Le Courrier de Paris* expressed amazement that shortsightedness was so much in fashion: "It is truly quite extraordinary that
half of Paris has been shortsighted until now, and no one knew anything about it." A week later, on 23 Messidor, *Le Journal de Paris* published what has become a well-known piece, in which it argued that
the recently diagnosed myopia was symptomatic of a degeneration
of the human race.

The pathognomonic symptoms of this degeneration are, first, a total relax-
ation of the optic nerve, obliging the patient to wear eyeglasses at all times,
the necessity increasing with the proximity of objects; and second, a cooling
of the normal body temperature which can be combatted only by wearing a
very tight-fitting coat, fully buttoned up, and a cravat wrapped six times
around the neck so that it completely hides the chin and threatens to mask
the patient's face right up to the nose.

Another symptom was "progressive paralysis of the organs of
speech":

The poor young men who suffer from this paralysis take great pains to
avoid consonants and thus end up deboning the language, so to speak. The
clear enunciation, the vigorous pronunciation, the accented inflexions that
give a voice its charm are all off limits to them. Their lips appear barely to
move ... There is nothing less intelligible than a conversation between two
sufferers of this malady. The only words that can be made out in the series
of vowels are *ma pa'ole sup'ême, inc'oyable, ho'ïble* and others similarly disfigured. An uncommonly clever man attempted to translate into French what

he thought he could grasp of these phrases, but the insignificance of what he managed to comprehend put him off continuing such a sterile task.

In the same ironic vein, an *Édit de Charette en faveur des agioteurs, accapareurs, avaleurs, escroqueurs et exterminateurs de la fortune publique* (Edict of Charette in Favour of Speculators, Hoarders, Swallowers, Swindlers, and Exterminators of Public Wealth) recommended "to our brave youths who are such avid purchasers of green cravats, square-cut coats, and fine leather boots" that they spew forth all imaginable curses against the Convention. Finally, there is the following comparison between the jeunesse dorée and the military, which appeared in *Le Bonhomme Richard*:

They comb their earlocks; we take ten thousand prisoners at one fell swoop.
They write little peevish articles in little dreary newspapers; we strip them of muskets, caissons, munitions, baggage, and equipment.
They squawk in the theatres; we crush them at camp.
They put on cravats; we have mustaches.
They cut throats in the prisons; our volunteer generals carry them to hospital on their shoulders ...
They fabricate royal letters and monarchical lamentations in Paris; we raise flags over their forts we have conquered.
They sing high mass and vespers in chapels filled with old bigoted women; we strike up "La Marseillaise" on the fields of victory.
They eat chocolates to console themselves; we fire a hail of withering shot at their phalanxes.
They busy themselves with their clique; we go on manoeuvres.
They await a king like a messiah; we shall have a republican Constitution.
They are a handful; we are millions.

But sarcasm was also backed up with concrete measures. On 10 Thermidor, Aubry had a decree passed in the Convention granting deserters a general amnesty on the condition that they return to their army units within ten days. However, it went unheeded because the war commissioner (as we saw in an earlier chapter) did not have the staff to enforce it. Whence the futile mockery of *Le Bonhomme Richard* on 26 Thermidor:

What wonderful gibberish they speak. How titillating is their conversation. What tender souls they are. What a lovely smile they put on to announce the happy news of the murder of some *te'o'istes* by a *Compagnie du Soleil*. How sincerely they deplore the misery of the people, while awaiting their modest repast that will cost them a mere three hundred livres each.

And on 27 Thermidor:

I saw (and I am telling the police so that they make it their business, too) numerous women dressed as men with *chouan* cravats, low coat collars, and turned-up cuffs at the wrists. They looked good enough to eat in those adorable costumes. I mistook them for chasseurs of the Royal Army of Artois in casual dress.

On 15 Fructidor, the Committee of Public Safety took further measures against young men of the first conscription who sought refuge in Paris and who were the butt of "much sarcasm," noted the police:

"Before, they would beat the call to arms to rally us," the young men were saying in the cafés and the foyers of the theatres. "Now, when the sections are about to meet to vote on the Constitution, the Convention thinks it can get rid of us. We want to see what will come of this. The Convention hopes to clear us out of Paris so that it can do with the people what it likes. We won't stand for it. We want to be here to see for ourselves. We won't be intimidated by any soldiers."

The situation would have been different had the Assembly still been able to count on the National Guard, but the laws of 28 Germinal and 10 Prairial had weeded out the lower-class element, the first stipulating that cavalrymen, gunners, and fusiliers would henceforth pay for their own arms, the second authorizing craftsmen, labourers, and other workers to get out of doing service simply by reporting to the staff officer in their section. The result was a bourgeois National Guard loyal to the sections. Against this force the Convention had no counterweight but the army, which remained the stronghold of the old Jacobin spirit and would prove to be the infrangible rock on which the attempts at royalist restoration in Vendémiaire would shatter. Army regiments soon began arriving in the Marly camp from the provinces. This caused a great stir in liberal circles in the capital. On 9 Fructidor, people were saying that the Convention wanted to force its adversaries to accept the new Constitution. On the thirteenth, it was rumoured that "the bourgeois" were going to be disarmed. On the fourteenth, it was being said, rather wryly, that the Convention, "which was letting the people starve to death," was about to make a show of strength to draw attention to its glorious exploits. On 11 Fructidor, the Mail Section appeared before the Assembly:

Why all these troops around Paris? Are we under siege or are we about to be ... Because we demand that our country's oppressors be brought to justice, we are accused of wanting a return of the Terror. Because we wear black or green collars, we are accused of being *chouans* ... Has the National Guard shown itself so disloyal that it must be surrounded by the army? People are saying that the Vendée rebellion is spreading. Well, then! Let our brothers in arms go win new laurels; we shall stand guard here at home.

This petition was given a noisy reception. Immediately afterward, a deputation from the Champs Élysées Section, led by the younger Lacretelle, was shown in. If the Assembly had been oppressed, it was because the tyrants had managed to find accomplices in its ranks. Whether it had successfully rid itself of these henchmen was up to the primary assemblies to decide. "Step forward confidently and let the people vote," concluded Lacretelle. "Earn their choice, rather than command it."

Amidst a complete uproar in the Assembly, Tallien – who now wore his hair straight, who had been deserted by the beautiful Thérésia Cabarrus, whom the jeunes gens had hounded to his very doorstep, and who was now regarded as a buveur de sang – shot back by accusing Lacretelle of being a deserter. He argued that Lacretelle was one of a coterie of former royalist deputies from the Legislative Assembly who had taken safe positions as journalists. Whenever there was any question of going to fight at the front, these men immediately asked to be conscripted into government administration. The only place they were courageous was in the theatres. Tallien, who had long been associated with the jeunesse dorée, knew his opponent's weak points. Lacretelle had to resign himself to responding by way of a pamphlet, in which he denounced Tallien as one of the butchers of the September massacres. On 16 Fructidor, the Le Peletier Section appeared before the Convention:

But, legislators, the more we trust you, the less we can believe that you have ceased to count on our courage to defend liberty against its enemies at home. Are you afraid that the citizens of Paris may have already forgotten the blessing of 9 Thermidor? ... Was it not in this very hall that they restored freedom of debate on 1 Prairial? Since the two expeditions of 4 Prairial, have they ceased to be worthy of the fond interest and paternal solicitude that you displayed toward them during those tumultuous days?

Seeing that they would not succeed in persuading the Assembly to order the withdrawal of the troops, the leaders of the sections attempted to win the good will of the soldiers. On 20 Fructidor the

Fidélité Section declared that it had found all the armed citizens on the outskirts of Paris to be "brothers and friends." On the twenty-second, the Panthéon Section addressed "its armed brethren in the camps around Paris" to warn them against treacherous insinuations from malicious sources. On the twenty-fourth, the Roule Section addressed "all soldiers of all ranks" in the armies of the Republic:

Brave soldiers, you want the Republic; we want the Republic. You have accepted the republican Constitution; we have accepted the republican Constitution. You want liberty and equality; we want liberty and equality. You want a stable government; we want a stable government. You want people and property to be respected; we want people and property to be respected. You do not want the scaffold to be raised again; we do not want the scaffold to be raised again. You do not want civil war; we do not want civil war. Thus we share the same opinions, the same sentiments, the same wishes. And yet we are being threatened with you!

On 10 Vendémiaire, Year IV, the Pont Neuf Section, making "an inviolable vow of friendship to its brothers in the armies of the Republic," warned them that dangerous groups were gathering in public places, that these gatherings were being used by malicious people to slander the young citizens of Paris, and that this slander was particularly insulting to men who had shown their bravery and courage during the turbulent events of Prairial by being the first to rally to the support of the Convention.

But it was farcical to suggest that the jeunes gens and the soldiers had the same political ideals. This was evident on 6 Messidor, when an adjutant-general got into a row with a group of black-collared youths at the Palais Égalité; likewise on the evening of 18 Thermidor, when a group of young men singing "Le Réveil du Peuple" set upon a soldier who was singing "La Marseillaise," and on 14 Fructidor, when a scuffle took place at the Palais Égalité between soldiers and green- and black-collared youths, a scuffle that would have turned very ugly had many people not intervened.

The primary assemblies opened finally on 20 Fructidor. The Convention had decreed that no citizen could be turned away from the assemblies and that a section card was sufficient for admission; but Zivy has found that in some ten sections the patriots were thrown out of the meetings, and in the others it is easy to imagine what kind of hearing they must have been given. Le Courrier des Amis de la Paix commented, "Look at all the thugs from Maillard's troop and the former Committee of General Security. Note their daunting, insolent air, as if they are already threatening the honnêtes gens. Under such circumstances, great governors, how can you blame the sections for driving away these men, men whose hands are stained with the blood of murder?"

The section leaders had a well-thought-out plan. They would accept the Constitution, reject the decrees, and then, before naming the electors, themselves decree that the deputies' powers would expire on 10 Vendémiaire; that the electors would meet as early as possible to hold elections, regardless of the decrees; and that the primary assemblies would break up only after the new legislative body had met.

The Le Peletier Section took the initiative. ("It was an affluent quarter, and yet a courageous one, too," quipped Lacretelle.) On 20 Fructidor the section adopted a "bill of safeguard" which left Parisians under the protection of their primary assemblies – as though they had been threatened by the Convention – and then informed the Convention that, since the people had now regained their sovereign rights, its legislative duties were over. Following its lead, most of the sections declared themselves in permanent session, and each thus became a source of revolt against the Convention. In the sessions, the jeunes gens whipped up the crowds "in an oratorical frenzy," urging on the cowards, firing up the fainthearts, and stoking the exasperation of the hotheads. All the leading lights of the jeunesse dorée did their bit: Lacretelle in the Champs Élysées Section, Chauveau-Lagarde and Bertin in Unité, Dussault and Léger in Tuileries, La Harpe, Beaulieu, and Lezay-Marnézia in Butte des Moulins, Ladevèze in Le Peletier, Michaud, Nicole, Fiévée, and Richer-Sérizy in Théâtre Français, Lebrun in Brutus, Brousse des Faucherets in Arsenal, Chéron in Roule, Souriguère in Piques, Isidore Langlois in Louvre, and elsewhere Dupont de Nemours, Pastoret, Vaublan, Quatre-mère de Quincy, Suard, Poncelin, Morellet, Marchéna, Martainville, and others. In all sections there were fierce attacks on the members of the Convention, "rogues reeking of carnage and awash in the spoils of plunder," "profoundly perfidious men, who thirsted for loot and incited slaughter." A Constitution adopted by twenty-five million men and defended by more than a million soldiers, asserted the Le Peletier Section on 26 Fructidor, did not need the support of five hundred individuals who had always led public opinion astray with their hireling journalists, their inflammatory posters, and their deceitful reports, not to mention the slander spread in the armies against the communes and in the communes against the armies. *Le Messager du Soir* warned "the old fraternity" that it would soon have to account for its crimes and deceit; a royalist pamphlet, *Mon Dernier*

Mot aux Parisiens (My Last Word to Parisians), denounced by Tallien on the third *jour sans-culottide*, urged people in no uncertain terms – "Kill them!" – to take up arms to exterminate the deputies. But the section leaders were in such a frenzy that they repeatedly menaced the Convention members, telling them that they would be duly punished as soon as they left the corridors of power, and were then astonished when the members delayed leaving their posts. After having convinced them, with very compelling evidence, that power was their aegis, the sections then accused them of seeking to cling to power! A similar frenzy had gripped the Convention's deputies, who likened themselves to defendants who fear a verdict and who, to prevent it from being rendered, occupy the judges' seats.

Meanwhile, the sections appeared one after another before the Assembly to announce that they had accepted the Constitution but rejected the decrees: the Unité Section on 25 Fructidor, the Place Vendôme, Nord, and Cité sections on the twenty-sixth, the Observatoire, Fidélité, and Théâtre Français sections on the twenty-seventh, and so on. The young man whom the Théâtre Français Section had chosen as its spokesman wound up his speech thus: "I warn the Convention that in just a few days the truth will be clear for all to see. You too will see it, but it will be too late!"

The awaited truth was the rejection of the re-election decrees, a result which seemed certain, since only one section, the Quinze Vingts, had accepted them. Consequently, when the deputy Gomaire appeared before the Convention on 1 Vendémiaire on behalf of the Decree Committee to announce the results of the voting in the 6,337 primary assemblies, and declared that the Constitution had been accepted by 914,853 votes to 41,892, and the decrees by 167,758 votes to 95,373, cries that the results had been tampered with resounded throughout the capital. Indeed, for Paris itself the votes of thirty-three sections had been counted as nil, on the pretext that the rejection had been recorded as unanimous, without any indication of the number of voters. The fraud was obvious, and it was said openly that the returns had been faked. "If the government were to proclaim today that two and two do not make four," asked the Le Peletier Section, "would the people of France be bound by that proclamation?" Following its lead, a dozen sections refused to recognize the "acceptance" of the Fructidor decrees. Throughout Paris the promulgators of the decree were jeered, caned, or arrested.

That evening, the Palais Égalité was calm save for a scene at the bookshop run by Brigitte Mathey: the patriot Gonchon shouted that he would whip the crowd of "royalists" who were there, just as he had whipped the Jacobin women when the Club had been forced to close. In itself this was a harmless incident, but it foreshadowed what was to come. In the days that followed, the entire Palais Égalité flared up. On 2 Vendémiaire, some Convention grenadiers had a set-to with a group of green- and black-collared youths – "men," explained Delaunay to the Assembly the next day, "whose only allegiance is to the Jardin Égalité, young men of the first conscription who, rather than be at the front with our brave brothers in arms, prefer to set up camp permanently in the garden."

The Marquis de Montaran, a noted skirt-chaser of twenty-two who had managed to land a safe post in military transport, was patrolling the garden toward late afternoon at the head of a group of fifteen or so youths when he had his henchmen give the Inspector-General of the Armies of Italy, Sylvain Matheron, a good thrashing for saying that "the deployment of the armed forces should not disturb those who cherish order and peace." The same treatment was meted out to the veteran Jean-François Arnaud: soon after applauding a crier's announcement about the capture of Mannheim, he appeared before the police commissioner of the Butte des Moulins Section, "his head wrapped in a kerchief and his clothes spattered with blood."

In late afternoon of the following day, the third, again at the Palais Égalité, Convention grenadiers were called bloodthirsty butchers and Swiss, and were told menacingly that they would get their throats cut, just like the Swiss Guards. Then someone fired a pistol at them and ran off to take refuge at the Café de Chartres. Shortly thereafter, at around eight o'clock, some two hundred young men marched along the rue de Thionville shouting "Down with the Two-Thirds!" And at nine o'clock, at the Pont au Change, a sizeable crowd of "terrorists" and "green collars" hurled abuse at one another, spoiling for a fight. Afterward, the jeunes gens split up and went through the sections, calling for people to take up arms and shouting that citizens were being shot at. While the youths had their own way in Butte des Moulins, where they set upon the saddler François Bucquet with their clubs, the Popincourt Section told them "that if it was true that shots were being fired, it could only be at Royalists, and that the section was going to halt its proceedings to fire too."

That night, a worried Convention sat until half past one in the morning drafting a proclamation to Parisians which condemned "a handful of schemers, agitators, anarchists, and murderers" who wanted to plunge the country into the horrors of civil war. "If the Convention, left without any support, were to perish within your walls," the proclamation read, "all of France would call you to account for your weakness."

This was followed by a decree rendering Paris answerable and responsible to the French people for the preservation of the national representative body and stipulating that in the event of a conspiracy the Assembly would move its deliberations to Châlons sur Marne. Then the order was given to the generals "to keep the republican columns ready to march." The Le Peletier Section retaliated immediately with an address to the Assembly:

The men we have just honoured with our trust you dare call schemers, anarchists, and murderers! Well, take a closer look at yourselves. Your clothes are stained with innocent blood. Thousands of your constituents have had their throats cut, cities have been destroyed, trade has been wiped out, probity outlawed, immorality, atheism, and brigandage deified, anarchy and famine organized, public funds squandered – this is your work.

Circulating around this time were many copies of a pamphlet entitled *Massacre horrible commis par les terroristes sur les jeunes gens au Palais-Égalité* (Dreadful Massacre of Young Men by Terrorists at the Palais Égalité). Yet, as Albert Mathiez has astutely pointed out, such slander was merely for the gallery. The real question at stake was not what type of regime – monarchy or republic – but which of two rival teams of politicians would win the legislative mandate.

Two minor incidents occurred on the following day, 4 Vendémiaire. At the Palais Égalité, Brigadier-General François Vachot, accused of being a Convention informer, was rescued by the guard at the last minute from a mob that was about to give him a beating. In Butte des Moulins, patriots who declared their support for the Convention and announced that "they would wipe their behinds with" the Sections' *billets de garde* (orders to report for National Guard service) were led off to the primary assembly by three men from the Mail Section, one of whom was a twenty-three-year-old dancer by the name of Jacques-Charles Joly. Meanwhile, at the Convention, grand, solemn statements were being made against the gilded youths, "*ces petits messieurs*," said Bentabolle, who were to be seen everywhere in public administration and government offices, where they did nothing, "absolutely nothing." Quirot added,

You have enemies, but who are they? Primarily the youths who meet at the Palais Égalité to take part in seditious gatherings ... I denounce these men who refuse to serve their country, these men who wear no other uniform than that of the *chouans*, who conduct their campaign solely at the Palais Égalité and in the theatres and who, though showered with favours from the government, declare themselves to be its greatest enemies.

Agreeing with his fellow deputies, Roux also denounced the jeunes gens as "the very ones" who spread slander. Merlin de Douai said that ever since he and Le Tourneur had been made responsible for the Guerre Section, they had "been rebuked endlessly" over their steadfastness in refusing requisitions. Special measures were obviously necessary. The Committee of Public Safety had a decree passed stipulating that any citizen of the first conscription arrested in a gathering prejudicial to public order would, on this account alone, be deemed an architect and promoter of a conspiracy to destroy the national representative body and would be handed over to the courts as guilty of conspiring against the security of the state. Subsequently, Tallien had a motion carried revoking all deferments of military call-up granted thus far. This was certainly a radical step.

Nonetheless, a few incidents did occur on the following two days: minor ones on 5 Vendémiaire, and rather more serious ones on the sixth. On the fifth, when the Quinze Vingts Section went to the Convention to declare its loyalty to the Republic, a thirty-year-old shopkeeper by the name of Paillier, known as Delille, of the Fontaine Grenelle Section, shouted from the public galleries that the Quinze Vingts was the section of the blind. Though said in jest, it was sufficient to warrant Delille's arrest. Also put under arrest was Louis-César Jardin, twenty-one, "engaged in the study of literature," who had asserted to people at the Palais Égalité that during the scuffle of the third the grenadiers had shot first. For the sixth, I found records of two arrests, that of a certain Crosnier, who was implicated in a chair-swinging brawl with soldiers at the Palais Égalité, and that of one Germain-André Goureau, of the Poissonnière Section, who was dragged before the Butte des Moulins police commissioner by four men who had heard him say "that he would make all the jeunes gens of Paris kiss his arse."

After the sixth, nothing more was reported. Indeed, things were so calm on the seventh that a worried deputy, Pocholle, had a decree passed instructing the Committees to report daily on the situation in the capital. "Whence comes this sudden calm, after the disturbances of the last few days?" he asked in puzzled astonishment. In my view, it can be attributed partly to the Convention's threatening legislation, but chiefly to the efforts of the primary assemblies to control the jeunes gens. Two documents testify to these efforts. The first, an *Invitation aux jeunes citoyens* (Invitation to Young

Citizens) from the Brutus Section, dated 4 Vendémiaire, urged the youths to work within the primary assembly, where "the large tribune would be made specially available to them," rather than in the streets and squares: "Brave youths, courageous vanguard of the battalions of 1 Prairial, you who defended the national representatives with an energy worthy of your age ... come into our midst. Avoid these hired informers who, dressed in your guise, would commit murder in your name." The other document, entitled *Aux jeunes gens* (To the Young Men), dated 7 Vendémiaire and originating in the Théâtre Français Section, is much harsher in tone:

Yet another incident at the Palais Égalité! Young citizens, will your petulance always lead you into the malicious traps set to cause not just your downfall but that of your family, friends, liberty, and the Republic? ... Young citizens, do you want to spark civil war over trifles, when your parents, in the people's assemblies, are content to proceed coolly with the agenda without regard to barbarous decrees that send them to their death as a recompense for their zealous defence of liberty! ... When the people are assembled, their rights are not to be defended in the city's streets and squares ... The Théâtre Français primary assembly urges you to avoid all gatherings in public places.

Thus it appears that the jeunes gens' reckless, wanton violence had become a cause of concern even for their supporters. The youths' unruly conduct negated the primary assemblies' attempts to circumvent the military and, what is more, drove the government Committees to consolidate the means of repression at their disposal in preparation for the revolt that the police reports said was growing increasingly likely. The young men were to transfer their fanaticism from the streets to the primary assemblies and, by pushing hyperbole and demagogy to the extreme, were to carry the liberal bourgeoisie much further than it would perhaps have gone without them. Now that the antagonistic political forces had polarized, battle lines were drawn, and insurrection was brewing.

VENDÉMIAIRE AND THE ROUT OF THE JEUNESSE DORÉE

On 7 Vendémiaire, a deputation representing twenty-three Paris sections went to the Convention to advise it that its powers, now that the people were meeting in primary assemblies, were de facto nonexistent and that its duties would henceforth be limited to those of a caretaker government, "because there always has to be one of

some sort." The deputation also intended to demand that the terror-
ists be put back behind bars and that the conduct of the government
Committees be investigated. But the Assembly, presided over by
Beaudin, refused to give it a hearing.

Unrest broke out in Châteauneuf, Chartres, Verneuil, and No-
nancourt, and on 10 Vendémiaire news arrived that the representative Duval, leading some two hundred men, had defeated a troop of
rebels at Dreux, killing ten and taking thirty prisoner. This time
there was no mistaking that a return to the Terror was imminent,
and the Le Peletier Section wasted no time in dispatching commissioners to the other sections to ask,

Is this oh so unhappy country soon to become a desert littered with human
remains? Are we to see a return to those days of horror and carnage that we
experienced? Are the scaffolds to be raised again, and the Bedouin fire to be
lit? Shall we again see old people and children disappear under the waves?
Shall we again hear the volleys of Collot's firing squads?

A decree read at the same time announced that a meeting of the
electors of the Commune of Paris would be held at the Théâtre
Français on the morrow, 11 Vendémiaire. This was an illegal meeting, since the Convention had set 20 Vendémiaire as the date when
the electorate would meet to name the deputies of the new legislative body. As a result, only eighty electors attended, representing
just fifteen or so sections, all of them centrally located: Théâtre
Français, Amis de la Patrie, Unité, Fontaine Grenelle, Mont Blanc,
Place Vendôme, Le Peletier, Arsenal, Champs Élysées, Brutus,
Droits de l'Homme, Butte des Moulins, Bonne Nouvelle, and Tuileries. Some thirty-three sections declined to participate, and thus
the strategy was a failure.

The meeting foundered in ridiculous pomposity. Some one hundred men – jeunes gens, lugging huge sabres, and a handful of chasseurs and grenadiers – formed an honour guard of sorts at the door
of the Théâtre Français. Inside, in the semi-darkness of a huge hall
where just the odd candle was burning, the rebel leaders put on solemn faces and pretended to be busy. The old Duc de Nivernais had
agreed to preside, after much hesitation. "You are leading me to my
death," he said to those who were pressuring him; then, caught up
in the enthusiasm, he declared "that on seeing the peril," he felt "the
ice of old age melting away," and finally accepted. Since there was
nothing else to do, wrote Lacretelle, the electors made exalted
pledges to the cause. Thus, Lallemant, the acting president, said, "If

you hear it said that someone has perished, I ask you to pray for me, because I shall be no more."

In the evening, two officials, flanked by six dragoons and trumpeters, appeared on the square in front of the theatre to proclaim a Convention decree ordering the assembly to disband immediately. They were booed by a crowd of young men with earlocks, and the electors responded to the proclamation by declaring themselves henceforth in permanent session. There being nothing for them to do, however, they eventually grew bored, and decided to go home to bed. When a column dispatched by the Committee of General Security arrived to disperse them late in the evening, it found the hall empty.

That evening, however, the Le Peletier, Butte des Moulins, Contrat Social, Théâtre Français, Brutus, Temple, and Poissonnière sections declared themselves to be in a state of rebellion. The Committees retaliated immediately by setting up a five-member commission responsible for "enforcing the law"; since the troops available seemed insufficient, they decided to arm the sans-culottes, who were organized into a unit with the pompous name of *Le Bataillon sacré des patriotes de 1789* (Sacred Battalion of the Patriots of '89). "There was no better way to fight adversaries such as these," said Barras of the jeunes gens, "than to set their natural enemies, the patriots imprisoned in the wake of Thermidor, against them." These were men who had been disarmed after the Prairial uprising, and who had just recently "escaped from their sections, where violent threats had been made against them." Some 1,500 sans-culottes were assembled and, like the regular troops, were given rations, brandy, weapons, and ammunition. But since Menou refused to command this "heap of rogues and murderers organized as patriots of '89," they were put under the command of General Berruyer. Their involvement was to prove decisive, but its initial effect was to spark an explosion. Hitherto, the jeunesse dorée had agitated unavailingly, chiefly because its royalist links made it suspect in the eyes of the shopkeepers of the lower-middle class. Only twenty-three sections had signed the address of 7 Vendémiaire, and a mere fifteen or so had been represented at the Théâtre Français assembly of electors. But in the rearming of the terrorists the honnêtes gens saw the reappearance of the horrifying spectre of the Year II. The Fontaine Grenelle Section feigned indignation at what it claimed was an attempt to debase the national representative body – "this plan to dishonour the National Convention by recruiting an army of cutthroats to protect it, this treacherous plan which suggests that crime alone has an interest in its defence, that the national representative body no longer represents France and that its real constituents are rotting in the prisons and rowing in the galleys."

The Gardes Françaises Section fulminated against the decision to arm "the hired killers of the decemvirate, whose presence in the ranks they regard as an appalling outrage." The government Committees thus created the very danger they had congratulated themselves on avoiding, and so brought about the insurrection by a measure aimed at suppressing it.

On the morning of Sunday, 12 Vendémiaire, the Le Peletier Section, followed by some fifteen others, proclaimed to the beat of the drum that the Committees were rearming the buveurs de sang and called all good citizens to arms. The government retaliated by ordering General Menou, assisted by the representative Delaporte, to march into the section with his troops. General Desperrière had come down with a sudden fever and had retired to bed, although just a few hours before he had appeared to be in very good health. In the meantime, the Committees suspended shipment of the main opposition newspapers to the departments and ordered the matrices and plates used in printing the assignats brought to the Convention. In the early evening, three columns marched on the section's administrative headquarters – the convent of the Filles St Thomas – the first by the rue de la Loi, the second by the rue Vivienne, and the third by the rue des Victoires. The entrance was guarded by a battalion of jeunes gens under the command of Delalot, the president of the primary assembly. When summoned by the deputy Delaporte to tell his men to lay down their arms, he replied solemnly,

What do you want from us? Our arms, which we have never used save in your defence. Who are your defenders? The rogues who cut your throats, whom we defeated fighting at your side, and whom we disarmed on your orders. What cannons are you lining up against us? Ours, which we surrendered to you voluntarily. Of what are you accusing us? The legitimate exercise of our rights. We paid with our own blood to defend the liberty of your deliberations, and you violate ours in defiance of all the laws.

The two sides advanced until they crossed bayonets, but they did not open fire. Delaporte preferred to negotiate, and proposed to the rebels that if they dispersed, the Convention's troops would withdraw. Menou, who sympathized with the section's insurgents, ratified the proposal by threatening to cut down the first soldier who took it into his head "to insult the good citizens of Le Peletier." So the troops withdrew, but no sooner had they marched off than the rebels took up their positions again. The government force had been duped, and with renewed courage the insurgents decided it was their turn to lay siege to the Convention.

They immediately set up an ad hoc organization consisting of a central committee, chaired by Richer-Sérizy; a military committee, which included among its members the former bodyguard Lafond, Dufaillant, and barons Delaporte and Defortisson; and an eleven-member special tribunal, on which sat, among others, Richer-Sérizy, Burgurieux, Mésange, Saint-Julien, Fitte, Delalot, Gérard de Bury, and Vasselin, allegedly "the most fearsome" of the lot. General Danican, whom Zivy describes as "a versatile but vain personage," was named commander-in-chief of the rebel forces; he arrived in Paris on 12 Vendémiaire and took up his duties on the morning of the thirteenth.

In the Convention, meanwhile, the representatives were voicing their indignation: "We have been betrayed! Arrest the traitor Menou!" Overcome with rage, the Committees relieved him of his command and replaced him with Barras, "the general of 9 Thermidor" who was regarded as a great military leader because he carried a large sabre. Barras immediately called on the services of General Napoleon Bonaparte, who was a total unknown at the time, as well as on other officers reputed to be Jacobins who had been put on reserve duty following Aubry's purging of the upper ranks in late Prairial. Then he set about preparing the defence of the Tuileries. At this point the Convention could count only on the regular troops of the Marly camp, the inchoate police corps, and a few detachments of grenadiers – perhaps five thousand men in all, for whom there were just eighty thousand cartridges. But Bonaparte had learnt from Menou that there were forty guns at the Sablons camp, and he wasted no time in dispatching Murat with three hundred cavalry to fetch them. A rebel force from the sections had already reached the camp, but Murat managed to beat it to the guns (this was later to prove decisive) and bring them back to the Tuileries, where provisions were being stocked in preparation for a siege. In the meantime, Fréron, whose nerve evidently knew no bounds, betook himself to the Faubourg Antoine to ask the Quinze Vingts Section for reinforcements, and returned with a contingent of 250 men. Calls had gone out to the Indivisibilité, Gravilliers, Gardes Françaises, and Panthéon sections, but without success. Lastly, even the representatives armed themselves with muskets.

Throughout the night of the twelfth to thirteenth, the drums beat the call to arms in the sections. At about half past midnight, the

Réunion Section's civil committee had a set-to with "some young citizens" who had seized the big drum and had begun to beat it. In Arcis, when it was heard that the other sections were calling to arms, a crowd of jeunes gens rushed off to the brigade leader's house to ask him to lead them. In the morning, an adjutant-general, who had gleaned the information from "some rather indiscreet young men," reported to Barras that the attack on the Convention was scheduled for four o'clock. "Why not four in the morning?" joked Barras, to which the reply was that "no doubt the estimable bourgeois of Paris, as in the days of the Cardinal de Retz, were incapable of changing their regular hours." It was rumoured that the bloodthirsty terrorists were preparing to cut the throats of women, children, and the elderly. On the afternoon of the thirteenth, some seven to eight thousand men from the rebel sections began surrounding the Convention. Danican was commanding on the left bank, Lafond on the right. Both sides had been ordered not to shoot first. When the Convention's troops and the insurgents found themselves face to face, at around four o'clock as expected, the initial impulse on both sides was to fraternize. For the Convention, such a turn of events could have been disastrous. Combat was absolutely essential. At about half past five, a shot was fired, possibly by Dubois-Crancé from the Vénua restaurant, and the battle was on. Thanks to the artillery from the Sablon camp, the Convention's forces quickly gained the upper hand, and by half past nine the insurgents had been crushed and had gone home to bed like good bourgeois. A Lieutenant Enée mockingly described them fleeing before a hackney coach that they had mistaken for a cavalry charge. A further attempt by the sections to mobilize the property-owners with the rumour that the Convention was going to allow its soldiers two hours of looting went unheeded. By the morning of the fourteenth, all that remained in session at the Le Peletier Section was the president's bell. There were some two to three hundred dead on each side, but the insurrection had been put down. "The Republic," concluded Lacretelle, quite rightly, "believed that it had triumphed, but it triumphed under the protection of a warrior who was soon to destroy it."

It remains to assess the jeunesse dorée's role in this last day of revolutionary struggle. To judge by the accounts of contemporaries, it must have been considerable. We know from Lacretelle that the young men had assisted in the preparations for the insurrection with "impetuous impatience." It is thus not surprising to hear Barras describe the insurgents as "fops in silk stockings, with long sabres at their sides; perfumed soldiers who thought they could handle gun carriages. These beardless Catilines, who sang the latest arietta instead of loading their weapons, were called *des pa'ole d'honneu' à la victime."*

Among the dead were many green and black collars but few shopkeepers, who, though carried along with the crowd, had remained at the rear. In a report on deserters dated 2 Brumaire, Year IV, General Loison recommended to the Committee of Public Safety that it take harsh measures against the jeunes gens who had fled military service and whom he described as the government's most relentless enemies. They had been the most ardent rebels on 13 Vendémiaire, he said. Police reports confirmed this: it had been "the electoral party, backed by *chouans*, journalists, fine ladies, and *queues retroussées*" (literally, hitched-up pigtails). The reactionary song-writer Ange Pitou was of the same opinion: "The sections' skirmishers are the government Committees' former militiamen." A variety of sources support this claim. The patriot Palloy, who on 5 Brumaire, Year IV, offered the Legislative Body a medal cast with the lead of Vendémiaire bullets, spoke of "royal grenadiers, Palais Royal chasseurs, the *Enfants Jésus* behind bars, and the *chouans*." The printer Bonneville boasted of having "foiled all the manoeuvres of those treacherous *cadenettes*." These remarks are corroborated by the *Almanach de Polichinelle*, which refers to the insurgents as "men with raised pigtails, green collars, green cravats, and fine boots, men who sing "Le Réveil du Peuple" and say *ma pa'ole sup'ême*." But the most telling testimony is that of J.-J. Dussault, Fréron's assistant, who after falling out with him vented his anger in a pamphlet dated Germinal, Year IV. In the pamphlet he claims to have written the speeches that Fréron delivered in the Convention and all the copy for *L'Orateur du Peuple*, while Fréron simply corrected the proofs. As for the Vendémiaire insurrection, Dussault asserts that the jeunes gens monopolized the sections' rostrums in the days preceding the rebellion and that the uprising failed because of their immaturity:

The youths who were called upon to fight in the insurrection were also given responsibility for the deliberations. The same fervour they showed, under your auspices, Fréron, and under your command, in repulsing the brigands of Prairial, they also took with them to the speaker's platforms of the deliberative assemblies, those tribunes that they alone occupied and from which they consistently excluded more mature men. This aroused a sort of secret envy among those who were reduced to the role of mere listeners – disciples, in effect – and while this envy did not sink the undertaking, it certainly did little to help it along. Whence the rash measures, the recklessness, and the mistakes.

Thus it was a bourgeois insurrection, but one which, had it been successful, might well have turned to the advantage of the royalists who were its chiefs of staff: Richer-Sérizy, Lacretelle, and their associates.

But the insurrection was put down with a restrained hand. The Convention, it was said, triumphed with moderation. Groups of insurgents surrounded at the Tuileries were sent home by Barras on the night of 13 Vendémiaire, while suspects brought before the Committee of General Security were released immediately. This clemency was pushed to such an extreme that on the evening of the fourteenth, Bordas and Taveaux had a decree passed against Collombel de la Meurthe suspending the releases. It was quashed, however, by another the next day which authorized the Committee of General Security to "release the individuals arrested in connection with the uprisings of 12, 13, and 14 Vendémiaire." On 22 Vendémiaire, Garrau disclosed to the Assembly that on the thirteenth the Committee of General Security, overwhelmed with work, had set up a five-member (actually six-member) commission "occupied solely with deciding the fate of the *chouans*, royalists, and rogues who sought to kill you." It was continuing to issue releases, he added. The president of the Convention even congratulated General Berruyer and a deputation of soldiers for the "moderation and generosity they had shown, after victory had been assured, in dealing with those who had dared to take up arms." The contrast with Prairial was striking, and a certain Roullin, on 22 Vendémiaire, wrote to Merlin de Douai, then a member of the Committee of Public Safety:

The people, who are not privy to the government's policy, are making very accurate comparisons between current measures and those of Prairial. Tread carefully ... Thus the people recall that after 1 Prairial the patriots were taken by the cartload to the scaffold and that now the rebels are travelling post on the highways. Deal a strong blow, but a fair one.

These remarks are corroborated by the same day's police reports:

Some people point out that the Prairial insurgents were less guilty than those of 13 Vendémiaire, since the former merely demanded bread, whereas the latter sought to attack and wipe out the national representative body. Yet, they say, the Prairial rebels were crushed much more swiftly and harshly than those of 13 Vendémiaire, with whom the Convention appears to commiserate.

On 15 Vendémiaire, the men from the insurgent sections went to hand over their arms, as women from the lower classes looked on derisively, recalling 4 Prairial, and shouted at them, "Come, lily-livers, your turn now!" Thirty-five thousand two hundred and two persons were disarmed that day, including 1,933 from Butte des Moulins, 1,637 from Le Peletier, 1,110 from Gardes Françaises, 1,095 from Théâtre Français, and 1,087 from Unité. With its militia-men disarmed, the National Guard was reduced to the realm of fiction. A decree was passed abolishing its general staff and its companies of gunners, and stipulating that it would henceforth consist only of infantry, that there would be only one drum per section, and that in future no proclamation would be made to the beat of the drum save by order of the general-in-chief of the Army of the Interior. This general-in-chief was no other than Napoleon Bonaparte, who had been an obscure figure only a few days before Vendémiaire. The history of the National Guard ends with him.

The repression also involved the proceedings of three military courts set up on 15 Vendémiaire to try the insurgents. Ironically, Barras had them sit in the administrative headquarters of the Théâtre Français, Le Peletier, and Butte des Moulins sections. Most of the accused – presidents and secretaries of the primary assemblies – had managed to flee thanks to the connivance of the Committee of General Security, which had left the city's gates open for a few days. Delalot, Castellane, Saint-Julien, Vaublanc, Ladevèze, Danican, and their associates were sentenced to death in absentia. Those who remained in Paris were given prison sentences or were fined. Menou, under Bonaparte's protective wing, was acquitted, and in the end only two men were executed: Lebois, the president of Théâtre Français, who, it was thought, after he had stabbed himself several times with a bayonet, would be better put out of his misery; and Henri Lafond, Louis XVI's former bodyguard, whom the president of the military court evidently tried to save, but who brought on his own demise by his unmitigated insolence:

"Do you admit that you led a troop of insurgents against the Convention on the thirteenth?"
"I would have a hard time denying it. My broken leg and this mean bed I am lying on are clear proof."
"But no doubt foreign influences pushed you to commit such an imprudent, reprehensible act?"

"Not at all. I acted of my own free will."

"But I believe that you did not act with the intention of overthrowing the government of the Convention?"

"I certainly did, and the only thing I regret is that we were unsuccessful."

"You are only saying that because you are distressed over your defeat, and perhaps because of the pain you are suffering."

"No. I had long found the domination of this assembly of cannibals to be quite unbearable, and I wanted to have done with them once and for all."

"Stop accusing yourself so. The Convention wishes to be lenient. Do not force us to pronounce a verdict we are not seeking."

"I do not want the Convention's leniency ... I have always loathed the Revolution, and now I loathe it more than ever, as well as those who conducted it, supported it, and continued it. A short time ago I ardently embraced the cause of the sections, in the fervent hope that we should succeed in crushing your abominable Convention. So sentence me now and be done with it. When my head is cut off, my leg will be healed."

In the face of such defiant arrogance, the court had no choice but to send Lafond to the guillotine. With the exception of Lebois and Lafond, however, those convicted were left in peace and, according to Lacretelle, would even appear, quite safely, at the Opéra, taking great amusement in the honour of being outlawed. This farce had become so obvious by mid-Brumaire that a fellow with a sense of humour remarked, standing before the list of those sentenced to death posted in the Place de Grève, "Gentlemen, all these dead men are in the best of health!"

While the Vendémiaire insurgents were excluded from the amnesty of 4 Brumaire, the Court of the Seine acquitted them the following year on the rather unexpected grounds that no insurrection had taken place on 13 Vendémiaire, Year iv! But there is nothing really surprising about such clemency. Like the members of the Convention, the rebels belonged to the Parisian bourgeoisie; as a social class, it was repelled by the idea of tearing itself apart. As Lamothe-Langon wrote, "There was something special about this revolt which made it both painful and unpleasant. It was not the rabble that rebelled, but the true people and the National Guard. This opposition by the enlightened population of Paris worried us a great deal."

But there was nevertheless the Commission of Seventeen, set up to purge the ranks of public administration. Apparently most government employees had taken up arms: 115 clerks out of 117, for instance, for the Legislative Committee. On 16 Vendémiaire, the Commission therefore decreed that those who had not been at their posts or who had not defended the Convention on the thirteenth would be dismissed. On 26 Vendémiaire, this measure was extended to all those who, though they had been in their offices on the thirteenth, had expressed anti-republican sentiments; department heads, who were liable to six months in prison for issuing false attestations of attendance, were given twenty-four hours to denounce their subordinates who had taken part in the insurrection. On 3 Brumaire, Tallien had a decree passed barring the insurgents from occupying public posts.

Also worthy of mention are the measures of redress taken in favour of the patriots. On the twentieth, the Convention voted to reinstate the military officers whom Aubry had relieved of their duties. On the twenty-first, a decree was enacted which forbade judges from passing sentence on the former members of revolutionary committees, municipalities, or administrations. Many indemnities were also granted to the patriots, notably to those of the Quinze Vingts Section registered by Gonchon who had come to the Convention's defence on 13 Vendémiaire. The battalion of the patriots of '89, which the authorities feared might turn into an unruly gang like the one led by the ruffian Maillard, was discharged quietly on 16 Vendémiaire on the grounds that the citizens had "business to take care of at home and that the Republic [was] no longer exposed to the dangers that [had] threatened it." The citizens were issued certificates honouring the "outstanding" service they had rendered to the Republic.

The insurrection of Vendémiaire, Year IV, the last in the series of momentous days of revolutionary struggle, ended with the intervention of the army, which had hitherto kept out of civil struggles for power. Once the National Guard had been disarmed, the government – which, in Mallet du Pan's view, was nothing but a "body of brigands who, after usurping supreme authority from the king in the name of the people, [was] now usurping the authority of the people to rule over them in spite of them" – found itself the undisputed master of the capital, which had been occupied by the army. The role of Paris as the driving force of the Revolution was over.

This was also the end of the jeunesse dorée. Its leader – not Fréron, who in reality was merely a figurehead, but Rovère, the actual organizer of the youths' escapades – was decreed under arrest on 24 Vendémiaire, and was vilified in the Convention by Legendre and, in particular, by Louvet:

Foreign powers wanted to prevent the government from governing. I call the members of the Committee to witness that Rovère spared nothing to achieve this: perpetual squabbling, petty quibbling, tiresome debates prolonged well into the night – he stopped at nothing to try our patience and waste our time. He never missed an opportunity to hamper our actions ... Well, then! Consider Legendre's denunciation that Rovère, on his own authority, was able to halt the royalist movements of these jeunes gens who, after the victory of Quiberon, wanted to prevent "La Marseillaise" from being sung at the changing of the guard, these youths who had succeeded in making the hall of the Opéra into their private club ... Consider these facts, and allow me to conclude with Legendre that whoever was able to halt such movements at will doubtless had the power to direct them. Furthermore, let him explain to us the strange coincidence whereby on the evening of 30 Messidor, just when the insurgents arrived in strength on the Petit Carrousel, he, Rovère, president of the Committee of General Security, suddenly abandoned his chair and vanished. Let him explain the incident reported by Calès, who once complained heatedly about the jeunes gens' audacity. Rovère said to him the following day, "Do you realize that you fired on my grenadiers?" These grenadiers are the men who beat the call to arms on 11, 12, and 13 Vendémiaire, and who on the thirteenth wanted to cut the throats of the members of the Convention ... Let Rovère explain why secret meetings were held under his roof. Why the parallel police force? Why, in particular, this meeting with a certain Vilambre?

Its meeting places wiped out by the abolishment, on 17 Vendémiaire, of the *décadi* general assemblies, its speculators harassed continually at the Perron, the threats that hung over the Palais Égalité, Lakanal wanting to tear it down, Louchet to convert it into barracks, its main newspapers the targets of a vicious campaign – the jeunesse dorée, which since Prairial had ceased to be required as a counterweight to the Jacobins, was broken up in just four months.

Though officially disbanded, the battalion of the patriots of '89 was secretly instructed to take its revenge on the jeunes gens and, under the leadership of two redoubtable ruffians, Sans-Gêne and Laborde, had it out with them in the streets. Witness the recriminations of one of their victims:

Oh, Executive Directory, what fateful coincidence is this whereby, with total impunity, French youth can be insulted, tormented – not to say murdered – daily under your very eyes? Should a man be outlawed simply because he wears a black collar? And by whom? By that abject, vile, contemptible class of beings, having neither morals nor property, who have sold themselves to the party which pays them, tramps whom the police should always keep a close eye on.

Absentee conscripts were hunted down mercilessly. "The orders recalling the youths to their battalions," noted an observer, "arouse impotent rage in these milksops and prompt cries from their shameless mistresses." In early Nivôse, Elléviou and Gavaudan were forced to rejoin the ranks. They could be seen in uniform at the Opéra, asserting that if they were the only ones to shoot at the Austrians, then the Austrians had nothing to fear. In Nivôse, the repression was carried to the theatres. On the ninth, the bands were instructed to play "tunes cherished by republicans" every evening – in other words, "La Marseillaise," "Le Chant du départ," and the "Ça ira" – and were expressly forbidden to play the "murderous" tune of "Le Réveil du Peuple." This caused a great stir in public opinion, with people expressing their amazement that the authorities should decree that they enjoyed some tunes more than others. But since many soldiers were present in the theatres, and civilians had been forbidden to carry weighted sticks, outright resistance was impossible. Yet ridicule was still an effective weapon. Republican couplets were sung by hoarse singers with cracking voices. On the twenty-second at the Théâtre Feydeau, musicians who were massacring the "Ça ira" by playing off-key quickly improved their rendition after receiving a few swats with the flat side of a sabre. So the jeunes gens began applauding ironically and cheering derisively at passages they disliked, such as the verse *"Tremblez tyrans, et vous perfides,"* which they wryly insisted referred to the people's representatives. But the Directory had it changed to *"Tremblez, chouans."* This form of dissent continued until mid-Pluviôse, when it was stamped out by harsher repression.

On 8 Pluviôse, the war minister directed his soldiers, "Go, scour all the areas to which you have been assigned. Snatch from the shame of idleness, from the crime of rebellion, this rash youth which, in the bosom of indifference, forgets that it has a country to defend, rights to uphold, and laurels to win." Raids became more frequent at the Café de Chartres, whose owner tried without success to renew his clientèle by throwing out speculators, and hundreds of arrests were made, even in the popular dance halls. Thanks to their earlocks, some jeunes gens reportedly managed to escape from the police by dressing up as women; others simply purchased their demobilization, or pulled strings by having a merveilleuse visit the war minister, who was soon given the title of *"ministre des jolies femmes."*

Outlawed in public places, including the cafés, the theatres, the galleries of the Convention and of the Revolutionary Tribunal, where Baron Cormatin, of the Royal Catholic Army, was being tried, the jeunes gens took refuge in the gambling dens that came to be known as "*étouffoirs*" (literally, stuffy rooms). A new card game was soon in fashion, invented by the card-maker Mandru, which consisted of five kings (the Directory), six jacks (the ministers), and many spades (the representatives) and diamonds (the people). There were no hearts. The game was a smash hit. The Boulevard des Italiens, nicknamed the Petit Coblentz, took over from the Café de Chartres as the idlers' agora. The fashionable folk of the day paraded up and down between six rows of chairs, and the titles of count, chevalier, and marquis were heard frequently. The Goncourt brothers described it as "a Paris within Paris. It was the meeting place of the malcontents, the protest of the elegant, the promenade of pretty women, the circle of good taste, the gallery of high fashion, the club of the honnêtes gens. It was a salon, a party, an army, a boudoir, a rebellion."

In late Pluviôse, the jeunesse dorée slipped into history. There would be further disputes in Nivôse, Year V, when the jeunes gens, in protest against the malicious caricatures showing them as incroyables, would don the old costume of the royal court: embroidered coat, lace jabot, purse, épée, and hat under the arm. There would be clashes with Augereau's soldiers in Fructidor, Year V, in the course of what was called the war of the black collars, and later the sanguinary Café Garchy expedition in Nivôse, Year VI. But these incidents were minor resurgences. After seeing its royalist hopes vanish in the smoke of Vendémiaire, the jeunesse dorée had ceased to be anything more than a topic of literary fantasy and, in four months, had faded into dandyism and society life.

Conclusion

The Thermidorian Reaction, as Albert Mathiez has rightly observed, was a process of disavowal: a fifteen-month period – from 9 Thermidor, Year II, to 4 Brumaire, Year IV – in which the men of the Year II were outlawed and their revolutionary work undone. The immeasurable denial and supreme renunciation involved in this piece-by-piece dismantlement of the economic, social, and political institutions of the Reign of Terror, combined with a severe famine, led directly to the popular uprisings of Germinal and Prairial, and soon thereafter to the bourgeois insurrection of Vendémiaire, Year IV.

As I have shown, the jeunesse dorée played a not insignificant role in these events. It therefore comes as a surprise to find that the subject, though given pride of place in popular history – witness the numerous biographies of Mme Tallien – has been curiously glossed over by academic historians. What could be called truly scientific knowledge of the jeunesse dorée has until now been sketchy at best. Standard history has never gone beyond an "impressionistic" treatment of the jeunesse dorée, with interpretations varying according to ideological obedience, from Pierre Gaxotte on the far right to Daniel Guérin on the far left. The first requirement of an in-depth study was to delimit clearly what was unknown territory, and the second was to explore this territory following the investigative methods of critical scholarship – that is, systematic scrutiny and rigorous interpretation of primary sources.

My aim in this was to reassess the jeunesse dorée's political and social influence on events during the Thermidorian period, as reflected in original archival material, and thus to determine whether the role ascribed to it in the memoirs of contemporaries of the Revolution, which had been accepted unquestioningly by standard history, was an accurate one.

First, I found that the jeunesse dorée played an essential role in galvanizing the reactionary movement. Its support was vital to the success of the still timid and indecisive Thermidorian party's first struggles in the Assembly, and its contribution considerable in the winning over of public opinion by the ideologists of the moderate camp. The surprising connection between the rate of prison releases and the renewal of rightist agitation in the sections is most revealing in this regard – not to mention the rout of the Jacobins, which was entirely the work of the jeunes gens.

No less crucial was the role played by the jeunesse dorée in the tremendous reactionary upsurge that occurred in French political life. This shift manifested itself in the renaissance of a sumptuous, decadent social life, the emergence of a new élite personifying the values of the day, the persecution of the patriots, and the sudden disrepute of anything associated with the Year II: the removal of Marat from the Panthéon, the disturbances in the theatres, from whose stages were banished the plays, actors, and actresses of the Year II, and the fête of 2 Pluviôse, which was conceived as a republican celebration but which the jeunesse dorée turned into an anti-Jacobin free-for-all. These developments were indicative of the level to which the Assembly had sunk, now that its actions were being dictated by the jeunes gens.

As the winter progressed, the jeunesse dorée likewise played a far from insignificant role in driving the populace to revolt. Scuffles in the streets and other public places between muscadins and sans-culottes matured the political consciousness of the common people and acted as a catalyst in mobilizing the masses. It was during this period that the trial of the "four ringleaders" was eagerly awaited, and strange, idealistic, futile attempts were made at conciliation between "workers" and jeunes gens. When the first hunger riot broke out, on 12 Germinal, the Assembly managed to escape the wrath of the "cutthroats" only thanks to the belated intervention of the jeunesse dorée. Then, from Germinal to Prairial, the food situation in Paris deteriorated from scarcity to outright famine, while social unrest grew ever more menacing. Although the jeunes gens were certainly fanning the flames of discontent, up to this point they had managed to prevent things from burning out of control.

The part played by the muscadins in the Prairial insurrection is more difficult to determine. Posted as the Assembly's praetorian guard on 1 Prairial, the jeunesse dorée broke ranks and fled at the rebels' first assault, and did not return until late in the evening to clear the debating chamber of the remaining rioters. The following day, the youths were put to work more systematically, as informers and as guards at the Hôtel de Brionne, where the Committees were sitting. On the evening of the third they were armed and, early the next day, the fourth, they were sent to attack the faubourg, whence they returned defeated and humiliated after a miraculous escape from a near massacre. The faubourg was then attacked from five different directions and, threatened with destruction, it surrendered. The jeunesse dorée's part in the Prairial insurrection had been to incite the insurgents, nothing more; the actual outcome had been decided by the military and the National Guard from the western areas of the city. In the ensuing repression, the jeunes gens were active in securing arrests in a significant number of sections – some fifteen, in all – while their vociferous interference at sessions of the ad hoc military tribunal was decisive in many convictions. In the last analysis, the jeunesse dorée provoked and aroused the anger of the populace but proved to be powerless against it, save in securing punishment of the insurgents after the rebellion had been put down.

With the sans-culottes ousted from the political arena, the jeunes gens were nothing but an unruly militia of which the Convention sought to unburden itself. This was the reason for the brief but acrimonious quarrel that the Committee of General Security picked with the youths through the pages of La Sentinelle, which ended with the closing of the Café de Chartres. Debates and clashes followed, like the inevitable action and reaction of some preset mechanism, leading ineluctably to the bourgeois revolt of Vendémiaire. Once again, the jeunesse dorée was at the centre of things. Café waiters, university students, servants, grocery clerks, government employees, members of the professions – the prison registers and arrest warrants bear out that it was indeed the jeunes gens who rose up against the Convention's attempt to establish its own feudal system and thus wrest power from the liberal bourgeoisie, and who were crushed by the Convention in the smoke of Bonaparte's guns. Consequently, there are no grounds for dismissing the assertions of standard history, which on the contrary my research showed to be well founded.

It would seem, then, that what have been regarded as two opposing theses are in fact capable of reconciliation. The proponents of the first thesis – Louvet, Fréron, Barras, Durand de Maillane, Larevellière-Lepeaux, Hyde de Neuville, Levasseur de la Sarthe, Rovère, and a few others – held that the jeunesse dorée was simply a political tool for furthering the Reaction, and was indeed used by the Thermidorians for precisely this purpose. According to the upholders of the second thesis – Lacretelle, Babeuf, Mallet du Pan, Thibaudeau, C.-F. Beaulieu, Lebois, Duval, and Louis Jullian – the jeunesse dorée, more than a mere tool of the government, was actually the driving force of the Thermidorian Reaction, carrying the Convention's deputies, who legislated at its behest, far beyond their political aims until Vendémiaire, which, significantly, marked both the end of the jeunesse dorée and the end of the Reaction as such.

To be sure, the jeunesse dorée was used by the Thermidorians, particularly at the outset, to galvanize and sustain the Reaction. Accordingly, it must be credited with the press campaign that turned public opinion against the Montagnards and the patriots, the proscription of the men of the Year II in the streets and the cafés, the subsequent closure of the Jacobin Club, the organization of a parallel police force, the Moderates' seizure of the sections, the purging of the sans-culottes from posts in government administration and arms workshops, and so on. While none of these developments actually exceeded the political aims of Tallien, Fréron, Rovère, and their colleagues, signs of the Assembly's debasement were already evident, as it shook off the domination of the Jacobins only to fall under that of the jeunesse dorée, and political and social life experienced another reactionary upswing. In the newly reopened salons, where the centrist people's representatives sold themselves to the Reaction, specifically republican values fell into disrepute. Even Rovère, one of the most fanatical reactionaries and the chief organizer of the jeunesse dorée, was harassed in the streets for having a small red cap on top of his hat. The journalist Delacroix dared to call for a king, while in the Assembly – where members delivered speeches written for them by their boudoir minions – a motion to have Marat's remains removed from the Panthéon was passed, one of the most dishonourable palinodes of parliamentary history. From Ventôse on, the muscadins' stinging provocations grew ever more frequent in a crescendo of agitation that saw a flurry of near riots and minor revolts. The violent response sparked among the lower classes legitimated in advance the retaliatory action taken against them, as though every move were part of a fateful chain reaction that would result inescapably in the explosions of Germinal and Prairial. This was the jeunesse dorée's real contribution to revolutionary history: from its initial role as the Committee of General Security's private militia, it gradually developed into one of the driving forces of the Reaction, and as such constituted the ultimate explanation of the Thermidorian phenomenon.

Several of the above theses had already been sketched out by other historians. What had been missing was the documentary evidence that would give them a solid foundation. My contribution was to examine the original documents and furnish standard history with the documentary evidence it was lacking. As a result, we may now accept the assertions of traditional historiography – hitherto merely appealing, logical hypotheses – without committing an act of intellectual temerity.

I wanted to highlight the driving role played by the jeunesse dorée in various revolutionary insurrections. Given this objective, I was forced to leave to others the atemporal attractions of non-event-oriented history in which, by definition, nothing happens in such a short amount of time. There is little justification, in my view, for the disfavour into which narrative history has fallen. Every event has its own ideological status, hence the importance of the narrative, a genre which deserves to be rehabilitated. Indeed, is not history narration of the specific and understanding of the singular? I thus proceeded by narration, description, dialogue, and judgment – the whole resting on the impressionistic perception of events that can be discerned in the primary sources.

However objective my investigation may be, I make no claims to neutrality. I feel genuine, committed sympathy for the common people who collapsed from exhaustion in the Paris streets of the Year III. But I do not consider this to be a hindrance to understanding the Thermidorian phenomenon in theoretical terms. In the secrecy of his study, the historian tells "the story of things worth remembering." Though a man of science, he never ceases to be just a man. And, as such, I trust that I shall not be begrudged my sympathy for the obscure, forgotten men who fought for the idea of liberty.

Bibliography

Baczko, Bronislaw. *Comment Sortir de la Terreur. Thermidor et la Révolution.* Paris: Gallimard 1989.

Bessand-Massenet, Pierre. *La France après la Terreur.* Paris 1946.

Brunel, Françoise. *1794, Thermidor, la Chute de Robespierre.* Brussels: Complexe 1989.

Castelneau, J. *Madame Tallien.* Paris: Hachette 1937.

Clarétie, Jules. *Les Derniers Montagnards.* 2 vol. Paris: Librairie internationale 1847–62.

Cobb, Richard. "Marat comparé à Jésus." *Annales historiques de la Révolution française,* 32 (1960): 312–14.

– "Notes sur la Répression contre le Personnel Sans-culottes de 1795 à 1801." *Annales historiques,* 32 (1954): 23–49.

– and Georges Rudé. "Le Dernier Mouvement Populaire de la Révolution à Paris." *Revue historique* (Oct.–Dec. 1955): 250–81.

Deville, G. *Thermidor et Directoire.* Paris, n.d. (Collection "Histoire socialiste de la Révolution française," Vol. 5.

Fassy, Paul. *Marat, sa Mort, ses Véritables Funérailles.* Paris: Éditions de Petit Journal 1867.

Furgeot, Henri. *Le Marquis de Saint-Huruge.* Paris: Perrin n.d.

Goncourt, Edmond, and Jules Goncourt. *Histoire de la Société Française pendant le Directoire.* Paris: Fasquelle 1864.

Houssaye, Arsène. *Notre-Dame de Thermidor.* Paris: Plon 1866.

Lafont, Paul. *Garat.* Paris: Calmann-Lévy 1900.

Lefebvre, Georges. *Les Thermidoriens.* Paris: Armand Colin 1937.

Lestapis, Arnaud de. "L'Assassinat de Tallien." *Revue des Deux Mondes* (1 November 1954).

Maricourt, Alphonse de. *La Véritable Madame Tallien.* Paris: Éditions des Portiques 1933.

Mathiez, Albert. *La Réaction Thermidorienne.* Paris: Armand Colin 1929.

Minnigerode, M. *The Magnificent Comedy*. New York 1933.

Tarlé, Eugène. *Germinal et Prairial*. Moscow: Éditions en Langues étrangères 1960.

Thureau-Dangin, Paul. *Royalistes et Républicains*. Paris 1874.

Tønnesson, Kare. *La Défaite des Sans-culottes*. Paris: Clavreuil 1959.

Wartelle, François. "Les Destinées du Jacobinisme entre la Chute de Robespierre et le Coup d'état du 18 Brumaire an V." *Bulletin de la Commission Départementale d'Histoire et d'Archéologie du Pas de Calais* 12, no. 2 (1987) 179–92.

Weigert, R.A. *Incroyables et Merveilleuses*. Paris: Rombaldi 1955.

Zivy, Henri. *Le 13 Vendémiaire*. Paris: Bibliothèque de la faculté des lettres de l'Université de Paris 1898.